Sounding the Depths

Sounding the Depths:

Tradition and the Voices of History

Victor A. Grauer

Self-Published via **CreateSpace**

For Alan Lomax, who lives . . .

I felt that their music came from the back of time, but also, to a certain extent, from my own depths.

Simha Arom

I have dwelt upon this extreme, rare and somehow utopian situation because it runs counter to most of the music we know and thus illuminates the rest of human musical activity in an extraordinary way. It points to the close bonds between forms of social and musical integration.

Alan Lomax

About the Author

Dr. Victor Grauer, based in Pittsburgh, PA, is a composer, musicologist, film-maker, media artist, poet and dramatist. He holds a Masters Degree in Ethnomusicology from Wesleyan University, with additional studies in that field at UCLA, and a Ph. D. in Music Composition from SUNY Buffalo. He was co-creator, with Alan Lomax, of the Cantometric coding system and worked on the Cantometrics Project for several years, under Lomax's supervision. His creative work has been presented in many venues worldwide, including Lincoln Center (the New York Film Festival), Carnegie Institute (Pittsburgh), The Kitchen (New York), The Mattress Factory (Pittsburgh), the Barbicon Center (London), etc. His writings on musicology and the arts have been published in journals such as *Ethnomusicology, Semiotica, Art Criticism, Music Theory Online, Other Voices, Millennium Film Journal, The World of Music* and *Before Farming*. He is a recipient of the Pittsburgh Cultural Trust's Creative Achievement Award. Grauer has taught at the University of Pittsburgh, Pittsburgh Filmmakers, the Pittsburgh High School of the Creative and Performing Arts and Chatham College. He is presently engaged in research linking his work with Lomax on Cantometrics with current developments in genetic anthropology and archaeology. Dr. Grauer may be contacted via email at: victorag@verizon.net.

Preface to the hard copy edition

Sounding the Depths was originally released on the Internet as a "Blog Book":

http://soundingthedepths.blogspot.com/

In that context, the many audio and video examples can be accessed simply by clicking links interleaved within the text. While the blog version is ideally suited to the multimedia nature of the project, many readers have complained about the difficulties of studying such a long and complex text from a computer screen and requested a printed copy. This version is designed for them.

For the benefit of hard-copy readers, I've added to the blog a set of cross-referenced multimedia links, on a page labeled "Audio-Visual Examples," located just under the chapter headings displayed in the "Blog Archive." (If you have trouble hearing or viewing any of this material, you may need to add the appropriate *plug-in* to your browser.)

The blog version of the book also contains a great many "figures," in the form of illustrations, photographs, diagrams, etc. In my opinion, the inclusion of such material in a volume of this sort is covered under the "fair use" provisions of the copyright law and need not require permissions. However, most publishers and their lawyers prefer to err on the side of caution — and since identifying the rights holders and obtaining permissions for all the many images would be an all but hopeless task, it's been necessary to remove from the hard copy edition all images for which I myself do not hold rights.

Therefore, as with the audio-visual examples, I've produced a specially designed blog page containing all the figures referenced in the text. The link to this page, labeled "Figures," can be found just below the "Audio-Visual Examples" link. (In case you're wondering about the rationale for such a procedure: in the event that any rights holders might object to my use of their images – or multimedia clips – it's much easier to remove such materials from an Internet site than from a printed text.)

While this hard-copy version does, in itself, convey all the basic ideas presented in the original, and can therefore be read as a stand-alone text, serious readers will want, from time to time, to access the images and multimedia materials available only on the blog. I apologize for the inconvenience entailed in such an arrangement, but see no alternative for those who prefer reading in a more traditional format.

Contents

Preface

Students and scholars of world music, technically known as "ethnomusicologists," have for some time been preoccupied with cultural studies, identity and gender politics, popular music, and the effects of change in an age of globalization, thanks to the (now venerable) influence of postmodernism. My focus, on the other hand, has always been on basic research into fundamental issues bearing on the nature, origins, meaning, and "deep history" of music, as revealed by the long-term survival of certain traditional practices among indigenous peoples. As the field turned increasingly away from what interested me most, I became more and more disenchanted, and ultimately abandoned ethnomusicology almost completely for many years.

My interest was rekindled around five years ago, as I began to read about what was going on in the field of population genetics, particularly the "Out of Africa" model of modern human origins, and realized that what I had learned about the shape of traditional music around the world seemed to fit remarkably well with what the geneticists were learning about the earliest migrations of our species. As a result of this "epiphany" I've done a lot of writing over the last few years, leading to publications in journals such as *World of Music, Before Farming* and *Ethnomusicology*. I also created a *blog* where I could explore some of these issues at greater length (http://music000001.blogspot.com/).

While most of what I'd been writing was concerned almost exclusively with music, I reached a point where I wanted to broaden my horizon to focus on what the worldwide musical picture can tell us about culture generally. The book I'll be presenting here is the result of that quest. My intention was definitely not to produce an academic tome, but what is called a "trade" publication, suitable for the sort of reader who enjoys books like Jared Diamond's *Guns, Germs and Steel*, Steven Mithen's *The Singing Neanderthals*, or the sort of popular anthropology books written in the past by people like Desmond Morris, Colin Turnbull, Margaret Mead, or Ruth Benedict. After some preliminary research on how to go about getting published, I dutifully wrote a book proposal and began querying literary agents who specialize in non-fiction.

Here's how I described the book to the first agent I contacted:

> What I've done is to use what I know about the musical picture and what I am learning about the genetic picture to propose what I believe to be a completely fresh and daring new approach to the "deep history" of homo sapiens and their (our) cultural evolution, in Africa, Out-of-Africa, and in the world beyond. The scope of my daring will be evident when I tell you that I have come up with a method for recreating not only the music but many aspects of the culture of our "most recent common ancestors" in Africa, ca. 100,000 years ago. I know this sounds pretty wild, but if you read my summary and the sample chapters I think you'll realize that my ideas are based on solid evidence and clearly derived inferences. I've worked hard to make my proposal as readable and engaging as possible and I think I've succeeded. In my humble opinion: the proposal rocks! :-) But I could be wrong and will certainly welcome your candid thoughts and suggestions.

This agent (who prefers to remain anonymous) had taken an interest in my blog, and had urged me to send him a book proposal. And while I'm at it, I want to take this opportunity to thank him, because he very thoroughly reviewed this earlier (now aborted) proposal of mine, giving me all sorts of valuable suggestions on what worked, what didn't, and how it could be improved. Unfortunately, his response to my latest proposal was not encouraging, as he felt my book was more suited to academic than trade publication. I was deeply disappointed, and responded as follows:

> I trust your judgment and must therefore assume you are right in seeing this as more of an academic project than something for the general public. Which creates a huge problem for me, because for me it's important to be able to reach the general reader. To be honest, I have little faith in the academics either in my own field of ethnomusicology or the social sciences generally. The premise behind my book will be anathema to the great majority of ethnomusicologists and anthropologists alike, since it flies in the face of what has become a mantra for them: "continual change is a universal of all culture, which means if you try to extrapolate the past from the present, you are way out of line."

Based on the agent's subsequent suggestions, and the many tips I was able to find in volumes such as *Selling Your Nonfiction Book, How to Publish*

Your Nonfiction Book, The Complete Idiot's Guide to Getting Published, etc., along with many of the websites devoted to the same topic, I rewrote the proposal and the sample chapters several times, to reflect what I assumed were the requirements for a successful trade publication.[1] To make a very long story short, nothing worked. Not even close. Of all the many agents and editors I queried, only two others bothered to even look at my proposal and both came back negative, for reasons that were never made clear.

In retrospect, I realize that I should have seen this coming, since literally every how-to book stressed, over and over, essentially the same message: if your topic doesn't fit into one of the prefabricated categories used by booksellers such as Barnes & Noble or Borders, no one will touch it. Sadly, my book is not easy to categorize by any standard. It's not really a music book, because music is only one part of the story I tell. It's not anthropology, because it deals mostly with societies that have long vanished. It's not archaeology, because it doesn't analyze a single artifact, stone tool, or fossil. It's not evolution, because it deals with cultural rather than biological evolution. It's not history, because it goes too far back into the past; and it's not prehistory, because it goes much farther into the past than what that term implies. It's about deep history, but that's not a category of which publishers and book sellers are yet aware.

There is also the little matter of sales volume. In the words of my old college friend, now a successful literary agent, Richard Curtis (from his book, *How to be Your Own Literary Agent*), "The pressures created by the [bestseller mentality] are exerted on writers, forcing them to write books of a certain kind or a certain length or a certain style, and in certain cases forcing them out of the writing profession entirely. . . . Whatever else your book may be, it must be profitable. And books that have little else to recommend them beyond being good are all too often marginally profitable or not profitable at all." I used to take such pronouncements with a grain of salt, but not any more. According to just about everything I've read and heard, it is almost impossible for someone with an offbeat idea, and no "platform" (i.e., no prior media exposure or pre-packaged audience), to be published in the trade market.

In desperation, I did what I had initially decided not to do: approach the University Presses. After all, I have a Ph. D., I've spent many years teaching in the halls of academe, and have published a fair amount in peer reviewed academic journals, so why not? University Presses are supposed to be more concerned with quality than profit, and innovative, multidisciplinary books of the sort I was pitching are supposed, so they all claim, to be just the sort of thing they want most in the whole world. Nevertheless, to make another long story short, my efforts with Oxford University Press, Harvard

University Press, Cambridge University Press, Indiana University Press, and The University of Chicago Press all came to nothing. Not one editor was interested in seeing the book proposal — I was turned down solely on the basis of my query letters. While the categories they had in mind might have been different from those in the trades, they were categories nevertheless – and the idea proposed in my query simply didn't fit. Or to put it in the terms of a typical rejection notice: my project looked "interesting, but is not a good fit for us at the present time."

Some Shameless Self-Promotion

Had any of these editors actually read my proposal, they would have learned that an earlier essay of mine on a closely related topic, "Echoes of Our Forgotten Ancestors," had been greeted with enthusiasm from leading figures in ethnomusicology and folklore. I'm not too modest to reproduce some of these endorsements here:

> Max-Peter Baumann, professor of ethnomusicology at Otto-Friedrich University of Bamberg, Germany, and editor of the journal World of Music: "Many thanks for sending me your manuscript 'Echoes of Our Forgotten Ancestors'. I have read it carefully and think it very exciting, challenging and fresh. . . . I am positively surprised by the new perspectives that you open with your approach, even if we still are aware of many theoretical and historical uncertainties referring to continuity and change."
>
> Akin Euba, leading African ethnomusicologist and composer; Andrew Mellon Professor of Music, the University of Pittsburgh: "I have read with deep interest parts of your fascinating paper; I feel that you are on to a very important line of research and I would like to urge you to continue to pursue it. The results of your research will be a major contribution to musicology."
>
> Rod Stradling, editor of the online journal, Music Traditions: "I . . . have spent the most exciting and intriguing three hours of my life, reading it all. This really is the most extraordinary stuff!" From his editorial in Music Traditions: "Whilst I'm no academic myself, I have to tell you that (assuming I've understood the somewhat technical nature of his arguments correctly) there are some truly earth-shattering ideas emerging from the work he's been doing with various genetic anthropology researchers. And I promise you that 'earth-shattering' is not an exaggeration!"

Jens Finke, author, The Rough Guide to Tanzania, the Rough Guide to Zanzibar, Chasing the Lizard's Tail: "Many thanks for your kind email, and for the link to the best, most enjoyable and most thought-provoking read I've had in months! Actually, it wasn't so much provoking as 'ah, of course...'"

Bruno Nettl, professor emeritus at the University of Illinois, formerly president of the Society for Ethnomusicology: "This is a magisterial work which takes on fundamental questions and issues of ethnomusicology . . . Grauer joins the likes of Carl Stumpf, Curt Sachs, Marius Schneider, and Walter Wiora, though he is immensely more sophisticated, thanks in part to advances in archaeology and biological anthropology." (From "Response to Victor Grauer," in World of Music 2/2006.)

Why Blog?

In the world of traditional publishing, trade or academic, all that matters, it would seem, is that your book fit into some narrowly defined, predetermined pigeonhole with which editors, publishers and booksellers feel comfortable. Well, maybe you can't blame them. They understand their market and if they deviate too far from what is expected, they will be out of business.

Fortunately, however, the world of publishing is currently undergoing some very fundamental changes. In fact, I would be so bold as to predict that both Barnes & Noble and Borders will have gone the way of Blockbuster Video in five years or so. Many of the big publishing houses will also have fallen by the wayside, along with most of the literary agencies, and literally all the university presses (and academic journals) will be operating in a totally different manner. Whether or not a book can find its way onto the shelves of some oversized book selling establishment will not matter a single whit. Internet booksellers have no shelves and all books can be accessed through very efficient, open-minded, and equable, search mechanisms. The stigma attached to self-publishing is starting to lift and will soon be gone entirely, as more and more books are published through alternative venues. The need for huge sales to justify a substantial investment will also be a thing of the past, since on-demand or online publishing will make it possible for books to be marketed to selective niche audiences with minimal up-front cost.

Since I have no desire for the dubious "prestige" of university press publication (I'm not a candidate for either tenure or promotion), and prefer in any case, as I've said, to reach a general, rather than a specialized, audience, I have no problem with self-publishing. (Though to be honest, I originally hoped I could wangle a fat advance from some big publishing house.) The question for me now is: which route to take? After giving the matter some thought, I rejected any of the usual venues, because what I really need is not a bound volume, but an efficient means of reaching as wide and varied an audience as I possibly can — what I will be discussing in this book is, in my opinion, something of real importance, which should be of interest to anyone with any curiosity at all regarding some of the most basic questions that can be asked about what it means to be human, and how we got that way.

I finally decided to do something unusual, to disseminate my book in the form of a blog, or what could be called a "Blog-Book" (B-Book ???). There were three reasons for this decision: 1. it's free; 2. publishing on a blog makes it easy to include any number of links to audio clips; 3. readers can easily add comments on a chapter by chapter basis, which might make this the first truly interactive book (unless someone else has already beat me to it, which would not surprise me). I'm hoping readers will take advantage of this opportunity to respond with comments and even criticisms. If you do, I promise to take your feedback very seriously and will consider making changes on the basis of valid criticisms and/or suggestions.

Face Flying

There is one more reason I decided to publish my book in this unusual manner. It openly challenges too many entrenched beliefs for it to be acceptable in just about any "respectable" format. The book is the product of my long-time interest in the broad-based comparative study of the traditions of indigenous peoples worldwide, with special attention to the possible survival of certain traditions from the deepest recesses of antiquity, in the hope that such study can provide us with important clues regarding the history and meaning of human culture, past and present. As I see it, musical traditions play a special role in this history, as will be evident as my story unfolds. While such an approach might seem perfectly reasonable to most people, it flies in the face of dogmas long cherished by specialists in almost all branches of the social sciences. And from painful experience I can attest that it's almost impossible to shake those with such a background out of their dogmatic slumber.

For the great majority of anthropologists and ethnomusicologists today, context is fundamental. One is expected to study the manner in which various aspects of culture function within a narrowly defined social context: a particular tribe, or set of closely related tribal groups, a village, town, religious community, age group, etc. Such an approach conveniently squares with the prevailing research model, i.e., field work within a small community. What is not encouraged is any effort to broaden the context beyond the fieldwork model. The prevailing assumption would seem to be that one cannot, and in fact must not, compare a certain practice in one place with what might look or sound like something similar in another place because that would entail the removal of both practices from their "context." And since it is only in terms of the local context that one can presumably assess the real meaning of any such practice – i.e., its function in the community — then any but the most cautious and limited attempts at comparative study would, literally, be meaningless – like comparing apples and oranges.

Needless to say, I see things quite differently. In my view, a recording of a musical performance already contains encoded within it a context of its own, a broader context, with a deeper meaning, than anything to be gleaned from an ethnographic study of how music functions in some specific community. If that were not the case, then listening to the music of another culture would have no more meaning for us than listening to a radio broadcast in an unknown language. It is this very deep well of shared meaning and emotion that sets music apart from most other modes of human behavior, and ought to have given the comparative study of the musical practices of the world a place at the center, rather than the periphery of anthropology.

A closely related dogma insists that we cannot read any aspect of the distant past into the current activities of any peoples living today. Assumptions along such lines were once the bread and butter of mainstream anthropology, but when too many assumptions went too far afield, and too many fanciful, untestable theories were being tossed around, an understandable reaction set in. However, this reaction, as I see it, went much too far, to the point that the proverbial baby was tossed out with the bathwater.

But things have changed rather dramatically over the last few years and anthropology is about to be shaken to its foundations — though you'd hardly guess it from the current state of the literature. Actually, it's already been shaken to its foundations. Just like the economy has already collapsed. Only no one knows it yet. It's the old Wile E. Coyote syndrome:

See Figure 0.1 (all figures may be accessed online at
http://soundingthedepths.blogspot.com/)

Wile E. is puzzled because he doesn't understand how he could be so far from our friend the Road Runner and yet not be hovering in empty space. What he doesn't yet realize is that he IS hovering in empty space.

What's about to change anthropology forever (and would already have changed it if it weren't for all those Wile E. Coyote types out there) is the revolution I'll be writing so much about in upcoming chapters – no, not the musical part, though that's important too. The population genetics part. Armies of vampiric geneticists have been drawing gallons of blood from innocent people all over the world for many years now, using it to do research of an absolutely extraordinary kind into the deepest depths of human history. We've all heard about it. But the meaning of this research hasn't really reached the groves of anthropological academe as yet – maybe everyone is still out in the field somewhere, engaging modernity, constructing identities, negotiating gender, or situating themselves in contexts (in-joke, sorry).

In the words of anthropologist Doug Jones,

> the situation has changed enormously in the last decade or two – so much that many researchers now argue that we are seeing the birth of an "emerging synthesis" in the study of prehistory. Rapidly accumulating information and new theoretical perspectives in population genetics, historical linguistics, and archeology seem to be coming together at last to tell a consistent story of the ancient human past, including the origin of modern humans, domestication and other innovations in subsistence, largescale demic expansions, genetic and cultural diffusion, and the origins and spread of major language families . . . based on significant correlations in the distributions of genetic, linguistic, and archeological variation. . . . [T]he emerging synthesis suggests parallel transmission has happened often enough to leave traces in current distributions of genes, language, and culture that point back to common causes in prehistory (Jones 2003:502).

Ghost Dance

This preface is almost complete, but there is one important thing I need to add. The book you are about to read is haunted. By the spirit of the man who inspired it, whose ideas are continually at work within it, my mentor and second father, whom I loved and admired; from whom I learned so much; with whom I sometimes also disagreed: Alan Lomax. You'll read more about Alan's role in the shaping of my thinking and my research in subsequent chapters, but what I want to say for now is that, as I see it, all my current work in the field of world music and comparative musicology can be understood as the continuation of a process pioneered by him.

Only he would not have seen it that way, and would, in all likelihood, have been opposed to what I am now doing. Alan was the first to see the music and culture of the African Pygmies and Bushmen as an all important "baseline," from which all of human history could be measured, and in this sense my work can be seen as a direct extension of his. However, he ultimately became obsessed with what seemed to me and many others as an overly rigid, complex, and outmoded theory, in which certain aspects of musical expression reflect evolutionary "stages" in subsistence and social complexity, beginning with relatively simple hunting and gathering societies and culminating with the highly sophisticated, irrigation-based, agricultural societies of the present day.

Alan argued that musical styles change systematically over time as various groups move in this way from simpler to more complex subsistence types, but I was never able to see any real evidence of that, and was therefore forced to reject his theory. Very sadly, he struggled in vain for the rest of his life to definitively establish his five-point, or sometimes eight-point, evolutionary "production scale," in the face of withering criticism, or outright neglect, from anthropologists and ethnomusicologists who saw it as a return to a sort of 19th Century thinking widely rejected long ago.

In my view, there are no universals that inevitably carry human culture from one evolutionary "stage" to the next, nor are there any hard and fast rules correlating musical style with social structure and/or culture, but a series of more or less unpredictable contingencies that have shaped certain societies, but not others, depending on who was in a particular place or situation at a given time. Although my approach in this regard is, on the surface, very different from Alan's (though certainly inspired by him), it does not, as I see it, constitute an outright rejection of his evolutionary thinking, which is in certain respects quite convincing. As I make clear in the book (see especially the chapter on Europe), there are certain basic insights, and also some very interesting correlations, that remain meaningful from both his standpoint and mine.[2]

Oh and One More Thing

The book being offered for your consideration here was not created out of whole cloth, but, very frankly, cobbled together from a variety of sources: earlier writings, both published and unpublished; old grant applications (all rejected); various and sundry emails, etc. Faithful readers of my blog, Music

000001, will recognize many passages lifted from certain posts more or less intact. As I worked on the blog, I realized that in some sense I was writing a book – and as I continued, I realized I was writing more than one, possibly several. So the present book is largely a sifting and compilation from various and sundry bits and pieces. My plan is to post one chapter at a time, and in the interim, continue to work on and polish the remaining chapters.

I believe I've managed to put together a coherent volume that is reasonably easy to follow, enjoyable to read, yet at the same time both comprehensive and scientifically sound. But this is in fact a very fine line to tread and I may not always be able to do so as gracefully as I would wish. There is a lot of ground to be covered and a lot of new ideas to get across, so I hope I will be forgiven if at times I get too carried away with certain details and/or arguments, or overwhelm the reader with material that might be more appropriate for an academic publication. (Most of the technical material has been placed in Appendices for the benefit of specialists who might want to delve more deeply into certain details.) Feel free to skip over anything that gets too dense or boring. And feel free to let me know through your comments when certain passages strike you as overly complex, convoluted or disjointed.

_____

1. I'd like to acknowledge the assistance of my old friend, Sam Reifler, and my sister, Rhoda Grauer, both of whom went over the proposal carefully, making some excellent suggestions, many of which have found their way into the book as it now stands.

2. To learn more about Lomax's approach, I recommend Chapter Six of the book *Folk Song Style and Culture* (Lomax et al. 1968). The most thoroughgoing and authoritative critique of his evolutionary theory was presented in a paper by one of his closest collaborators, Edwin Erickson: "Tradition and Evolution in Song Style: A Re-analysis of Cantometric Data," *Cross-Cultural Research*, November 1976, vol. 11 no. 4, pp. 277-308. (http://ccr.sagepub.com/content/11/4/277.abstract). An excellent biography, *Alan Lomax: The Man who Recorded the World*, by John Szwed, has recently been published by Viking Books.

Introduction

An Overwhelming Question

A single question, broken down into three fundamental parts, asked by the great French painter Paul Gauguin in an obscure corner of his final masterpiece: *"D'où venons-nous? / Qui sommes-nous? / Où allons-nous?"* "Where do we come from? Who are we? Where are we going?"

> See Figure 0.2 (all figures may be accessed online at
> http://soundingthedepths.blogspot.com/)

We all ask ourselves more or less the same question, don't we? But isn't it one of those metaphysical questions that can't ever really be answered? As I see it, Gauguin's words should not be interpreted in the context of Western metaphysics, but as a reflection of the much more down to earth mode of thought we find, time and again, in the words of indigenous people.

A religious Westerner might respond that we come from God; a scientific Westerner might be more matter of fact: we come from our mother's womb; but for most indigenous people, there is one response: we come from the ancestors. As for "who are we"? What the ancestors want us to be. "Where are we going?" Back to join the ancestors. What suggests to me that this was Gauguin's intention is the mysterious bird we see on the lower left, next to the old woman contemplating her death. In Tahitian mythology, large white birds were seen as messengers of *Ta'aroa*, the most powerful of the ancestral gods (*http://www.tahitiguide.com/@en-us/584/articlepopup.asp*).

So. Our question should not be understood as the usual Western, "metaphysical" question to which we have for so long become accustomed, but the more down to earth *historical* question of interest to *all* humans: who were our ancestors, what were they like, what part of their legacy has survived, and what lessons can we derive therefrom? My claim is that such questions are now, for the first time, actually open to serious study, thanks largely to evidence from the two fields that will be highlighted throughout this volume: music and genetics.

A Baseline

The basic argument can be summarized as follows:

1. the Pygmies and Bushmen of Africa, now recognized by population geneticists as carriers of the most ancient lineages in the world, share a remarkable musical language, despite thousands of miles of separation in completely different regions of Africa, with totally different environments — strongly suggesting that this musical practice is a survival from the time the geneticists tell us the two populations most likely diverged, tens of thousands of years ago.

2. thus, astonishing as it might sound, by listening to a recording of traditional Pygmy or Bushmen music, we are, in a sense, entering a kind of time warp, hearing the sort of sounds our African ancestors may well have been making anywhere from 70,000 to over 100,000 years ago.

3. and if their shared musical traditions, like their genetic "clades," have a common root, deeply buried in the heart of the Paleolithic era, then it's possible to infer that other traditions shared by both groups might also be survivals of cultural practices inherited from the same ancestral population.

The logic outlined above enables us to go beyond the realms of music and genetics to postulate a hypothetical *baseline* representing the culture of this ancestral population, from which, in theory at least, all subsequent cultures are derived. On this basis, drawing upon a wide array of evidence, the book takes the reader on a journey through some of the deepest recesses of human history, suggesting solutions to mysteries that, until recently, were thought to be completely beyond the reach of systematic investigation.

An Outline of History

Chapter One relates the stories behind the discovery of key bodies of evidence from each of the two realms on which the book draws most heavily: 1. the shared musical language of the African Pygmies and Bushmen, whose music and culture will be significant points of reference throughout; 2. the revolutionary new research of the population geneticists, for whom both groups uniquely represent the deepest branches of the human family tree.

Chapter Two deals with a key question of population genetics: what can it mean to say that the Pygmies and Bushmen are somehow special because they stem from a 'common root,' if that same root is the one we all sprang from? In response, I consider some of the most recent and convincing genetic evidence. Most of the statistics are expressed via "phylogenetic trees," or, in less technical terms, family trees, which distill the genetic findings in diagrams that are relatively easy to grasp. In each case we see three specific populations, Western Pygmies, Eastern Pygmies and Bushmen occupying the deepest branches, implying that all three populations diverged from our "Most Recent Common Ancestor" well into the Paleolithic era.

Chapter Three takes us from the realm of music and genetics to that of culture generally. If indeed we are transported tens of thousands of years into the past by the distinctive sound of Pygmy and Bushmen music, we can take its hand, so to speak, to be led inexorably from the aesthetic to the social, from musical style to cultural style, from the distinctive organization of sound to the equally distinctive social structure appropriate to the production of that sound. The intimate connection between Pygmy/Bushmen musical style and the values that form the core culture of all three populations (Western Pygmies, Eastern Pygmies and Bushmen) is revealed through the eyes of anthropologists and ethnomusicologists who have studied such groups extensively.

If such correspondences are indeed meaningful, and the ancestral group represented in the phylogenetic trees displayed in Chapter Two did indeed vocalize in Pygmy/Bushmen style (P/B), then this very distinctive mode of musical behavior would have reflected the ancestral social structure in precisely the same manner as it reflects the social structure of contemporary Pygmies and Bushmen. And if this is in fact the case, we cannot ignore the possibility that other traditions also held in common by representatives of all three populations (Eastern Pygmies, Western Pygmies and Bushmen) could also be grounded in the culture of the group ancestral to all.

Taking the evidence and arguments presented in the previous chapters to their logical conclusion, Chapter Four proposes a methodology of "triangulation," operating as follows: *"Any distinctive value system, belief system, artifact or attribute not likely to be the result of outside influence, found among at least three different groups representing each of the three populations with the deepest genetic clades, i.e., Eastern Pygmies, Western Pygmies and Bushmen (EP, WP, Bu), may be regarded as a potential survival from an older tradition traceable to the historical 'moment' of earliest divergence."*

On the basis of such commonalities a "Hypothetical Baseline Culture" (HBC) is postulated, representing the subsistence strategies, dwellings, bodily ornamentation, language, music, rituals, kinship system, behavior and core values of the common ancestral group. While these are certainly not the only traditions that could be considered, they pertain to some of the clearest commonalities found among all three populations, and thus constitute a baseline, however provisional, incomplete and hypothetical, for the exploration of cultural history. The various elements of the baseline should not, of course, be seen as proven facts, but rather as testable hypotheses to be employed as exploratory tools.

Chapter Five considers the relation between the baseline established in the previous chapter and the traditions of various groups of often very differentiated and distinct hunter-gatherers in various parts of the world, with an eye to evaluating the possibility that certain of their traditions might be survivals from the ancestral culture (HBC). An especially important difference will also be stressed: the strongly competitive, violent and warlike characteristics evinced by so many of these groups, in contrast to the largely egalitarian and pacifist traditions of almost all Pygmy and Bushmen societies.

Chapter Six addresses confusing and contradictory notions regarding the lifestyle and values of our so-called "stone-age" ancestors, related to the idea that the popular view of today's indigenous peoples is some sort of myth, based on romantic notions of "noble savages" living an idyllic, "utopian" existence at one with themselves and nature. To this end, the chapter will begin where the previous one left off, with a further examination of competition and violence among hunter-gatherers.

In this context, I argue that the Pygmy and Bushmen societies on which the baseline is modeled are certainly not Utopias, in the sense of ideal societies where everyone gets along perfectly, women have full equality, disputes are rare, and always settled fairly and without violence. Nevertheless, at least two aspects that stand out as especially important for the developed world, in this time of economic and social turmoil, are well worth noting: first, the avoidance of war, vendetta, or any other type of socially sanctioned violence; second, the imperative toward social equality in terms of individual autonomy, mutual cooperation, and the equitable sharing of goods.

Chapters Seven through Fifteen tell the story of the Out of Africa migration, from the initial exodus across the Red Sea, to the long march along the Asiatic coast, to the subsequent populating of East and Central Asia, the Middle East, Europe, Oceania and the Americas. In each case, I focus on the manner in which traditions associated with the baseline culture and its music either persisted or were altered in response to outside forces, both environmental and social; forces which have, in turn, given rise to new and, in some cases, highly competitive and violent societies quite different from HBC.

4

This will not be a smooth progression by any means, since both the musical and genetic evidence reveal a major gap, centered in what is now India, suggesting that, at some point very early on, the Out of Africa migrants must have encountered a catastrophic event, so devastating as to produce a major turning point in human history.

Chapter Sixteen looks backward to consider evolutionary processes that might have led to the development of the musical style on which I've been focusing so much attention, reminding us that HBP (the Hypothetical Baseline Population) represents the *Most Recent* Common Ancestor, *not* the earliest. It's only logical to assume, therefore, that HBC must have evolved from simpler practices that preceded it.

This chapter speculates rather broadly on the possibility that the music of the ancestral group might have evolved from an equally interactive, but far less complex, mode of vocalization, resembling the "duetting" and "chorusing" characteristic of certain contemporary ape and gibbon populations, which may well be perpetuating primate "traditions" developed long before the advent of modern humans. In the course of the discussion, some tantalizing clues will be considered, bearing on the origin and evolution of music, its meaning for early humans, and the possibility of a close association with the origin of both religion and language.

Chapter Seventeen begins with a playful discussion of an ancient Chinese myth, the story of the "Yellow Bell," concerning the creation of a system of tuned pipes that became the basis of not only the Chinese musical system, but some of the most fundamental aspects of Chinese culture generally. My own version of this myth takes us from China to Africa, as I speculate rather broadly on the possible relevance of tuned pipes to the origins of both music and language, ultimately linking this chapter to the previous one as part of a grand evolutionary "metanarrative." This is by far the most speculative chapter in the book, whose value lies more in the possibilities it suggests than any solutions it offers.

The final chapter is an extended meditation on, and response to, the challenging questions posed at the beginning of this introduction: "who were our ancestors, what were they like, what part of their legacy has survived, and what lessons can we derive therefrom?" As such, it will serve as both a retrospective summary of the book as a whole and a forward looking discussion of the role of indigenous peoples in the world of today, with special emphasis on the importance of the ancestral legacy bequeathed to us through their enduring traditions.

Sidebar 1 — Preliminary Considerations

Before I continue to Chapter One, it's important that I make my position clear regarding what may well be the two most problematic aspects of my research: the emphasis on musical evidence, which is rarely if ever taken seriously in the literature on anthropology and cultural evolution; and my notion of cultural continuity, which departs radically from what has become a persistent dogma of the social sciences, the insistence that continual change pervades all aspects of cultural history.

The Musical Dimension

Typically, when confronted with musical evidence, most anthropologists simply throw up their hands, as if to say "what do you expect of us, we are not musicians and are therefore not in a position to comment one way or the other." The fact that most are not linguists either, or archaeologists, doesn't discourage them from taking that sort of evidence very seriously. But linguistics and archaeology are part of the standard anthropological quadrivium, while musicology is not.

This is unfortunate, because musical traditions clearly occupy a position in most cultures comparable in importance to language, or even moreso, as evidenced by the strong tendency in many societies to retain a traditional musical style even in the face of significant cultural and linguistic change. Moreover, music has much in common with language, and can even be considered a language in its own right, as reflected in many semiotic studies. The relationship between the two has been expressed by a great many different thinkers, from ancient times to the present, in many different ways.

Clearly a great many people have attached considerable importance to music, as evidenced by the enormous number and range of writings devoted to this topic by some of our greatest thinkers over thousands of years. So why are musical traditions so shamefully neglected by anthropology? More to the point, why isn't music considered at least as important to the study of culture as language?

Cultural Continuity

Many social scientists see the perpetuation of a tradition from one generation to the next as something like the reproduction of a tape recording, which loses a certain amount of information each time it's dubbed. From one generation to the next, hardly anything appears to have been lost. But over the course of several dubbings, the original may no longer be recognizable. A favorite analogy is with the well known game of "Rumor," where someone whispers something to his nearest neighbor, who repeats the message to the next in line, until, after several repetitions, the original message may well be distorted beyond recognition.

In both cases, communication is based on the linear transmission of a signal from a sender to a receiver through an "analogue" process. But cultural transmission operates in a very different manner. For one thing it is not linear. Culture is not simply passed on from a sender to a receiver, because culture is not so much a message as a multivalent lattice or field. Nor is it simply a means of communication, but a generative and regenerative process through which reality itself is constructed. Each new generation is immersed in this "reality" from birth, and its effects accumulate very rapidly to the point that most children are thoroughly conditioned by the time their first sentences are spoken.

Unlike analogue recordings (or archaeological artifacts), culturally transmitted information won't necessarily diminish or get distorted over time, because, as with digital recording technology, what is preserved is not only the information itself, but the process by which the information is stored and retrieved. Transmission errors can certainly occur during digital encoding, but most can be caught and corrected through the use of a checksum, or similar self-correcting scheme. The cultural equivalent of the checksum is the process by which the entire community is continually available to assist and correct the novice whenever a "transmission error" occurs. What we have, therefore, is not simply communication from generation to generation but an integrated and continually reinforced network; not a chain held together link by link, but a chain-link lattice of tightly interwoven connections with multiple self-correction mechanisms.

In light of the above, it is not that difficult to understand how a particular tradition can be "handed down" from "generation to generation" over thousands, or tens of thousands, of years with only minimal or superficial change. Because, for one thing, it is not really "handed down," but maintained as part of a cultural field that permeates the awareness of everyone in it. And secondly, the generational aspect is almost irrelevant, since there is never a point in time separating one generation from another, but, again, an ongoing temporal field within which individuals of all ages are engulfed. Consequently, there is never a moment of transmission when something is handed down but a continual process of cultural imprinting, enforcement and re-enforcement.

And if such a process can suffice to maintain a certain tradition for a hundred, or two hundred, or five hundred, or a thousand years, then, if the society is sufficiently isolated, or capable of resisting external pressure from neighboring groups, there is no reason to assume the same process can't continue for two thousand, five thousand, ten thousand or, indeed, one hundred thousand years, or more. Once such a process gets going there is no intrinsic reason for it to stop. There is in fact no provision for significant change in such systems, which, especially among the most tradition-minded indigenous societies, are designed in such a way as to resist any innovation not directly associated with survival.

This is not to say that a certain amount of "drift" is out of the question. We know very well that cultural dialects can be and are being produced on a regular basis. But such dialects tend to develop via localized linear transmissions that are almost always subsumed within the overall, nonlinear, field. Thus the innumerable variants of particular folk songs have no effect on the overall structure and performance style of all such songs, which remain essentially fixed within prescribed norms.

According to this model, traditions are likely to change only when confronted by powerful external forces capable of distorting or destroying the cultural fields that maintain them. If such forces are never encountered, then both the fields and the traditions will tend to persist. The model should be understood as applying most strongly to non-specialized, indigenous peoples, whose attachment to ancestral traditions is demonstrably stronger than that of more specialized societies, where competition between specialists can over-ride traditional constraints in favor of innovation.

Chapter One: The Pygmy-Bushmen Nexus

A Musical Journey

What if I told you I had a time machine, enabling you to listen in on events from thousands of years in the past? Naturally, you'd smile and discreetly change the subject. "Humor me," I'd insist, flashing a smile of my own. I'd then draw a small device out of my pocket to wave slowly and mysteriously before your eyes, like a magician's wand. "But this is just an mp3 player," you'd protest. "I don't see any time machine." I'd silently produce a small headset, plug it in to the device, press the "start" button, and hand it to you. You'd place it over your ears and listen. "Hmmm, what's this?" (see Audio Example 1)

For Mickey Hart, drummer of the legendary rock band, *The Grateful Dead*, "these magnificent sounds . . . lit my imagination, suggested possibilities, and opened a strange new world to a kid growing up in the city. . . I was sort of listening to the roots of the roots. Deeper than the blues. What the blues was formed from" (From interview with Brian Handwerk, for *National Geographic News*, June 6, 2003.) Marie Daulne, founder of the innovative vocal group *Zap Mama*, expressed her feelings in simpler terms: "it was like an illumination, like a light" (from article on *Zap Mama*, in *Wikipedia* — *http://en.wikipedia.org/wiki/Zap_Mama*).

For ethnomusicologist Simha Arom, "It was a shock . . . It made my spine tingle. How could these people play such complex music without a conductor?" According to composer Marc-André Dalbavie, "this is currently one of the richest musics in existence. The complexity of the polyphony and polyrhythms is absolutely marvelous."

"OK," you say, "I get it. There is definitely something special about this music. But I have no idea what you mean about the 'time machine' part. How are these recordings a time machine? And what, exactly, am I listening to?"

Sorry, but the first part of your question won't be fully answered until you've read the entire chapter, right up to the last sentence. As for the second part . . .

From the Back of Time

What you've been listening to is *Diye* (from *Musical Anthology of the Aka Pygmies, Ocora Records* 560171/72, CD2, Track 9), a divining song of the Aka (also known as the BaAka or Biaka), a group of African Pygmies, as recorded by a man who has spent much of his life studying their music, ethnomusicologist Simha Arom. "Right from the beginning," he wrote, "I sensed that this music existed in us all, like some Jungian archetype." Of his first experience of hearing Pygmy music, from a hotel room in the capital of the Central African Republic, Arom wrote:

> I felt that their music came from the back of time, but also, to a certain extent, from my own depths. Yet I could never have known it, never having heard anything like it before. It was insane. How did the musicians achieve this? I was dumbfounded. (as quoted in "No Small Triumph," in *The Independent*, Oct. 6, 2003 — *http://www.independent.co.uk/arts-entertainment/music/features/no-small-triumph-582413.html*).

Music "from the back of time." Music from "my own depths." Music that already "existed in us all." Music that functioned "like some Jungian archetype." Bold words. But what can they mean? Linguists would love to reconstruct the very first language, based on what is known about the nature of all the various language families in existence today. There's not much hope that any such effort could be successful, as there are very few (or perhaps too many) clues to work with and the whole process of reconstruction would have to be based on a long series of untestable assumptions and speculations. However, music would seem to operate in a very different manner than verbal language and as a result there may be no need to reconstruct the "archetypal" music of our ancestors. If it is still being performed today, we can simply listen to it! But how can that be? If languages have changed so much over time, wouldn't musical styles also have changed? One would think so, certainly. But the evidence would seem to tell a different story. What is that evidence?

If all we had were some recordings of Aka Pygmies, the music itself would tell us nothing about the tradition behind these intricately interwoven musical counterpoints. But there is more to the story, much more. Many other groups of Pygmies also sing in a strikingly similar manner, including populations thought to have been isolated from one another for many thousands of years. Even more remarkable, essentially the same, almost identical, style of vocalizing can be found among certain "Bushmen" groups, based in a completely different region of Africa.

Rouget's Discovery

The first to take note of this unlikely association was a remarkable Frenchman by the name of Gilbert Rouget, who, after a long and distinguished career as a tireless documenter and interpreter of world music and dance, is still active at age 94, hard at work (as of 2010) on a new book. While Rouget is probably best known today for his path breaking research on the relation between music and trance, he is also a formidable master of the art of field recording and a pioneer of documentary film. In 1946, Rouget took part in a Musée de l'Homme- sponsored expedition to the *Oessa* region of the Congo, home of the Babinga (aka Babenzélé) and Bagombé Pygmies.

The recordings he and his colleagues made on this expedition seem to have been among the first examples of Pygmy music ever published. A few years later, Laurence Marshall, a successful businessman and adventurer, took his family to live among the *!Kung* Bushmen, in the Kalahari desert. For eleven years, beginning in 1950, the Marshall family, Laurence, his wife, Lorna, and their children, Elizabeth and John, lived with, studied, filmed and recorded many aspects of their lives, producing some of the first recordings of Bushmen music ever made.

When Rouget heard the Marshall's recordings, he was startled at the striking resemblances between the musical style of these hunter-gatherers of the southwest African desert and the Pygmies he'd recently recorded, based in the tropical forest region of the Congo, in Central Africa, many thousands of miles to the north. When he played his own recordings for the Marshalls, they agreed that "the resemblance of the Bushmen and Pygmy music was so striking that it deserved to be underlined." (Rouget 1956, p.2)

Out of their mutual effort, a now-historic LP disc was published, under the title *Bushman Music and Pygmy Music*, designed as a direct comparison between the musical styles of the two groups. In an accompanying booklet, Rouget expresses his puzzlement over the "troubling relationship" between the music and dances of peoples "belonging to races entirely distinct" and separated by such great distances, "as much geographic as climatic." Pointing to "resemblances constituting a system too complex and too coherent" to be explained on the basis of "convergence," i.e., independent invention, he wondered whether it was "necessary to believe, then, that the Pygmies and Bushmen are of common stock, and that their dance and music represent the remainder of a common cultural heritage?" (Rouget 1956)

To get a better idea of what Rouget found so interesting, let's do some listening of our own. We've already heard an example of Aka Pygmy music, the divining song *Diye*, as recorded by Simha Arom (see reference above): *Audio Example One:Diye*. Compare with the following recording of two Ju/'hoansi Bushmen women singing a "Giraffe Dance Song" (from *Healing Dance Music of the Kalahari San*, recorded by Richard Katz, Megan Beisele and

Marjorie Shostak, Folkways 4316, side 1, track 2): *Audio Example Two:Giraffe Dance Version One*.

While Diye begins with a solo voice, interwoven with one or two others, more voices join in as the performance continues, to form a complex web of sound: *Audio Example Three:Diye Part Two*. Compare this with another version of the Ju/'hoansi Giraffe Song, as sung by a large group of approximately 35 males and females (Op. Cit., side 1, track 3): *Audio Example Four:Giraffe Dance Version Two*. Here is another Aka Pygmy song, from Michelle Kisliuk's book, *Seize the Dance*, CD2, track 9: *Audio Example Five:Elanda Dance*. Compare with this Ju/'hoansi Bushmen performance, from the CD *Mongongo*, recorded by John Brearly, track 3: *Audio Example Six: //Kaa*.

The Aka, living in the Central African Republic, represent the Pygmies of west central Africa. The Mbuti Pygmies, made famous by Colin Turnbull's popular book, *The Forest People*, are located far to the East, in the Ituri Forest of the Congo. Yet their music shares essentially all the most distinctive characteristics of both the western Pygmies and the Bushmen. Here is an Mbuti "Elephant Hunting Song," as recorded by Turnbull (from *Mbuti Pygmies of the Ituri Forest, Smithsonian Folkways SFW40401*, track 3): *Audio Example Seven:Elephant Hunting Song*.

Compare with the following Ju/'hoansi Bushmen performance, from Rouget's original LP, *Bushman Music and Pygmy Music*, Peabody Museum and Musee de l'Homme, side 1, track 3: *Audio Example Eight:Giraffe Medicine Song*. Finally, I'll add one more example, from a different Bushmen group, the Qwii (from *Bushmen: Qwii - the First People*, track 10): *Audio Example Nine:The Ostrich*.

In all these examples, we can hear many of the striking points of stylistic similarity shared by the three populations, western Pygmies, eastern Pygmies and Bushmen: delicate, extremely relaxed and fluid vocalizing, often highlighted with yodels; interlocking parts; a frequent tendency for one part to be completed by another part, with the effect of a melody tossed back and forth between two or more voices, a practice similar to what, in Medieval Europe, was called "hocket" (or "hiccup"); the extraordinarily well matched and fluent blending of the voices; intricate, precisely executed, polyrhythms; the predominance of meaningless vocables, usually open vowels, such as "oh" or "ah"; highly repetitive, but also varied, melodic structures, based on short motives (but with an underlying melodic phrase as an implied, but often unheard basis); frequent imitation of parts, as in a canon or round; wide melodic leaps; a continuous flow of interwoven sound with no pauses. In most cases, singing is accompanied by complex, often polyrhythmic clapping, stick beating, or rattle patterns, and, among Pygmies especially, we sometimes hear drumming, though the drum is not a traditional Pygmy or Bushmen instrument.

Roots, Shallow and Deep

For many it might seem strange to make so much of a musical affinity between any two African populations, regardless of how far apart they might be living. Aren't *all* Africans "of common stock"? And doesn't all African music sound more or less "the same"? A great many Africans do, in fact, have much in common, biologically, culturally and musically, due to an important historical development called the "Bantu expansion," thought to have taken place relatively recently by archaeological standards: roughly 2,000 to 4,000 years ago. To simplify a complex history: Bantu speaking farmers seem to have originally been confined to a relatively small region of West Africa, at a time when much of the vast central African rainforest was occupied by Pygmies, speaking a language now lost, and most of southern Africa dominated by Bushmen, speaking a "click" language thought by many to be the oldest in existence: *Khoisan*.

When the Bantus expanded, roughly three or four thousand years ago, most likely in search of fresh farmland, those Bushmen unwilling to alter their traditional hunter-gatherer lifestyle were either killed off or marginalized to the Kalahari desert, a dry, harsh environment for which farmers had little use. For a long time, the Pygmy hunter-gatherers were safe within their forest retreat, far to the north, since most Bantus feared forest spirits.

But as the expansion progressed, some of the less powerful Bantu groups were forced into the margins of the forest, where they managed to develop symbiotic relationships with neighboring Pygmies. Eventually most of sub-Saharan Africa became dominated by Bantus, their languages, their culture and their music. I've presented a simplified overview of a complicated history, and there were other groups involved, speaking languages from other families, such as Nilotic and Cushitic, but suffice it to say that the Bantus appear to have been the most successful, widespread, and dominant, group.

What is now understood by most non-Africans as "African music," is actually based on certain typical features of Bantu music: call and response choral singing; relatively simple vocal harmonies; many types of plucked string instruments, often performed by gifted musician-poets known, in West Africa, as "Griots"; various wind instruments, such as flutes, pipes, horns, trumpets, etc.; a wide array of percussion instruments, from simple "bells" to sticks, rattles, xylophones, etc.; and, of course, an elaborate subculture built around the drum, featuring an incredibly complex array of drumming techniques and traditions.

Here is a fairly typical example of Bantu "call and response," from the Kamba people of Kenya, as recorded by Hugh Tracey (*Dance songs of the Kamba people from Machakos district, Kenya*, ILAM, track 1): Audio Example 10: *Nthambi wa Mutwana*.

In this sense, music from one part of Africa can, crudely speaking, be said to resemble music from many other parts of Africa — all indeed stemming from a common root, based in the West African Bantu homeland of two to four thousand years ago. While of enormous significance in the history of Africa and indeed the world, that root is relatively shallow – and fairly well understood. No mystery there.

The Pygmies and Bushmen on the other hand, occupy a very different musical universe, far more complex vocally, and far simpler instrumentally, with no indigenous string instruments other than the mouth bow, no percussion other than hand clapping and stick beating, and no drums, at least traditionally (as we can hear, some Pygmies and Bushmen have become expert performers on drums borrowed from neighboring Bantu groups). Both peoples have long been thought to occupy a much older historical layer, with far deeper roots – though until recently no one had any idea *how* deep. More significantly, they are based in completely different parts of Africa, within totally different environments, and are thought to have remained isolated throughout most of their history from all other humans – and certainly from one another – for many thousands of years.[1]

Their isolation is reflected in both their genetic makeup (see Chapter Two) and their completely different physiognomies (though both are unusually short in stature), to the extent that each group has been considered a unique "race" unto itself. Under such circumstances, assuming — as most anthropologists do — that all cultures inevitably change over time, one would not expect their musical traditions, or in fact any of their traditions, to have much in common. It's not surprising, therefore, that Rouget, an experienced Africanist, would be astonished by the striking resemblances he discovered.

The Lomax Code

Rouget's prophetic words landed on deaf ears as far as the majority of anthropologists and ethnomusicologists were concerned. Both fields were in the process of moving away from comparative studies, in response to a general trend in academia toward ever more narrowly focused specialization. Perhaps because he was neither an academic nor, strictly

14

speaking, an ethnomusicologist, a notable exception to this trend was the American folklorist Alan Lomax, for whom Rouget's juxtaposition of Pygmy and Bushman music came as a revelation.

While Lomax is primarily associated in the public mind with American folk music, his boundless energy and enthusiasm eventually took him much farther afield, to produce what are now recognized as major collections of traditional music from the West Indies, Great Britain, Spain and Italy. His career took a decisive turn when he entered into an agreement with Columbia Records to produce an unprecedented collection of eighteen LP discs, representing traditional music from many obscure corners of the world: the *Columbia World Library of Folk and Traditional Music*.

As it happened, Gilbert Rouget was enlisted as co-editor of volume two of this series, devoted to the music of what was then called "French Equatorial Africa." Meeting with him in Paris, Lomax was introduced to the remarkable music of the Pygmies and Bushmen, and infected with Rouget's intense interest and curiosity regarding the "troubling relationship" between them. "Pygmy/Bushmen style," highly distinctive, highly integrated, almost Utopian in its non-hierarchical, freely flowing counterpoint, in which every voice had an equal "say," was to become a core component of his research from then on.

Ever since his experiences in Spain and Italy, Lomax had been contemplating a radically new approach to the comparative study of music, based largely on stylistic features immediately apparent from recordings, as opposed to the painstaking analysis of melodic patterns and scales based on music notation, which had dominated the research of folklorists and musicologists for many years. Rouget's examples clearly demonstrated the power of recordings to vividly convey what was most essential, since both the highly distinctive qualities and striking resemblances of the two musical realms seemed clearly apparent, even on a first hearing.

But Lomax was keenly aware of the difference between subjective interpretation and scientific method. If recorded performances were to yield convincing results, a systematic approach to encoding and comparing them would need to be developed. Thus was born the methodology that Lomax was to call "Cantometrics," at once the systematic "measure" of song and the use of song as a "measure" of culture.

While Lomax had always been deeply involved with music, he lacked a formal musical education and thus felt the need for a trained musician as collaborator in the development of the Cantometrics method. At the time, I was completing a Master's Degree in ethnomusicology at Wesleyan University, under the supervision of David McAllester, a leading ethnomusicologist, outstanding teacher and kindred spirit. I still recall his words, informing me of Lomax's search for a suitable collaborator, and his surprise at my enthusiastic response to his rather diffident question: "Do you think you might be interested in this sort of thing?" I jumped at the chance — an interview with Lomax was arranged, and in short order I was informed that I got the job.

The following summer, I sublet a tiny basement apartment in New York's Greenwich Village, a few blocks from Lomax's densely packed and somewhat chaotic combination office, studio and living quarters, on West Third Street. We spent the summer together, one of the most challenging and memorable periods of my life, intensely focused on our efforts to produce a coding system flexible enough to encompass the entire range of folk and traditional vocal music throughout the world.

Listening Cantometrically

Don't panic. This book is not going to be about Cantometrics, though I'll be referring to certain Cantometric findings from time to time. And I certainly won't expect you to learn the system. However, the treatment of music throughout this book is deeply influenced by the innovative approach pioneered by Lomax, which represented a profound break with the methods then prevalent among students of both Western and non-Western music.

Unlike those methods, focused on details of the various tonal and rhythmic components of a musical "composition," Cantometrics represents a deliberate simplification, emphasizing certain very broad, clearly audible parameters of musical *performance*. Lomax's innovation was to put aside traditional music notation, with its focus on the technical aspects of scale and structure, in favor of a more generally applicable, informal, behavior oriented, rating system which could do justice to the sort of large-scale *stylistic* patterns that seem to reflect the overall shape of the musical picture worldwide.

Since the strategy behind Cantometrics is to examine music more or less as a listener with no formal musical training would tend to hear it, we can use aspects of the coding system as tools in helping us hear all sorts of details we might ordinarily miss, without the need to know much about music theory or even read musical notes. Readers who want to hear for themselves what I've been running on about, and learn something about the way Cantometrics works should consult the "Evidence from Cantometrics" section of *Appendix A*, in which a Pygmy performance is systematically compared with a Bushmen performance, using Cantometrics as a guide. If you'd rather not get bogged down in such details, feel free to ignore the Appendix and read on.

Supporting Evidence

Very early on, during the course of our work together, I too became infected with Lomax's enthusiasm for the music of the Pygmies and Bushmen, which became the topic of endless conversations speculating on what "Pygmy/Bushmen style" (P/B), as we called it, might mean. For Lomax, both their music and their "Utopian" social structure and values were to become the "baseline" from which the evolution of all human culture ultimately stemmed.

The close affinity subjectively noted by Rouget was, indeed, supported by some of our earliest results, as Lomax reported the following year, in the journal *Ethnology*:

> Perhaps no two peoples, so far separated in space (3,000 miles), living in such different environments (desert and jungle), and belonging to different racial and linguistic groups, share so many stylistic traits . . . as far as Cantometric analysis is concerned, the styles are, indeed, identical. (Lomax 1962).

Some years later, in 1971, ethnologist/ethnomusicologist Charlotte Frisbie conducted an independent analysis of the same traditions, with results "practically identical with those achieved by the Cantometrics system . . . Thus, at least in one instance, a Cantometric profile can be replicated by using a non-Cantometric, more traditional comparative approach." Noting that "[t]he comparative analysis of Bushmen and Pygmy music shows overwhelming similarities . . ." she arrived at a conclusion in perfect accord with Rouget's original insight: *"in view of the attributes of music which make it a valid tool in reconstructing culture history, these findings would present a serious problem to anyone who tried to deny an earlier historical connection between the two groups"* (Frisbie 1971:285,287 – my emphasis).

Our excitement over the possibilities opened by this line of research was enhanced by a string of related discoveries. Echoes of Pygmy/Bushmen style could be found among a wide variety of different indigenous and "peasant" peoples, also marginalized, for the most part, to various "refuge areas," both in and out of Africa, reinforcing some of Lomax's earliest suspicions that the style could be among the oldest on Earth. But many questions remained and, as far as I was concerned, we still had a long way to go before fully understanding the meaning of this remarkable musical style and its unexpected distribution in so many obscure corners of the world.

Aftermath

I left the Cantometrics project early in 1967, to enroll as a graduate student in music composition at the State University of New York at Buffalo. As the years went by, Lomax, his co-director Conrad Arensberg, and a remarkable group of musicologists, dance analysts, anthropologists, linguists, statisticians and computer programmers, enlarged the scope of the project to include equally innovative research in related areas, such as movement and dance (Choreometrics), popular music, speech (Phonotactics and Parlametrics) and the relation of performance style to cultural evolution.

Supported over a period of more than thirty years by substantial grants from the National Institute of Mental Health, the National Endowment for the Humanities, the National Endowment for the Arts, the National Science Foundation, the American Council of Learned Societies, the Rockefeller Foundation, the Apple Foundation, etc., Lomax's research on Cantometrics and other aspects of performance style was very possibly the most heavily funded humanities-oriented project in history.

Nevertheless, despite his best efforts as both researcher and promoter, Cantometrics and its sister methodologies were ultimately rejected by Lomax's colleagues in both ethnomusicology and anthropology, as both fields moved away from comparative studies toward new approaches inspired by developments in cultural studies and postmodernism, in which the principal focus moved from far ranging speculations regarding the evolution of timeworn traditions to more locally oriented, hands-on studies of adaptation and change.

I never lost interest in either world music or Cantometrics, and maintained a close friendship with Lomax over many years. But my personal goals had changed, and for a long time I did no research at all in any aspect of ethnomusicology. It was only within the last few years, after becoming aware of exciting new developments in the field of population genetics (see below), that the full significance of what we had been calling "Pygmy/Bushmen style" began to dawn on me.

Delving once again into the ethnomusicological literature, I discovered, moreover, that considerable progress had been made in the understanding and analysis of both Pygmy and Bushmen music since the time Lomax and I had worked together, filling in many of the gaps needed to fully assess the relation between the two traditions. After careful study of remarkably thorough research on Bushmen music by Nicholas England, an important book on Pygmy music by Michelle Kisliuk, and pioneering research on Pygmy and Bushmen music by Simha Arom and his students, Susanne

Fürniss and Emmanuelle Olivier, I felt ready to undertake a systematic comparative review of the two traditions.

A Shared Language

Several transcriptions of Pygmy and Bushmen polyphonic vocalizing are systematically analyzed and compared in the paper that grew out of my studies, "Concept, Style and Structure in the Music of the African Pygmies and Bushmen" (Grauer 2009). At the heart of this effort is a demonstration that the many similarities that seem so striking to the ear are not merely an auditory illusion, as some have asserted,[2] but are based on deeply rooted conceptual and structural affinities. The research reported in my paper went beyond the limitations of Cantometrics to reveal an extensive list of highly distinctive shared features, some of which are unusually complex and even quite subtle. For a thorough examination of this, and other relevant musical evidence, see *Appendix A.*

In addition to the many purely musical affinities, there is also a compelling psychological association that cuts deep into the mindset of both groups. Among the Ju/'hoansi Bushmen, as reported by both Emmanuelle Olivier (1998:366) and Nicholas England (1967:61), certain songs are given to healers during a dream or trance by the spirits of dead ancestors who join the dreamer in a multipart performance. Upon awaking, the healer teaches the basic melody to his or her spouse, who teaches the song to others in the group, who then reconstitute the song in its original multipart form, with multiple variations.

A remarkably similar process of dream transmission, also from the dead to the living, and across genders, has been noted among the Aka Pygmies by Michelle Kisliuk (1998:177-178). An "eboka" (a type of performance combining song and dance) was transmitted in a dream to an Aka woman by her deceased brother. The woman was then expected to teach it to her husband, who then taught it, in turn, to a group of young men from the same band. According to Kisliuk, "an eboka can emerge as a mystical, dreamed gift within a family, transferred across genders and across the threshold of death."

In sum, I feel confident that careful examination of the relevant literature, from Rouget to Lomax to Frisbie to more recent studies of my own, based on additional research by England, Kisliuk, Arom, Fürniss and Olivier, will reveal that the musical affinities — structural, conceptual and contextual — are clear and decisive. All the evidence points quite strongly to the same surprising conclusion: despite the huge disparities, geographical, environmental and temporal, the various Pygmy and Bushmen groups covered in the research cited above clearly share essentially the same musical language. Consequently, if, as suggested by Rouget, their musical practices must therefore be understood as stemming from a common root, it is possible to conclude that all the many shared stylistic, structural, conceptual, and cultural attributes enumerated above may well have been present in the ancestral model.

A Fresh Perspective

When Rouget and Lomax originally asked themselves why the singing styles of so many Pygmy and Bushmen groups were so strikingly similar, despite the enormous geographical distances among the many populations involved, there was no easy answer. And despite all the evidence that's accumulated since, musical research in itself can take us only so far. If Pygmy/Bushmen style originated among the common ancestors of both groups, we would still have no idea when they lived – or where. Although many anthropologists suspected that these African hunter-gatherers could be perpetuating the life style of some of our earliest homo-sapiens ancestors, their thinking was based largely on assumptions. There was little in the way of solid evidence to support such a notion and there were many skeptics.

It was only since the late Nineties, with the advent of the "Out of Africa" theory, based on new and very exciting genetic research, that the real significance of this remarkable musical affinity became evident. Over and over again it is the Pygmies and Bushmen of Africa whose DNA is being referenced as representative of some of the oldest populations in the world.

The book, *Mapping Human History*, by Steve Olson (2002), summarizes in a fascinating manner much of this research, including some very intriguing genetic findings regarding both groups. Based on such evidence, Olson concludes not only that "the ancestors of the Bushmen had to be one of the first groups to become established in Africa," but "several tribes of Forest Dwellers [Pygmies], who today live in scattered remnants in central Africa, [also] have very old mitochondrial [female line] and Y [male line] lineages. And like the Bushmen, the Forest Dwellers seem to have been much more widely distributed at some time in the past...." (*ibid.*:50-51).

What Olson is saying is that both the Bushmen and Pygmies might well represent the original inhabitants of Africa. According to a widely quoted study led by geneticist Yu-Sheng Chen,

> these data showed that the Biaka [Aka] Pygmies have one of the most ancient . . . sublineages observed in African mtDNA [mitochondrial DNA] and, thus, that they could represent one of the

oldest human populations. In addition, the Kung [Bushmen] exhibited a set of related haplotypes that were positioned closest to the root of the human mtDNA phylogeny, suggesting that they, too, represent one of the most ancient African populations" (2000:1362).

Chen et al. estimate that the ancestors of the Biaka diverged from a hypothetical founder population that lived in Africa between 76,200 and 102,000 years ago, with a divergence time for the Kung Bushmen between 41,000 and 54,100 years ago. A sampling of Senegalese Bantus is given a much more recent divergence time of between 17,900 and 23,200 (Chen *et al.* 2000:1371).

In a more recent overview, published in *African Archaeology*, an important mainstream collection encapsulating some of the newest research in the field, Curtis Marean and Zelalem Assefa report that "both the fossil and genetic records target Africa as central to the origins of modern humans. A consistent result of these studies is that African people of Khoi [Bushman] and Pygmy ancestry represent some of the most ancient populations on this planet" (Stahl 2005:97). In the following chapter, we'll learn more about the methodology of the population geneticists, and more closely evaluate the unique role played by Pygmies and Bushmen in the unveiling of our shared "deep history."

As should now be clear, it is only in the light of genetic evidence that did not become available until many years after Lomax and I worked together, that the musical findings can now be tied to what is being discovered about the human family tree, strongly suggesting that "Pygmy/Bushmen style" could date all the way back to the time when the ancestors of every human now living were a single population. In other words, by listening to a recording of traditional Pygmy or Bushmen music in the style I've been describing, we are, in a sense, entering a kind of time warp, hearing the sort of sounds our African ancestors may well have been making anywhere from 76,000 to over 100,000 years ago.

1. For an update based on new genetic evidence suggesting the possibility of "relatively recent contact" between certain Pygmy and Bushmen groups, see Sidebar 4.

2. For a discussion of a conflicting interpretation offered by two of Simha Arom's students, Susanne Fürniss and Emmanuelle Olivier — and my response — see *Appendix A*.

Chapter Two: A View from the Trees

"Whichaway whichaway does that blood red river run,
From my back window straight to the rising sun."
Rising Sun Blues, as sung by Sonny Terry and Brownie McGee

The Diego Gene

While a student at UCLA, I took a class in the anthropology of the South American Indians with one of the outstanding authorities in that field, Johannes Wilbert. At that time (probably 1962), Wilbert was especially interested in a biological marker, the so-called "Diego gene," and had recently published a study of its distribution in South America (Wilbert and Layrisse 1961). Wilbert identified the "Diego blood group" as "an exclusive Mongoloid gene marker." As such, it was commonly found in most Native American populations. However, it was either absent or rare in a small group of "Marginal Indians," the Waica, Warao and Yaruro, who were thought to represent some of the oldest populations on the continent. On the basis of his study, he suggested that such "Diego-negative populations were the first to arrive and to extend throughout South America, while the Diego-positive tribes came later" (p. 1077).

As he discussed his findings in class, I found myself getting increasingly intrigued and excited. I had spent the previous summer working with Alan Lomax on Cantometrics, listening to hundreds of recordings from all over the world, discussing the distributions of certain musical styles and what they might mean. It was clear to Lomax that these distributions must reflect historical events from the distant past, but there seemed no reliable method for reconstructing that past. Now, Wilbert's research was pointing the way to a completely new approach to the problem, via the study of genetic markers — which in some strange sense reminded me of the musical "markers" we'd been puzzling over. At some point during class discussion, the possibility of carrying this sort of research much farther through the study of DNA was raised, and Wilbert noted that DNA did in fact hold great promise as a tool for reconstructing human pre-history.

Cavalli-Sforza

The structure of DNA had been revealed only a few years earlier, however, and DNA studies were still in their infancy. For a long time afterward, studies of what came to be called "population genetics" were

22

confined to the so-called "classical markers," mostly derived, as with the Diego gene, from the analysis of blood types. A pioneer in this field was Luca Cavalli-Sforza, whose monumental, *The History and Geography of Human Genes* (written in collaboration with Paolo Menozzi and Alberto Piazza) (1994), relates the development of this sort of research from its earliest, relatively primitive stages, when the focus was on classical markers, to the far more advanced research now being done with DNA. Interestingly, the book dates the first such attempts to early research on blood types done by Cavalli-Sforza and A. W. F. Edwards in 1964 (p. 68), ignoring the pioneering work published by Wilbert in 1961. Wilbert's name does not appear in the extensive bibliography.

Cavalli-Sforza and his associates were apparently the first to develop "methods of reconstruction of trees of descent, based on simple genetic theories" (p. 68), what we now usually refer to as "phylogenetic trees." And, already in 1994, they produced such a tree for Africa, with Mbuti Pygmies occupying the deepest clades (i.e., branches), followed by "Khoi" (a group closely related to Bushmen), Somalis and San (i.e., Bushmen) (p.169). The Mbuti interested Cavalli-Sforza so much that he made a special trip to Africa to study them (pp. 177-180). Thanks to a presentation given by Lomax in the mid nineties, Cavalli-Sforza became interested in Cantometrics and made an attempt to contact him, but by that time Lomax was in poor health and unable to respond.

Thanks to the efforts of Cavalli-Sforza and a growing host of colleagues and students, great strides have been made in the field of population genetics (also known as "anthropological genetics" or even "archaeogenetics"). DNA has been extracted from the blood of many thousands of people all over the world and an ever clearer (though still, in some quarters, controversial) picture of modern human origins and early human migrations is emerging – and, as pointed out in the previous chapter, a growing consensus gives a special place to certain Pygmy and Bushmen groups .

Roots and Branches

Many who follow popular accounts of this research have been puzzled by what appears to be a very difficult and confusing question: what can it mean to say that people such as the Pygmies and Bushmen are somehow special because they stem from a "common root," if that same root is the one we all sprang from? To get a clearer picture of this particular root, and the branches stemming from it, we'll need to examine some trees, the aforementioned "phylogenetic" trees, modeled by population geneticists as an aid to understanding the intricacies of our common ancestry.

In a recent paper, Sarah Tishkoff et al. (2007) present the following chart, based on those "haplogroups" (related sets of genetic markers) closest to the root of the mitochondrial (i.e., exclusively female) phylogenetic tree:

See Figure 2.1

The uppermost row of the table, just under the diagram, lists each of the most important haplogroups, with those representing the deepest (thus oldest) branches to the left. The leftmost column lists the various African populations studied, grouped according to language family.

The first four haplogroups, labeled LOd, LOk, LOf and LOa, are, as you can see, offshoots from the leftmost branch of the tree. Under the first column, LOd, among the most ancient of surviving human mtDNA haplogroups, the !Kung Bushmen (also known as *Ju/'hoansi*) are represented by fully 96% of their sample. The groups listed under the names !Xun/Khwe and !Xun are also represented by large percentages, 61 and 51 respectively. Since !Xun is actually a variant spelling of !Kung, I'm assuming the two groups probably represent two nearby villages with essentially the same language and culture, with !Xun/Khwe representing a mixed sample of !Xun and Khwe speakers. Together, the !Kung, !Xun and !Xun/Khwe are the only Bushmen groups in the sample, though the other two *"Khoisan"* speakers, *Hadza* and *Sandawe*, are also hunter-gatherers. Note that no other population on the list is represented by more than 5% of its sample for this haplogroup. Moving to the next, LOk, we see that this haplogroup, also among the oldest on the tree, is found only among the three closely related Bushmen groups.

Moving down to the next language family, *Niger-Kordofanian* (of which the very widespread Bantu language family is a subgroup), we find three of the Western Pygmy groups, Mbenzele, Biaka and Bakola. With only one very minor exception (2% of the !Xun sample), none of these groups share any of their haplogroups with any of the Bushmen groups. In fact the great majority of the Western Pygmy sample (97%, 77% and 100%, respectively) can be found under haplogroup L1c, stemming from a completely different branch of the mtDNA tree than LOd or LOk. And in this case also, no other group is represented in this haplogroup by more than 5% of its sample.

Moving down the first column, we see, under the *Nilo-Saharan* family, the sole instance of Eastern Pygmies in the sample, the Mbuti. The majority of Mbuti (55%) are represented by yet another haplogroup, L2, not found at all among the western Pygmies and in only relatively small percentages among the !Xun/Khwe and !Xun (17% and 16% respectively), possibly reflecting an archaic link to a remote common ancestor. In other words, when we compare the three groups, the Bushmen, the Western Pygmies and the Eastern Pygmies, we find that each has its own distinctive haplogroup or groups that set it apart from the other two, while the great majority of the Pygmy groups cluster along completely different branches of the phylogenetic tree (L1 and L2, as opposed to L0) from all the Bushmen groups.

The only important exception to this pattern appears to be haplogroup L0a, which cuts across several groups of both hunter-gatherers and farmers. While this haplogroup could conceivably stem from a truly archaic ancestor, it is among those haplogroups whose distribution seems, in the view of the authors, largely due to relatively recent gene flow (p. 2191). Given what we know about African history, most of the gene flow in such cases can be attributed to the relatively recent (over the last few thousand years) movements of large and aggressive farming populations across vast regions of the continent known as the "Bantu expansion", and is not likely to reflect direct, face-to-face associations among the much smaller and more reclusive hunter-gatherer bands.

More recently, Tishkoff and her collaborators completed a monumental study of 121 African and African American populations, by far the most extensive and ambitious project of its kind (Tishkoff et al 2009). This time, Tishkoff concentrated on nuclear microsatellite and insertion/deletion sites, a much richer, but also more complex, set of genetic markers than the mitochondrial and Y chromosome haplotypes that have dominated earlier studies (*The Genetic Structure and History of Africans and African Americans*).

Figure 1 from this paper is a neighbor-joining phylogenetic tree, including all populations studied. I've reproduced the lowest, deepest, segment of this tree below:

See Figure 2.2

Once again, the Bushmen groups, labeled in this case *San* and *!XunKxoe*, occupy the lowest, thus deepest, branches of the tree, with the Pygmy groups just above them — though, as before, stemming from a different branch. Here again, the Eastern Pygmies, represented by the Mbuti, occupy a branch of their own, with the Western Pygmies stemming from one sub-branch, and literally the rest of the world stemming from the other.

We haven't yet seen any results representing purely male lineages, so let's take a look at a phylogenetic tree based on a comprehensive re-evaluation of the Y chromosome, published (in 2002) as Figure 1 in *A Nomenclature System for the Tree of Human Y-Chromosomal Binary Haplogroups*, by the "Y Chromosome Consortium" (2002):

See Figure 2.3

While group names are not included in this diagram, an accompanying table reveals that the deepest branches are occupied almost exclusively by either Bushmen or Pygmies, with Bushmen classified under either A or B (see large letters on the left) and almost all Pygmies (Aka and Mbuti) under B. With the exception of one Zulu individual, none of the other groups included in the study belongs to A or B. All non-African populations occupy only the lower branches, C through R. From the perspective of this particular survey of male lineages, therefore, we find a picture remarkably similar to what we've already seen from the mtDNA (i.e., female) and autosomal trees, with Bushmen represented at the root of the tree (A), and Pygmy groups occupying the next deepest clade (B).[1]

The results of several Y Chromosome studies are summarized as follows in *Wikipedia* (http://en.wikipedia.org/wiki/Khoisan#cite_ref-13):

> In the 1990s, genomic studies of different peoples around the world found that the Y chromosome of Khoisan men (using samples drawn from several San tribes) share certain patterns of polymorphisms that are distinct from the genomes of all other populations. As the Y chromosome is highly conserved from generation to generation, this type of DNA testing is used by geneticists to determine when different subgroups separated from one another and hence their last common ancestry. The authors of these studies suggested that the Khoisan may have been one of the first populations to differentiate from the most recent common paternal ancestor of all extant humans, the so-called Y-chromosomal Adam by patrilineal descent, estimated to have lived 60,000 to 90,000 years ago. . .
>
> Various Y-chromosome studies [have] since confirmed that the Khoisan (or Khoe-San) carry some of the most divergent (oldest) Y-chromosome haplogroups. These haplogroups are specific subgroups of haplogroups A and B, the two earliest branches on the human Y-chromosome tree.

Additional information from the same Wikipedia article, drawn from both archaeological and linguistic evidence, also supports the hypothesis that the Kalahari Bushmen represent a lineage of great antiquity:

From the beginning of the Upper Paleolithic period, hunting and gathering cultures known as the *Sangoan* occupied southern Africa in areas where annual rainfall is less than a meter (1000 mm; 40 in), and today's San and Khoi people resemble the ancient Sangoan skeletal remains. These Late Stone Age people in parts of southern Africa were the ancestors of the Khoisan people who inhabited the Kalahari Desert. . .

The evidence of the Khoisan's original presence in South Africa in fact can be seen in the distribution of their languages today, which often show extreme differences in structure and vocabulary despite close proximity, demonstrating a long period of settlement and co-evolution of languages in the same region. In contrast, the languages of Bantu-origin peoples in the region such as the Zulu and Xhosa are all relatively very similar to one another.

Here is one more mitochondrial tree, from a recent (2008) paper, *The Dawn of Human Matrilineal Diversity*, by Doron Behar et al., a project sponsored by the Genographic Consortium of the National Geographic Society:

See Figure 2.4

The most obvious aspect of this tree is the emphasis on the striking division between the two deepest clades, L0 and L1, and the clear division between "Khoisan" and "Non-Khoisan" populations, with the Khoisan groups limited to the deepest branches of the tree, L0d and L0k (consistent with Tishkoff's mtDNA tree, as we've already seen). In this case, the term "Khoisan" can be regarded as equivalent to what we've been referring to as "Bushmen." (N.B.: LSA stands for "Late Stone Age".) From our perspective, the most interesting aspect of this report are the references to the deep antiquity of the Khoisan lineages, as summarized in the abstract:

> We paid particular attention to the Khoi and San (Khoisan) people of South Africa because they are considered to be a unique relic of hunter-gatherer lifestyle and to carry paternal and maternal lineages belonging to the deepest clades known among modern humans. Both the tree phylogeny and coalescence calculations suggest that Khoisan matrilineal ancestry diverged from the rest of the human mtDNA pool 90,000–150,000 years before present . . . (p. 1).

27

While not represented specifically on this diagram, African Pygmies occupy some of its deepest branches: LOa and L2 (eastern Pygmies) and L1c (western Pygmies).

To understand the full, and indeed rather staggering, significance of the population genetic evidence, let us pull back to consider all the evidence in context. We have three populations consisting of nomadic hunter-gatherers with the simplest of material cultures, no permanent residence, no iron or steel tools (until very recently), without domesticated animals, moving about on foot, and located in three distinct regions of the African continent, at least 1,000 miles from one another: the Pygmies of eastern central Africa, the Pygmies of western central Africa, and the Bushmen, in the Kalahari desert of southwestern Africa. Yet they have musical traditions that, for most of the musicologists who have studied them, are so close as to be almost indistinguishable. Since, as we have seen, the genetic evidence so strongly points to all three groups stemming from the oldest branches of the same ancient root, it seems likely that this very distinctive musical practice must date from the time when the ancestors of all three were part of the same population, a history that, according to the Genographic Consortium tree, may go back as far as 200,000 years into the past.

It is important to understand that what concerns us in this context is not the earliest humans nor even the earliest *homo sapiens*, but a very specific founding group, the Most Recent Common Ancestors (MRCA),[2] from which the ancestors of the Pygmies and Bushmen diverged. Were they the only "modern" humans alive in their day? Probably not, but the genetic evidence strongly suggests that they were the only such group whose lineage has survived to the present era. Did all other humans alive at that time resemble them, sharing the same culture, the same traditions, the same music? We have no way of knowing, because whatever traditions they might have practiced may have died out with their lineage. Because their descendants would not have survived until the present, then, aside from very fragmentary and possibly misleading archaeological evidence, we have no basis for drawing inferences about what they were like. What the evidence suggests is that only this one specific ancestral group, which might well have been a tiny band, can be regarded as the common ancestors, not only of the Pygmies and Bushmen, but of everyone now living on this planet.

----

1. Another Y Chromosome study from roughly the same date reveals a genetic association between Khoisan speakers and certain Ethiopian populations, which also show up, although in far smaller percentages, in some of the deepest branches of clade I (equivalent to A, above): Khoisan 41%; Ethiopians, no more than 14.6 %. (Semino et al., "Ethiopians and

Khoisan Share the Deepest Clades of the Human Y-Chromosome Phylogeny." *Am. J. Hum. Genet.* 70:265–268, 2002.)

2. Strictly speaking, the genetic research has produced two MRCAs, based on either the mtDNA evidence, for the female line, or the Y chromosome evidence, for the male. In each case one specific founding individual is inferred, rather than a general group or population — and current coalescence methodologies have dated "Mitochondrial Eve" and "Y Chromosome Adam" to two different eras. What I refer to in this text as MRCA is neither Eve nor Adam, but a founding *group*, whose existence is inferred from both the genetic *and* the cultural evidence. As I see it, the preponderance of evidence from both sources, taken together, strongly suggests the existence of a single ancestral population.

Chapter Three: The Cultural Connection

Once upon a time, it was not unusual for anthropologists to see all hunter-gatherers as "primitive peoples," still living in the "stone-age," whose lifestyles were assumed to be more or less identical to those of our paleolithic ancestors. The field has changed drastically since that time, and today's anthropologists know better than to express such "hopelessly naïve" and "reductive" opinions.

Nevertheless, "stone age hunters" are still with us as far as the popular media is concerned, as is evident from an article that appeared on the Worldwide Web in July, 2007, *Face to face with Stone Age Man: The Hadzabe tribe of Tanzania*. In this account, the authors describe "a four-day quest covering thousands of miles by light aircraft, Land Rover and, finally, on foot," to "reach back in time and meet our living human ancestors from countless millennia ago. . ." The Hadzabe (aka Hadza) are described as a "mysterious Stone Age tribe . . . whose way of life has scarcely changed since human evolution began."

> These nomadic hunter-gatherers live as all humans once lived: wandering the plains with the changing seasons, killing game for survival, constantly avoiding aggressive wild beasts, and, finally, dying as they were born, under the sun and the stars.

This is exactly the sort of thing that inevitably causes professorial eyes to roll and heads to wag sagaciously. The "myth" of the "stone-age hunter-gatherer" is always fair game for even the most politically incorrect of social scientists, what everyone in the field feels duty bound to "deconstruct." But why, exactly? Doesn't it seem reasonable to assume that the Hadza are in fact living in more or less the same manner as all humans were living, back at the evolutionary stage when we were all hunter-gatherers?

Political correctness considerations aside, the real problem with such thinking lies with two key words: "assume" and "stage." We can assume all sorts of things about the lifestyle of "early man," but such assumptions tend to be based only minimally on evidence, and maximally on something halfway between educated guessing and wishful thinking. It may certainly seem as though the Hadza are living in "the stone age," but what can we really know about the lifestyle of humans who existed tens of thousands of years ago — and what do we really mean when we talk about the "stone age," as though all of human history could be neatly divided into stages?

While significant advances in our understanding of prehistory have certainly been made by physical anthropologists and archaeologists, the fragmentary and often controversial "stone and bone" evidence can take us only so far. A frustrating gap yawns between such evidence — tangible, datable (sometimes), and unquestionably representative of some past situation, but also fragmentary and difficult to interpret — and the evidence gathered from living peoples through anthropological field work, which can be plentiful, rich in meaning, and somewhat easier to understand (through direct questioning of informants), but much more difficult to assess historically. Thus the skepticism of today's anthropologists is certainly justified in the face of the seemingly insurmountable difficulties inherent in any of the usual attempts to reconstruct our distant past.

While most anthropologists are willing to accept, or at least consider, the implications of genetic evidence retrievable from the DNA of contemporary populations, there has been great reluctance to consider the possibility of a cultural correlate, retrievable through the comparative study of contemporary indigenous peoples. It stands to reason that all sorts of changes must have taken place among all human lineages over the last 150,000 years, even the most isolated. And there is no lack of evidence for that.

If, for example, the ancestors of the Bushmen were the original inhabitants of southern Africa, their lifestyle would have been quite different in a great many respects from that of their Kalahari descendants, displaced to the desert by the relatively recent migrations of Bantu farming peoples over the last two to four thousands years, and thus forced to adapt to one of the most challenging environments on Earth.

And if the ancestors of today's Pygmy groups lived as "pristine" tropical forest hunter-gatherers during the Old Stone Age, their lifestyle would have been significantly different from that of their modern descendants, symbiotically tied to neighboring villagers, on whom they have long relied for farm produce, tobacco and metal tools. But an important question remains: did such groups alter their lifestyle and their value system entirely, or make only those changes absolutely necessary for survival?

The Hunter-Gatherer Paradigm

The perennial debate has centered on the question of whether, and to what extent, certain groups now dubbed "hunter-gatherers" or "foragers" can be regarded as in any way representative of ancestors from the distant past. The great majority of today's anthropologists would no doubt insist that all living peoples must be seen as fully modern and thus as fully evolved as "we" are.

What has too often been lost in the debate is the fact that there is, in any case, really no such thing as "hunter-gatherer" culture in general, but a great many different such cultures, with certain things in common and other things not in common, so in order to claim "hunter-gatherers" represent our earliest ancestors it is necessary to universalize them first, which means removing most reference to specifics and in effect "essentializing" them out of any real existence and into some idealized evolutionary "stage" — i.e., turning them into a myth; which has, of course, become a standard complaint among the many skeptics.

In this context the genetic research emerges as a welcome beacon of hard evidence and specificity in a sea of vague assumptions, generalizations, claims, counter-claims and denials – and the beacon is very clearly pointed in one direction. Not "hunter-gatherers" in general, but a very specific group of hunter-gatherers, with a remarkable "pedigree."

Over and over again, as we have seen, it is the African Pygmies and Bushmen who are singled out in the genetic literature as uniquely representative of the ancestral group from which all living humans descend. But what can this mean in cultural terms? Since they currently live in totally different environments, both natural and social, separated by vast distances, isn't it safe to assume that each population has long since adapted to its environment in completely different ways since their ancestors diverged, tens of thousands of years ago?

Foragers and Farmers

A recent genetic study by Etienne Patin et al. (2009) provides us with a useful clue by raising important cultural issues pertaining explicitly to the question of adaptation:

> The sequence of the divergence events underlying the current differentiation of Western Pygmy, Eastern Pygmy and agricultural groups remains unclear. All Pygmy groups share idiosyncratic cultural and phenotypic traits, but substantial linguistic and genetic differentiation between Pygmy groups is also observed. These observations call into question the postulated common origin of African "Pygmy" populations. Indeed, if Western and Eastern Pygmy groups share a more recent ancestry with their respective agricultural neighbors than with each other, then they may have acquired their shared specific traits by convergence rather than by shared ancestry. (Patin et al. 2009:5)

32

The language of each Pygmy group is derived from that of neighboring Bantu farmers, a pattern found over and over again among Pygmies throughout central Africa. Certain other cultural differences between the various Pygmy groups have also been noted. It has been suggested therefore, in the words of linguist Roger Blench (1999), that the whole notion of Pygmies as a distinct, culturally unified population could be an ethnographic "fiction," and that each Pygmy population may be more closely related, both genetically and culturally, to the farmers with whom it has become associated than to any other Pygmy group.

Indeed, significant cultural differences between Pygmy populations, due largely to their association with different farming villages, have been noted by Barry Hewlett, who concluded on that basis that the many "patterns of diversity" make it "difficult if not impossible to refer to an African 'Pygmy' culture" (Hewlett 1996:244).

Since Hewlett concentrated almost exclusively on the current state of Pygmy life, characterized by varying degrees of external influence, dependency, and change, with little or no attention paid to those aspects of their culture most likely to be survivals from a common past, the broader significance of such a finding is difficult to assess. Regardless, interpretations of this sort reflect a deep-seated reluctance on the part of many anthropologists to acknowledge that anything particularly meaningful might lie behind the so-called "myths" so often associated with Pygmy and Bushmen foragers.

In such a context, the conclusions of Patin and his associates take on a special importance. On the basis of their analysis of the genetic evidence, "Western and Eastern Pygmies share a recent common ancestry, indicating that their shared specific traits, such as hunting and gathering in rainforest ecosystems and short stature, were acquired by shared ancestry rather than by convergence" (Patin et al.:8). Specifically,

> we show that the ancestors of Pygmy hunter–gatherers and farming populations started to diverge ~60,000 years ago. This indicates that the transition to agriculture—occurring in Africa ~5,000 years ago— was not responsible for the separation of the ancestors of modern-day Pygmies and farmers. We also show that Western and Eastern Pygmy groups separated roughly 20,000 years ago from a common ancestral population. This finding suggests that the shared physical and cultural features of Pygmies were inherited from a common ancestor, rather than reflecting convergent adaptation to the rainforest (from the Author's Summary, Patin et al.:2 – my emphasis).

While the Patin group focused on cultural practices associated with subsistence, such as hunting, gathering, honey collecting, etc., their findings suggest that other cultural features might also be due to inheritance from the same common ancestor identified in this, and so many of the other, genetic studies. But which features, exactly? And what of the Bushmen, whose genes are apparently rooted in the same deep ancestry?

Music and Language

The possibility of a long lost linguistic connection between Pygmies and Bushmen has been proposed by genetic anthropologist Sarah Tishkoff, whose research suggested that "[t]he shared ancestry, identified here, of Khoesan-speaking populations with the Pygmies of central Africa suggests the possibility that Pygmies, who lost their indigenous language, may have originally spoken a Khoesan-related language . . ." (Tishkoff et al. 2009:1041)

If certain Pygmy groups had languages that could be related to Khoisan, the family of languages spoken by most Bushmen groups, or even if they only had the clicks so closely associated with Khoisan languages, then such a commonality would have to be taken very seriously, as it would strongly suggest a common origin stemming from the culture of a common ancestral group. While, on the basis of the genetic evidence, this same group could be considered ancestral to all living humans, the fact that African Pygmies and Bushmen have been isolated for so long that their genetic markers occupy the deepest branches of the human family tree suggests that this same isolation might have preserved aspects of the ancestral culture as well.

Realistically, however, though Tishkoff's reasoning is sound, the linguistic association is simply not there — and the fact that Pygmies and Bushmen currently speak totally different languages, from completely unrelated linguistic families, has contributed to the general tendency among anthropologists to treat these two populations as though they had no more in common culturally than any other hunter-gatherer groups anywhere in the world.

Partly for this reason, partly due to extreme skepticism regarding the possibility that any tradition could survive more or less intact over many thousands of years, the full impact of the genetic discoveries has yet to be felt among the great majority of today's cultural anthropologists. Without actually being able to return to the archaic past in a time machine, the skeptics insist, we have no way of knowing what the culture of our ancestors was like.

But we do have a time machine, remember? In the form of a language, of sorts — the very special musical language I've been referring to as Pygmy/Bushmen style, or P/B. We have already examined some of the implications P/B has for the study of our earliest musical traditions, but the same evidence can take us even farther, because it holds a vital clue – a remarkable piece of the puzzle of human history that is, in my view, both incontrovertible and decisive.

Just as the various phylogenetic trees represent the most compelling evidence for a deep biological connection between certain groups of Western Pygmies, Eastern Pygmies and Bushmen, the most compelling evidence for a comparably deep cultural connection can be found in their music — or, more precisely, the highly distinctive stylistic and structural qualities of what is clearly a shared musical language.

If, in fact, we are transported tens of thousands of years into the past by the distinctive, unmistakable sound of African Pygmy and Bushmen music, we can take its hand, so to speak, to be led inexorably from the aesthetic to the social, from musical style to cultural style, from the distinctive organization of sound to the equally distinctive social structure appropriate to the production of that sound.

A Musical Mirror

The distinguished French-Israeli musicologist, Simha Arom, began his career playing French Horn with the Kol Israel Symphony in Jerusalem. Bored with the routine of an orchestra musician, Arom eagerly accepted an invitation from the Israeli Ministry of Foreign Affairs to work with musicians from the Central African Republic, as part of a cultural exchange program.

I've already related the story of how, while in Central Africa, he heard some music that would change his life, the sound of a group of Pygmies singing in the street beneath his hotel window. From then on he was to work tirelessly, recording and analyzing both the music of the Aka Pygmies and that of other tribal groups in Africa with similarly intricate instrumental traditions involving the complex interweaving of independent parts.

On the surface, it might seem as though Arom were focusing exclusively on the purely musical aspects of Pygmy performances, the sort of thing that can be completely represented on the five lines of the musical staff, at the expense of the social and cultural contexts that motivate all the notes and make them meaningful.

On the contrary, Arom's unusually deep absorption in the music itself enabled him to more fully appreciate the manner in which the contrapuntal interweavings of Pygmy music were a reflection of their richly interwoven social life, and the deeply ingrained egalitarian values that grounded it. I want to dwell for a while on some of Arom's observations, which provide us with useful insights on the intimate relation between these two seemingly very different realms: Pygmy music and Pygmy culture:

> [Aka] music is collective and everyone participates; there is no apparent hierarchy in the distribution of parts; each person seems to enjoy complete liberty; the voices swell out in all directions; solo lines alternate in the same piece without any preset order, while overall the piece remains in strict precision! It is this which is perhaps the most striking thing about this music, if one had to sum it up in a few words: a simultaneous dialectic between rigor and freedom, between a musical framework and a margin within which individuals can maneuver. This moreover reflects perfectly the social organization of the Pygmies — if only mentioned in passing — and it does so perhaps not by chance [my emphases] (as quoted in Kisliuk 1998)
>
> The social activity of a Pygmy encampment has no apparent hierarchy. Each person appears to enjoy total liberty; however, life is rigorously organized according to implicit plans, imperceptible to the uninitiated observer. As we shall see, Pygmy music, in the image of all their social activities, presents very similar characteristics, that is to say, relative autonomy of each participant within implied but strict structures [my emphases]. (Musical Anthology of the Aka Pygmies)

I'll now expand on certain passages from the above which I find particularly telling. In each case we find terminology that can equally be applied to both music and culture.

• "The music is collective," i.e., it is an expression of a group consciousness, which also to be the case with Pygmy culture generally, where important decisions are made collectively.

• "Everyone participates" i.e., music making is an occasion for all present to join in. While certain rituals are limited to males or females only, there are no musical specialists. All participants are expected to add their voices to the musical fabric.

• "There is no apparent hierarchy in the distribution of parts." This is an extremely important aspect of P/B style that is often overlooked. Whereas

36

much Bantu music is based on solo-chorus interaction ("call and response") with the soloist choosing the song, setting the tempo, improvising, and generally playing a leadership role, solo-chorus antiphony among Pygmies is relatively rare (and probably the result of Bantu influence). Most Pygmy music is built around the interlocking or interweaving of essentially equal parts, and anyone can choose to sing any part at will, entering or dropping out as he or she pleases. While much Bantu singing is accompanied (and often dominated) by drumming, a highly specialized skill mastered by a relatively small number of specialists, Pygmy music is traditionally accompanied by an especially intricate type of polyrhythmic handclapping or stick beating, with everyone participating according to his or her degree of skill. Non-hierarchical organization, both vocal and percussive, is the aspect of Pygmy music most consistent with the egalitarian nature of Pygmy society generally.

• "Each person seems to enjoy complete liberty." In other words, there do not appear to be explicit rules that anyone has to follow when participating in any song. While there are certainly implicit rules, these are so ingrained from childhood that they don't have the psychological effect of rules, just as the rules of grammar are not felt as conscious restraints when we speak. Anyone may choose to join in or drop out of the singing at will. This atmosphere of complete individual autonomy is instilled in BaAka children from an early age.

• There is "a simultaneous dialectic between rigor and freedom, between a musical framework and a margin within which individuals can maneuver." While such a dialectic can be found in many types of music, P/B style music-making tends to be simultaneously more highly organized, in a more intricate manner, than just about any other traditional music anywhere in the world; yet is, almost paradoxically, far less regimented, with a remarkable degree of individual autonomy. Combining intricately coordinated group interaction and synchronization with a remarkably fluid social context, within which anyone can improvise his or her own part at will, at any time, Pygmy music does indeed appear to embody a social situation characterized on the one hand by "sharing and cooperation" and on the other by individual "autonomy."

Not only does the music mirror some of the most basic elements of the culture, but more significantly, as Arom's comments suggest, a musical practice of this degree of complexity and precision requires a degree of highly synchronized interpersonal coordination and musical skill that only a certain type of culture can provide.

Comparable results can be achieved in the Western classical tradition only through a significant period of preparation on the part of especially trained ensembles. Yet, according to Arom, his recordings "bear witness not only to the extraordinary variety of the musical patrimony common to all the Aka, but, also — and this is particularly notable — to the perfect knowledge of this patrimony by each of the members of the community." The intricate musical technique required of all participants "is the fruit of long apprenticeship. As soon as they are able to walk, the children take part in the life of the community and thus in one of its principal manifestations, music." (Musical Anthology of the Aka Pygmies).

Utopian Voices

Thanks to his enduringly popular book, *The Forest People*, Colin Turnbull is probably the best known of the many anthropologists who have studied Pygmy culture. While music was not the focus of his studies, his musical training (he was a skilled organist) enabled him to appreciate and, at times, write quite eloquently, on various aspects of Pygmy music, which, like Arom, he recorded extensively.

While Arom's observations are based on his study of western Pgymies, especially the Aka, Turnbull writes in very similar terms of the strong association between music and social structure among the Mbuti Pygmies of the eastern group. Turnbull has been accused of idealizing the Mbuti and their life in the forest, and indeed there are passages in The Forest People that suggest an almost Utopian view of Pygmy life:

> The Pygmies were more than curiosities to be filmed, and their music was more than a quaint sound to be put on records. They were a people who had found in the forest something that made their life more than just worth living, something that made it, with all its hardships and problems and tragedies, a wonderful thing full of joy and happiness and free of care. (p. 26)

His tendency to hear Mbuti music as an expression of the same worldview is clearly apparent when he waxes lyrically on

> the sound of the voices of the forest people as they sing a lusty chorus of praise to this wonderful world of theirs – a world that gives them everything they want. This cascade of sound echoes

among the giant trees until it seems to come at you from all sides in sheer beauty and truth and goodness, full of the joy of living (1961:13).

Regardless of what one might think of Turnbull's supposedly idealized view, for which he has often been criticized, passages such as this strongly suggest the existence of an intimately reciprocal relation between Mbuti music and culture. In the following passages from his lesser known companion volume, *Wayward Servants*, he writes of this relationship in more down-to-earth terms:

> An examination of Mbuti song form not only reveals areas of concern to the Mbuti, such as their food getting activities, life and death, but it also reveals the concern of the Mbuti for cooperative activity . . . The songs are most frequently in round or canon form, and the hunting songs, in order to heighten the need for the closest possible cooperation (the same need that is demanded by the hunt itself), are sometimes sung in hoquet (p. 256).
>
> It is certain that an acute analysis of Mbuti music would reveal much that parallels the structure of Mbuti society. The extraordinary level of polyphonic achievement is surely related to a highly developed individualism that would hardly tolerate the confines of unison. The Mbuti musical categories of berai and imaia, chorus and solo song, indicate a system of recognized relationships between the group and the individual, and the technique of hoquet, already mentioned, further mirrors social relationships . . . [as well as] social values (Colin Turnbull, Wayward Servants, p. 257, footnote 7).

A similarly intimate relation between musical structure and cultural value among the Bushman has been noted by ethnomusicologist Nicholas England:

> As they severally alternate the musical materials in what might be called an extended *Stimmtausch* [part crossing] technique, the singers bring into being a contrapuntal complex that constantly changes throughout the performance as the musical period . . . is repeated again and again until the performance is terminated. This interchanging of melodic phrases is a common method of music making in Bushmanland, and it is a principle that, to my mind, epitomizes the Bushman way in general: it *clearly reflects the Bushmen desire to remain independent (in this case, of the other voices) at the same*

time that he is contributing vitally to the community life (in this case, the musical complex) (England 1967:60 – my emphasis).

Many reports on Bushmen culture and values reflect a "Utopian" view remarkably similar to that of Turnbull. Witness this passage, from the *Cambridge Encyclopedia of Hunters and Gatherers*:

> Ju/'hoan political ethos abhorred wealth and status differences. No one should stand out from the rest of the group. If someone returned from a successful hunt showing excessive pride, he was put firmly in place, even if the kill was large. Emphasis on sharing and lack of status roles produced a high degree of egalitarianism. . . . Anger and resentment were low as each person's opinion was respected. Conflicts could be terminated by a disputant leaving to join another group (p. 208).

Since, as we've seen, Bushmen and Pygmies vocalize in essentially the same manner, it's not difficult to conclude that their "Utopian" cultures are also mirrored by a no less "Utopian" style of music making. Or, in more realistic terms, the Utopian aspects of their musical language would seem to mirror an equally Utopian ideal at the heart of their value system – an ideal more easily achieved, no doubt, in music than the realities of day to day life. (I'll be having more to say about Utopia, and its discontents, in an upcoming chapter.)

Ancestral Voices

It's difficult to imagine how the conditions variously described above could hold among so many groups of contemporary Pygmies and Bushmen unless both their musical style and the cultural characteristics we've been considering had not also been present in the culture of their (and our) mutual ancestors. We are speaking, therefore, not only of a very deep musical heritage but of the opening of a door through which music can lead us, step by step, to certain insights regarding an equally deep cultural heritage. What are these steps? Let's review:

First, as far as the musical evidence in itself is concerned, P/B is a practice traceable all the way back to a "common root," i.e., the music of the common ancestors of the Pygmies and Bushmen, as identified by the genetic evidence.

Second, since the great bulk of the genetic evidence points to the lineages of certain Pygmy and Bushmen groups as diverging during a time frame well within the Old Stone Age, it seems reasonable to conclude that P/B is at least that old, very possibly much older.

Third, as attested by the observations of experienced musician/ethnographers, such as Simha Arom, Colin Turnbull, Nicholas England, etc. (see above), the musical organization of P/B appears to reflect certain aspects of Pygmy and Bushmen social structure in such a manner as to take us directly from the realm of music to that of culture.

There are two aspects to this association: 1. the organization of P/B in such a manner that it reflects the organization of Pygmy and Bushmen societies generally; and 2. the organization of Pygmy and Bushmen societies in such a manner as to make some of the most remarkable and distinctive characteristics of P/B possible.

In the light of all the evidence presented so far, it seems logical to conclude that the very distinctive mode of musical behavior we've been considering would have embodied the ancestral social structure in precisely the same manner as it embodies the social structure of contemporary Pygmies and Bushmen. And if this is indeed the case, we cannot ignore the possibility that other traditions also held in common by representatives of all three populations (Eastern Pygmies, Western Pygmies and Bushmen) could also be grounded in traditions stemming from the group ancestral to all. Remarkably, the musical evidence has led us to a point where we can begin to consider the much broader question of culture in general, the question that has eluded so many for so long: what were our ancestors like?

Sidebar 2: Deconstructing the Postmodern Condition

From Wikipedia
(http://en.wikipedia.org/wiki/JeanFran%C3%A7ois_Lyotard):

> [I]n *La Condition postmoderne: Rapport sur le savoir (The Postmodern Condition: A Report on Knowledge)* (1979), [Lyotard] proposes what he calls an extreme simplification of the "postmodern" as an 'incredulity towards meta-narratives'. These meta-narratives - sometimes 'grand narratives' - are grand, large-scale theories and philosophies of the world, such as the progress of history, the knowability of everything by science, and the possibility of absolute freedom. Lyotard argues that we have ceased to believe that narratives of this kind are adequate to represent and contain us all. We have become alert to difference, diversity, the incompatibility of our aspirations, beliefs and desires, and for that reason postmodernity is characterised by an abundance of micronarratives.

Christopher Norris on postmodernism and deconstruction:

> Postmodernism amounts to a generalized scepticism (or cynicism) about the whole idea of disinterested, truth-seeking enquiry; whereas deconstruction is a critical probing and analysis of the presuppositions behind it. ("Two Cheers for Cultural Studies," in *Interrogating Cultural Studies:Theory, Politics and Practice*, 2003, p. 90).

So what does it mean when these two formidable idea-systems collide? What can it mean to deconstruct post-modernism? Is such a thing even possible?

As I see it, Lyotard's original conception makes considerable sense. In the 1970's we had reached a point where too many were struggling to produce grand unifying schemes that could account for everything while history was moving in multiple directions at once and such accounts seemed increasingly academic and pointless. Unfortunately, however, what began as a healthy and long overdue "incredulity towards meta-narratives" soon became what can only be described as a ruthlessly puritanical inquisition, and a very nasty one at that.

Somehow, Derrida's extremely sophisticated, far more radical, but at the same time balanced, cautious and circumspect, notion of "deconstruction" became hopelessly confused with an equally misleading and rigid notion of postmodernism, to the point that they became, as far as the academic world was concerned, practically interchangeable synonyms for a relentless process of demystification, i.e., debunking, that has literally taken over and is now smothering the social sciences, from archaeology to anthropology and yes, even ethnomusicology, where it is practically forbidden to generalize about anything but the most trivial aspects of culture, social structure and history — and comparative research beyond any but the most narrowly conceived boundaries has become almost unthinkable.

What it means to deconstruct such an unfortunate "condition" is, first of all, to remind ourselves that deconstruction itself is not by any means the same as demystification or debunking. So, second of all, we need to distinguish the extremely complex, intricate, and ultimately impossible (Derrida's word, not mine) task of teasing out the presuppositions that have enabled any particular construct to construct itself from the all too easy temptation to simply dismiss such a construct as "essentialist," "reductive," "reified," etc. It may well be all of these things. But it is foolhardy to assume we can purge such problematic elements from any meaningful thought process, *even our own*.

What is necessary, as I see it, is to put all these things into perspective, to try to understand what sort of demand they are attempting to satisfy, and finally to put *our own* biases into perspective as well, so we can properly appreciate what can be *accomplished* by even the most problematically constructed constructs, even as we struggle to deconstruct them, i.e., understand the intellectual infrastructures that precipitated their construction in the first place, along with the traditions that have caused them to be perpetuated even after the original conditions no longer exist.

Chapter Four: The Baseline

Based on what we have learned in the last three chapters, we are in a position to move beyond the realms of music or genetics into completely new territory. Drawing on evidence gleaned from ethnographic studies of contemporary Pygmy and Bushmen groups, I will propose a hypothetical model of the cultural landscape, both material and non-material, of MRCA, our most recent common ancestors, the population from which, according to the most widely accepted interpretation of the genetic evidence, everyone now living is descended. Our model can then serve as a baseline for studying the history of human culture generally. I will refer to this population as the Hypothetical Baseline Population, or HBP. The culture of HBP will be referred to as the Hypothetical Baseline Culture, or HBC.

Our consideration of the genetic, musical and cultural evidence suggests a straightforward, though necessarily provisional, method for reconstructing HBC: *Any distinctive tradition, in the form of a value system, belief system, performance practice, behavior pattern, artifact or attribute, not likely to be the result of outside influence, found among at least three different groups representing each of the three populations with the deepest genetic clades, i.e., Eastern Pygmies, Western Pygmies and Bushmen (EP, WP, Bu), may be regarded as a potential survival from an older tradition traceable to the historical "moment" of earliest divergence, and thus ascribable to HBC.*

This strategy of "triangulation" is based on the unlikelihood of essentially the same tradition developing independently in all three regions due to either convergent evolution, given such contrastive environments; or mutual influence, given the considerable evidence, archaeological, historical and genetic, that each of the three populations has been isolated from the others for many thousands of years.[1]

Before we continue, it is important to understand that the Pygmies and Bushmen of today may, on the whole, be no more similar to the common ancestors than any other indigenous groups, hunter-gatherers or otherwise. They are most certainly not "stone age" relics or "living fossils." What makes them special is not the fact that they more closely resemble our ancestors than anyone else, which is certainly debatable, but that there are clues to the nature of the ancestral culture that only they possess. For this reason, what I have been focusing on is not the Pygmy and Bushmen groups themselves, as we know them today, but *only* those traditions held in common among representatives of all three exemplary populations.

Core Values

Since we have already discussed, in some detail, the manner in which the musical organization of P/B reflects the value system of all three populations, a consideration of core values generally would seem the most appropriate place to begin constructing our baseline. An understanding of core values is especially important in the light of significant differences among various groups of Pygmies and Bushmen, largely based on their responses to relatively recent external pressures, to the point that certain "revisionists" have dismissed all attempts to define "Pygmy culture" or "Bushmen culture" as dangerous essentializations.

A sensible corrective to this shortsighted view has been offered by anthropologist Cornelia M. I. van der Sluys, who decries the influence of those who

> focus almost exclusively on ecological-economic issues and pay little attention to the forces inside these cultures that tend to perpetuate their reproduction from generation to generation. . . An instance demonstrating that long-time contacts with "outsiders" do not necessarily imply a profound change in a hunter-gatherer culture's *core premises and embedded values* can be found in Turnbull's (1965) description of the Mbutis, hunter-gatherers in Zaire. Despite relationships with their agriculturalist Bantu neighbors, the Mbutis safeguard the reproduction of *the core of their own culture* by adopting certain Bantu customs and taking part in Bantu rituals. Similar strategies are also used by other hunter-gatherers . . ." ("Gifts from Immortal Ancestors," in *Hunters and Gatherers in the Modern World*, ed. Biesele and Hitchcock, 2000, p. 427-428 — my emphases).

When we move from a consideration of such strategies of compromise to "the forces inside these cultures that tend to perpetuate their reproduction from generation to generation," based on "core premises and embedded values," we find that it is indeed possible to speak not only of "Pygmy culture" and "Bushman culture," but of a single set of *core values* held in common by almost all Pygmy and Bushmen groups. While, as van der Sluys implies, many other hunter-gatherer societies worldwide share many of the same values, I'll be limiting myself for now to evidence drawn from the study of WP, EP and Bu only.

Considerable evidence for shared core values among representatives of all three populations can be found in the ethnographic literature. Aka

Pygmies are described as having "an 'egalitarian' sensibility, coupled with individual autonomy"; as being "fiercely egalitarian and independent," with "no chief in the sense of a person commanding ultimate authority"; valuing "sharing, cooperation, and autonomy" and "intergenerational equality." "Aka infancy . . . lacks negation and violence"; "male-female relations are extremely egalitarian by cross-cultural standards"; "physical violence in general is infrequent"; "the Aka are probably as egalitarian as human societies get." (Hewlett 1991:Chapter Two).

In *The Cambridge Encyclopedia of Hunters and Gatherers* we find a very similar description of Bushmen values:

> Ju/'hoan political ethos abhorred wealth and status differences. No one should stand out from the rest of the group. If someone returned from a successful hunt showing excessive pride, he was put firmly in place, even if the kill was large. Emphasis on sharing and lack of status roles produced a high degree of egalitarianism. . . . Anger and resentment were low as each person's opinion was respected. Conflicts could be terminated by a disputant leaving to join another group. (Biesele and Royal-/O/OO 1999:208)

Essentially the same values are attributed to the Mbuti Pygmies in Turnbull's *The Forest People* (1961:124). For example,

> Cooperation is the key to Pygmy society; you can expect it and you can demand it and you have to give it. . . As soon as the hunters return they deposit meat on the ground and the camp gathers to make sure the division is fair. Nobody acknowledges that it is but in the end everyone is satisfied.

And from his more complete study, *Wayward Servants*:

> All major [economic] decisions are taken by common consent, as in other realms of Mbuti life. Men and women have equal say . . . Any tendency toward charismatic leadership is countered by ridicule . . . (Turnbull 1965:179-180). A woman is in no way the social inferior of a man, and there is little absolute division of labor along sex lines (Turnbull 1965:270).

Much has been made of instances of violence, sexism, and self interested behavior among individual Pygmies and Bushmen (see for example, Lee 1984:192; Liazos 2008; Turnbull 1965:189-217) that might seem to contradict

46

the "Utopian" picture painted by anthropologists such as Colin Turnbull, leading to the dismissal of all such reports as promulgating an idealized "myth" of egalitarian, non-competitive and non-violent "Noble Savages."

However, as suggested in the more balanced view of Bushmen violence presented by Patricia Draper (1978), the fact that everyone doesn't always conform to a particular value system does not mean that the value system isn't a pervasive and important force for the society as a whole, where all behavior is judged, if not necessarily controlled, according to long established norms.

In sum, if an ancestral ethos can be inferred from both the values and the behavior of EP, WP and Bu, then we might want to characterize HBC as a culture similarly torn between a Utopian ideal and an all-too-human reality determined to test its limits. What has, nevertheless, been preserved from generation to generation, the many exceptions notwithstanding, is the cultural ideal, the "core values" through which society as a whole constructs its identity. And if there are any doubts regarding the efficacy of such a heritage, we may look to the many violent and destructive practices reported among so many other indigenous peoples, hunter-gatherers included, yet rarely if ever found among Pygmies or Bushmen.

What we do *not* see, and would not therefore expect to find in HBC, are evidences of: cannibalism, head-hunting, endemic warfare, exploitation of women or children, female mutilation, prostitution, slavery, blood-feuds, raiding. While witchcraft and sorcery have been reported, such beliefs appear to have originated with neighboring farming peoples. (see Turnbull 1965, p. 59 et seq.)

Shamanism ???

At the core of a society's value system is its system of beliefs and rituals, sometimes subsumed under the rubric "religion," which for most indigenous peoples has generally been characterized as "animistic," a handy catch-all for a wide variety of beliefs and practices. A bit more specific is the notion of "shamanism," though this too has been the source of great confusion. The term "shaman" originated in Siberia, and there has been ongoing controversy regarding the appropriateness of that term when similar practices from other regions are being discussed. Nevertheless, most researchers agree that very similar practices are found among indigenous peoples in many parts of the world. According to Mathias Guenther,

> While in a strict ethnographic sense the shaman's cultural province is Siberia, the term and category are used in a generic sense by most writers. . . Shamans everywhere enter altered states of consciousness,

in order to gain spiritual inspiration or divinatory guidance, or to effect their mystical cures. . . . A classic example is the Kalahari Ju/'hoansi Bushmen . . . (*The Cambridge Encyclopedia of Hunters and Gatherers*, p. 427).

Rituals of a shamanistic nature have indeed been frequently reported for various Bushmen groups where, according to some reports, more than half the males, and also some females, are "shamans." According to Megan Biesele and her Ju/'hoansi Bushmen collaborator, Kxao Royal-/O/OO,

> Ju healers have access to supernatural powers such as *n/om*, magical energy/potency with which Ju/'hoansi can counter malevolent ghosts, heal the sick, and resolve conflicts. When one sings special songs, Ju say, *n/om* comes out. Ju/'hoan ceremonies feature intense, exhilarating, all-night healing dances, where the power of *n/om* heals, protects and gives well being (*The Cambridge Encyclopedia of Hunters and Gatherers*, p. 208).

Specialized healers known as *Nganga* are reported among the BaAka, though it's not clear to what extent their activities could be characterized as "shamanistic" in the strictest sense — see Barry Hewlett, *Aka Pygmies of the Western Congo Basin*. In *Seize the Dance*, Kisliuk describes a ritual dance called Njengi, where the dancer, who becomes possessed by the Njengi spirit, is completely covered by a mask made of leaves. The mask itself is strictly "off limits to women," who are expected to believe the leaves are inhabited by a spirit.

Spirit possession of a similar sort is an essential aspect of the Mbuti *Molimo* ceremony, as described by Turnbull in *The Forest People* (see especially Chapter Four). The molimo is understood to be both a musical instrument and an animal and, again, the women are expected to believe that it is in fact a spirit-animal. As with the Njengi mask of the BaAka, they are forbidden to see the instrument itself.

Though Turnbull never refers specifically to shamans, shamanism or even healers among the Mbuti, there are instances where individuals fall into trance, which, according to Michelle Kisliuk, is not unusual among Pygmy groups generally (personal communication).Mauro Campagnoli refers to spirits which dance along with the Baka Pygmies and dances which are healing rituals led by Baka healers. Again it's hard to say whether these healers are in fact bona fide "shamans," though they would seem to perform at least some of the same functions. According to Barry Hewlett, "all the [Pygmy] forager groups have traditional healers, and several of them (e.g., the Aka, Baka, and Mbuti) recognize the supernatural abilities of great hunters, who can communicate with the supernatural world, make themselves invisible, and take the forms of various animals" (From the *Encyclopedia of World Cultures: Tropical Forest Foragers*).

One of the most common techniques in the repertoire of shamans, healers, "medicine men," etc. is the method of curing the sick by literally *sucking* the sickness out of their bodies. Often it emerges in the form of a small stone, bone or dart. Among the Aka Pygmies,

> witches or sorcerers (the Aka make no distinction) practice secretly and are unknown to the general population, although ngangas (healers) are highly suspect. The witches send poison darts (ndoki) into the body of their victim, and the person eventually dies from the poison unless the nganga can extract the dart, usually by sucking it out (Hewlett 1991).

Similar cures performed by Bushmen healers have been described by Richard Katz and Elizabeth Marshall (as quoted in the Wikipedia article, *Bushmen Healing and Rock Art*
(http://en.wikipedia.org/wiki/Bushmen_healing_and_rock_art):

> Katz . . . states that the people can only heal when they learn to control their boiling n/um, or energy. The healer learns to "pull out sickness" from the people. When they do this, they use !kia, or enhanced consciousness, to see the things they need to pull out, like "the death things God has put into the people", and they get them out.
>
> According to Elizabeth Marshall, to cure people and get the evil out of them the medicine man, or healer, will begin by washing his hands in the fire. He then will place one hand on the person's chest, and one on their back, and will "suck" the evil from them. The medicine man often shudders and groans as he does this, and then will suddenly "shriek the evil into the air."

Though I haven't been able to find any reference to the "sucking cure" among Mbuti healers, the importance of this method among both the Aka Pygmies and Ju/'hoansi Bushmen seems consistent with a tradition that might indeed date all the way back to HBC. It's also possible that sucking could have been introduced relatively recently by neighboring Bantu healers, though the centrality among the Ju/'hoansi of both the method and the belief system associated with it makes such a hypothesis unlikely.

The fact that we find instances of supernatural healing, trance, and spirit possession among representatives of EP, WP and Bu, strongly suggests that practices very close to shamanism, at least in certain respects, are likely to have been part of HBC. The evidence also suggests that the ancestors of the Bushmen subsequently went farther in this direction than the ancestors of the Pygmies, since rituals of a shamanistic nature would appear to play a much greater role among the former than the latter.

Possession, trance and healing appear to be treated much more casually and informally among Pygmies than among Bushmen. The roots of shamanism are of course a very complex and difficult topic. All I'll say at present is that it looks like some form of shamanism or proto-shamanism was part of HBC, but to what extent or what this might mean is hard to say.

Kinship

Kinship has traditionally been one of the major preoccupations of anthropology, and for good reason, as it reflects some of the most fundamental aspects of human relationship in a manner that appears, at least on the surface, to be systematic, consistent and logical, thus particularly amenable to scientific study. Unfortunately, the promise that kinship in itself might tell us something important about cultural history has been largely unfulfilled.

According to Barry Hewlett (1996), all four Pygmy groups he studied (two each, from EP and WP) "have Hawaiian kin terms, patrilineal descent and patrilocal post-marital residence," as do the farmers with whom they have long been associated. "However, beyond the surface patterns the differences between foragers and farmers are striking," Pygmy kinship terminologies being more classificatory and generalized, and residence patterns more flexible.

Among the Mbuti, as described by Colin Turnbull,

> kinship does not have the same importance as a focal point of social control as it may in other African societies. . . Together with this lack of emphasis on the biological aspects of kinship, and the accompanying generational system of terminology goes a lack of formal restrictions on behavior between different kin categories, and a marked unwillingness to clearly define kin relationships between individuals (Turnbull 1965:109, 112).

Compare with Mathias Guenther's description of Bushmen kinship practices:

> A number of social institutions are flexible sui generis, a result of . . . the 'organizational lability' of society. Neo-locality and highly classificatory (indeed universalistic) kinship systems are both social patterns that obscure genealogical detail . . . Absence of status differentiation and vaguely defined leadership and ritual specialization, unstable, tenuous marriages in early to mid-adulthood, and loose and informal child-rearing practices . . . allow for a wide margin of individual action as none is an institution or practice based on cut-and-dried jural rules but, instead, all are tentative and open-ended. (in Kent 1996:78)

Or this, from a leading authority on Bushmen culture, Alan Barnard:

> In studying Khoisan kinship, I have found that the rigid application of traditional models drawn from other parts of the world or from anthropological, rather than indigenous, discourse, obscures interesting features. An approach which takes into account similar features across society boundaries can reveal *underlying structures which add much more to our understanding of kinship than the surface structures which are the subject of conventional methods of formal analysis* (*Hunters and Herders of Southern Africa*, p. 6 — my emphasis).

Thus, while it's possible to categorize Pygmies and Bushmen within formally defined, traditional kinship models that are, in fact, different from one another (i.e., "Hawaiian" among the Pygmies and "Eskimo" among Bushmen), the "underlying structures" they have in common may be of greater significance. For our purposes, the differences in formal kinship terminology, naming and marriage customs, etc. between Pygmy and Bushmen groups, largely due to external influences, can be put aside in favor of the underlying commonalities, because it is what they all have in common that is most likely to stem from HBC. And what they all appear to have in common is very little system at all.

Moving from the world of values, beliefs and kinship to more material concerns, we find certain very interesting artifacts and practices, apparently held in common by all three populations, which are well worth examining in some detail.

Bows and Arrows

Within the three populations under consideration, EP (Eastern Pygmies), WP (Western Pygmies) and Bu (Bushmen), some groups hunt primarily with poison-tipped arrows and others with nets. Interestingly, we find net hunters among representatives of both EP (Mbuti) and WP (Aka), while those that hunt primarily with bows and arrows can also be found in both tropical forest regions (Hewlett 1996). No Bushmen group, to my knowledge, hunts with nets. Poison arrows, however, are in fact used for hunting by groups from all three populations, even when they are not the principal method. (While the Aka and Mbuti use nets as their primary hunting tool, they also use poison arrows for certain types of prey.)

Therefore, regardless of the net evidence, the presence of bows and arrows equipped with poison in all three major populations completes our triangulation and thus makes hunting with poison-tipped arrows a strong candidate for inclusion in HBC.[2]

However, bows and arrows are commonly found among many of the farming groups that have had contact with either Pygmies or Bushmen for a very long time. And there have been reports of the use of poisoned arrows among such groups. Thus, as far as bows, arrows and poison are concerned, we have an interesting test case, in which the criteria of triangulation have been met, but which might nevertheless be falsified through additional research into the history of such weaponry.

If convincing evidence can be found that non-foragers learned to use poison arrows from Pygmy and/or Bushmen groups, that would point to the use of such weapons by HBP and we could at least provisionally accept this technology as a part of HBC. If no such evidence can be found, or if it is determined that the Pygmies and Bushmen learned it from more "advanced" farmers, then either it was never a part of HBC or its status must remain indeterminate.[3]

Beehive Huts

A characteristic type of dwelling, known as a "beehive" hut, has been commonly found among representative groups from all three Pygmy and Bushmen populations. As is apparent from photographs, the similarities are striking.

See Figures 4.1, 4.2, 4.3

The similarities in the manner in which these huts are constructed are also quite striking. Here, for example, is a description of how a Bushmen hut is made (from *Patterns of settlement and subsistence in southwestern Angola*, by Alvin W. Urquhart (1963?), quoting Vedder):

> The poverty of the Bushman existence is very clearly indicated by their huts. *It is the women's task to erect them.* At a distance of from six to eight feet apart, two strong poles are planted in the ground in such a way that the points meet at the height of about five feet. The tops are tied together with the soft bark of a tree. This archway forms the door to the Bushman hut and it is never closed. *Further poles are now planted in an irregular semicircle and joined at the top to form a sort of domed roof. This framework is covered with branches with leaves on and dry grass*, and the Bushman hut is complete (p. 17 — my emphasis).

Next the Baka (from *The Baka Pygmies of Cameroon* — http://www.articlesbase.com/online-education-articles/the-baka-pygmies-of-cameroon-67733.html):

> They live in huts they call mongulu which are one-family houses *made of branches and leaves* and *nearly always built by the women*. After a frame of very flexible, thin branches is prepared, *recently-gathered leaves are fit in the structure*. After the work is complete, *other vegetable materials are sometimes added* to the dome in order to make the structure more compact and *waterproof*. (My emphasis)

Finally, the Mbuti (from *The Forest People*):

> Now she squatted down making her own home, driving the saplings into the ground with deep thrusts, each time in exactly the same place, so that they went deeper and deeper. When she had completed a circle she stood up and deftly bent the fito over her head, twisting them together and *twining smaller saplings across, forming a lattice framework*. Then she took the *leaves* we had collected and slit the stalks toward the end, like clothespins, hooking two or three of them together. When she had enough she started hanging them on the framework like tiles, overlapping each other and *forming a waterproof covering* (pp 64-65 — my emphasis).

The Mbuti are EP, and the Baka are WP, thus both photos and written descriptions represent all three groups, EP, WP and Bu. Since there are so many striking similarities in the way these huts look, the way they are constructed, and also the cultural context of their construction, i.e., in almost all cases constructed as temporary shelters, in hunting camps, and by women, it would seem very difficult to argue that they could have been independently developed. And since the three groups appear to have lived in completely different regions of Africa, with no possible means of contact, and no evidence of contact (remember that their genetic profiles are completely different), the only remaining explanation would be on the basis of shared ancestry, stemming from the use of similar huts by HBP.

Unlike poison arrows, which are found among at least some Bantu groups, this particular hut design is not found among Bantus. And for good reason, since Bantu tribes live in sedentary settlements and thus require more permanent dwellings. It is thus highly unlikely that this type of hut design was the result of Bantu influence. Independent invention is a particularly weak alternative in this case since most instances of independent invention are driven by environmental adaptation, and Pygmies and Bushmen live in two totally different environments, tropical forest and desert.

Finally, I'm going to invoke Occam's Razor, a well known though little understood scientific principle that goes like this: *"pluralitas non est ponenda sine necessitate* ("plurality should not be posited without necessity")." In other words, if there is no necessary reason to do so, it is better not to assume that any particular phenomenon (such as the striking similarities among EP, WP and Bu huts) has a plurality of causes (i.e., multiple independent inventions), when a simpler explanation (shared heritage) fits the evidence equally well. In this case, as should be clear, the simpler explanation fits the evidence far better than independent invention, or indeed any other explanation I can think of.

Putting together all of the above, on the basis of evidence gleaned via triangulation, I would say that it is possible to make an especially convincing case that the construction of this type of hut is a tradition inherited from HBC.

Scarification, Body Painting

The inscription of symbols on the body, in the form of scarification, painting or tattooing, is a practice found among indigenous peoples in just about every corner of the world. And, as one might expect, such practices are an important aspect of both Pygmy and Bushmen culture:

> The principal element in the [first kill] rite is the scarification of the boy. The purpose of this is to put into the boy's body, through

little cuts in his skin, substances that, in !Kung belief, will make him a successful hunter. The scarifications remain visible on the skin for a lifetime; they show that the man has been "cut with meat". (Lorna Marshall, *Nyae Nyae !Kung Beliefs and Rites* 1999: 154).

The evening before I left, before the singing started, three of the great hunters took me off into the forest. They said they wanted to be sure that I would come back again, so they thought they would make me "of the forest." There was Njoho, the killer of elephants; his close friend and distant relative, Kolongo; and Moke, an elderly Pygmy who never raised his voice, and to whom everyone listened with respect. Kolongo held my head and Njobo casually took a rusty arrow blade and cut tiny but deep vertical flits in the center of my forehead and above each eye. He then gauged out a little flesh from each slit and asked Kolongo for the medicine to put in. . . [He rubbed the black ash-paste hard into the cuts until it filled them and congealed the blood that still flowed. And there it is today, ash made from the plants of the forest, a part of the forest that is a part of the flesh, carried by every self-respecting Pygmy male. And as long as it is with me it will always call me back (Colin Turnbull, *The Forest People*).

Pygmy and Bushmen bodies are also painted for various reasons, including, of course, magic:

[*Anjo*] is a paste made from the heart, brain and eyes, sometimes from other parts as well, of some highly prized game. . . The paste is put on the body, most often the forehead, of the hunter and of members of his family (Turnbull, *Wayward Servants*, p. 155).

As at birth, there is a certain amount of decoration of the body with what might be considered as forest charms, and toward the end of the [Elima] festival the girls paint each other with a white forest clay (ibid., p. 135).

Pigment is still used for body painting among the few remaining Bushmen of the Kalahari in the context of rites of passage and other ceremonies central to the well being of the group (Berghaus 2004:115).

Language

Almost all Pygmy groups speak Bantu languages derived from those of neighboring farming societies, and most Bushmen speak click languages deriving from a completely different family, Khoisan. They all have something in common, however, because both Bantu and Khoisan languages are tonal; i.e., they make use of pitch to distinguish lexical or grammatical meaning. In fact, almost all languages to be found in SubSaharan Africa are tone languages. Given the Out of Africa model, and assuming that all languages have a common root, as implied by the model, then the almost complete domination of tone language in Africa strongly suggests that the language of the ancestral group may also have been tonal. I'll be returning to this issue later on, when discussing the Out of Africa migration.

Honey

Almost all hunter-gatherers have a passion for honey, wherever it's available, and EP, WP and Bu are no exception. It might seem easy to challenge the distinctiveness of this trait, since honey is prized as a treat just about everywhere. However, the hives of wild bees are not easily accessible in either the tropical forest or the desert, where honey-gathering is both a challenge and an art, as can be inferred from the following description of honey gathering among the Efe Pygmies of the Ituri Forest:

> Honey gathering, like hunting, is man's work. Karambodu's honey tree is an old ndau (Irvingia gabonensis), and the hive is located in a rotten branch some twenty meters (sixty feet) from the ground. A colony of *Apis mellifera* bees lives in this tree, which is good because hives of stinging bees always seem to contain more honey than the stingless variety (*Meliponula bocandei*). Gathering honey is a dangerous pursuit, but the rewards are potentially enormous. Kebe hands his twelve-year-old son Ndikpa an apopau, a small machete, with which to open the hive. He helps Ndikpa up to a notch on an adjacent tree that he will climb to reach the lowest branches of the tall ndau. As Ndikpa maneuvers across to the hive, smoke from the tilipi parcel of hot embers and green vegetation swirls around him and keeps the now agitated bees somewhat at bay. He cuts the hive open with three quick hacks and pulls out and throws down sections of honeycomb, which we catch in mitts of sini leaves, a smaller forest version of tilipi. The bees are everywhere, sticking to the comb, sticking to our skin. I keep my arms away from my body so as not to trap an irate bee under my armpit, and Ndikpa makes short snorts as bees sting his honey-coated hands and arms. ("An Efe honey gathering trip," Ituri Forest People's Fund

http://www2.bc.edu/~morellig/IturiForestPeoplesFund/HTML/hone
y.htm)

Before the hive can be raided, it must be located, which is even more of a
challenge, given the tendency of wild bees to nest high up near the treetops.
To this end, both Pygmies and Bushmen make use of a remarkable bird
called the "Honeyguide": "The Honeyguide gets its name because it finds
bee habitations, directs other animals there, and then feeds on beeswax, one
of few birds known to do so. Many Bushmen report traditions of using the
honeyguides to find bee colonies and honoring the birds with the kill."
(TropicalBirds.com *http://www.tropicalbirds.com/honeyguide.php*) Since both the
technology of honey gathering and the use of the Honeyguide are commonly
found among literally all Pygmy and many Bushmen groups, the same
traditions may well have been a part of HBC.

The HBC Model Thus Far

The full array of characteristics I've come up with so far is summarized in
the following list, which can serve, for now, as a provisional baseline:

◎   Subsistence: hunting and gathering. Honey is an especially prized
food. Use of the Honeyguide bird to locate the hives.
◎   Social Organization: division into small bands; nomadism.
◎   Kinship: most likely flexible and loosely applied; possibly universal
or even nonexistent.
◎   Economics: communal.
◎   Political structure: acephalous.
◎   Location: unknown. Possibly tropical forest or East African
savannah.
◎   Physical characteristics: morphology unknown; stature short.
◎   Dwellings: beehive huts.
◎   Weapons: wooden spears; very possibly bows and arrows with
wood or bone arrow tips; very possibly poison-tipped spears and arrows,
but more evidence is needed.
◎   Tools: wooden, bone and stone implements (the last based on
archaeological evidence — metal tools and weapons are currently in use).
◎   Language: unknown, but probably some type of tone language.
◎   Music: P/B vocal style (see Chapter One); certain songs originating
in dreams or trance; musical bow; hocketing pipe ensembles; few other
instruments; no drums.

◎ Ritual/Spiritual Life/Religion: possibly proto-shamanistic. Supernatural healing, trance, possession, contact with spirits via dreams, initiation rituals, funerary rituals, strong orientation toward ancestors.

◎ Healing: extraction of harmful objects by suction.

◎ Bodily Ornament: body painting, scarification.

◎ Core values: strong emphasis placed on egalitarianism, cooperation, non-violence, conflict avoidance, individualism, sharing of vital resources.

◎ Gender relations: relative equality, based on male-female complementarity. Women and men have different, though sometimes interchangeable, roles.

◎ Behavior: mostly cooperative, unaggressive and peaceful; however, sometimes contentious, sexist and/or violent in spite of relative gender equality and strong social sanctions against violent behavior.

◎ Warfare: nonexistent.

Headhunting: nonexistent.

Cannibalism: nonexistent.

Blood feuds: nonexistent.

Raiding: nonexistent.

Slavery: nonexistent.

Prostitution: nonexistent.

Sexual mutilation: nonexistent.

Many anthropologists will no doubt object to at least some of the hypotheticals listed above, since 1. exceptions can be found among certain Pygmy and/or Bushmen groups (where, for example, violent and warlike behavior and even slavery have been recorded); 2. "revisionist" anthropologists have cited archaeological and historical evidence that both Pygmies and Bushmen have been strongly influenced by farming and/or herding societies for thousands of years (Barnard 2006; Grinker 1994); 3. certain characteristics (such as egalitarian social structure) are widely found among hunter-gatherers worldwide.

To understand the meaning of the proposed baseline, it's important to remember that it is not based on a general overview of Pygmies and Bushmen, or hunter-gatherers generally, nor on the recorded history of any of these groups, nor on any assumptions about the way they might have lived in the distant past, but, very strictly, on specific commonalities identified among certain representative groups from the three populations with the deepest genetic roots. If, for example, we currently see evidence that violent behavior is strongly discouraged among at least one eastern Pygmy, one western Pygmy, and one Bushmen group, that satisfies the triangulation method and justifies (provisionally) characterizing the value system of HBC as non-violent.

To make the point as strongly as I can: if we were to learn that certain Bushmen groups had erected skyscrapers and were driving over paved roads on home-made bicycles two hundred or even two thousand years ago, that would have no bearing on the method I am describing here, which is based on the identification of specific traits or traditions *currently* shared by specific groups from each of the three populations. Whether some also have other traits or traditions related to their contacts with other groups, based on past history, recent or ancient, has no bearing at all on the chain of logical inference grounding my argument.[4]

The presence of similar traditions or value systems among other hunter-gatherer societies in various parts of the world, while certainly meaningful and relevant for future research, also has no bearing on the argument presented here. Too often, anthropologists will tend to lump all hunter-gatherers together, as though there were some universal ahistorical force that unites them, simply because they maintain hunting and gathering traditions. As we will learn from the following chapter, this is far from the case. All "immediate-return" societies do *not*, in fact, look alike.

In terms of the argument presented here, those practices and values that certain (though certainly not all) hunter-gatherer groups *do* appear to have in common may most simply be explained neither as universals nor environmental adaptations, in agreement with functionalist doctrine, but according to a paradigm long since rejected but, in the light of the Out of Africa model, well worth reconsidering: cultural survival. Thanks to the "triangulation" method proposed here, we need not survey all such groups for commonalities, but can concentrate our efforts on the three African populations (EP, WP, Bu) whose genetic history and musical affinities make them especially useful in the attempt to recreate the social structure and value system of HBC.

A Cultural Observatory

The baseline represented above is a hypothetical model, a tool for future research, open to testing and revision, and not (yet) a full-blown theory of human origins. But it isn't just any model. HBC is intended, ultimately, to represent the culture of the most recent common ancestor of all living humans, a very real, very specific society that existed prior to the earliest divergence of the modern human family tree, as inferred from both the genetic and the cultural evidence. Any physical or cultural attributes that can be associated with HBP should be understood as in some sense, and of course provisionally, ancestral to all subsequent populations and societies — or, to be more accurate, all such groups that have survived to the present time.

In terms of the Out of Africa model (assuming its validity, of course), each and every tradition that can be attributed to our baseline must be understood therefore as a potential source of any similar tradition found anywhere in the world, since every extant population can be understood as deriving, however remotely, from HBP. Thus, any attribute found to be shared between any society now in existence and HBC is open to investigation as a possible survival from the ancestral culture.

We have arrived, however provisionally, at a baseline of human cultural history, a point zero from which we can consider everything we now see in literally every human society in the world around us, from the most "primitive" to the most "advanced." Think of the baseline as a kind of observatory.

-----

1. For an update based on new genetic evidence suggesting the possibility of "relatively recent contact" between certain Pygmy and Bushmen groups, see Sidebar 4.

2. Note, by the way, that the discrepancy in the use of nets and bows as principal hunting technologies, which for Hewlett (1996) amounts to an important cultural difference among Pygmy groups, has no bearing on our method, which depends only on the *presence* of certain traditions, not their degree of importance, especially under relatively recent conditions.

3. In this case, the practice of hunter-gatherers outside of Africa could be relevant, since many of these groups also employ both bows and arrows and poisoned tips. Since the "Out of Africa" exodus of ca 60,000-80,000 years ago clearly predates the Bantu expansion of ca 2,000-4,000 years ago, it seems unlikely that such weaponry originated with Bantu farmers. Of course, the possibility of independent invention cannot be completely ruled out, especially given the possibility that the bow and arrow could have been independently invented in the Americas.

4. Even if involvement in warfare or the presence of local "chiefs" could be identified among certain groups in all three populations, this would not satisfy the triangulation method either, since the rubric pertains *only* to attributes *"not likely to be the result of outside influence."* Since such practices are invariably associated in the historical record with relatively recent external influences and pressures, they would be excluded from the baseline.

Chapter Five: Hunter-Gatherers

On a Clear Day

Well, the view from HBC is very interesting, I must say. From this great height of possibly 100,000 years ago, or more, we can look down for years and years through millennia after millennia of human history. The view is admittedly a bit foggy. But with a little more research we might be able to see forever. Or at least as far into the future as now.

What I want to do next is take a close look at certain specific hunter-gatherer groups in an attempt to determine, however tentatively, which aspects of certain cultures could be survivals from HBC and which might represent a variant or divergence from the ancestral model.

Traditionally, as we've seen, anthropologists have tended to assume that there are certain people out there who can be grouped together as "hunter-gatherers" or "foragers," because they appear to have so many things in common. And since the notion of cultural survival was long ago discarded as some sort of myth, anthropologists now tend to think of such shared traditions as due to some universal characteristic that we could call, I suppose, "hunter-gatherer-ivity." If they hunt and gather, and have no other visible means of support, that means they must belong to some mysterious cultural sub-species of the human race that for some mysterious reason shares all sorts of interesting beliefs, attitudes, methodologies, etc.

From our newly constructed baseline observatory, however, what I now see, through a glass darkly, is the likelihood that what all so called "hunter-gatherer" groups might have in common is their connection with HBC. Now that we have a baseline, we can not only reconsider the possibility of cultural survivals, but speculate with much more precision regarding their nature and their origin. It's not so much a matter of proving that some particular instance is in fact a survival, because that would be almost impossible to do, as opening the door on a fresh approach to comparative studies of the sort that could help us organize and systematize our search for history and meaning.

The Hadza

Let us consider, for example, the Hadza, a group of "hunter-gatherer" bands, some of which are still living an apparently traditional lifestyle in what is now Tanzania (formerly Tanganyika and Zanzibar). A recent issue of *National Geographic* contains a very interesting article by Michael Finkel, titled *The Hadza* (*http://ngm.nationalgeographic.com/2009/12/hadza/finkel-text.*), and subtitled as follows:

> They grow no food, raise no livestock, and live without rules or calendars. They are living a hunter-gatherer existence that is little changed from 10,000 years ago. What do they know that we've forgotten?

The subtitle is misleading, "10,000 years ago" refers simply to the general estimate among Archaeologists that the earliest signs of agriculture date from roughly 10,000 years in the past. The assumption being that 1. the Hadza have lived as hunter-gatherers during the entire period since the earliest advent of agriculture; 2. hunting and gathering in itself is a principal determinant of culture, and 3. all hunter-gatherers are now living as our ancestors lived. These are *huge* assumptions.

Nevertheless, we have good reason to believe that certain *aspects* of Hadza life haven't changed much over a period anywhere from 40,000 to very possibly well over 100,000 years ago. How can we make such a statement? Not on the basis of loosely defined assumptions, but very specific evidence pointing to strong socio-cultural affinities with HBC, the ancestral culture we've constructed as our (hypothetical) baseline.

We learn toward the beginning of the article that one of the Hadza males is "maybe five feet tall." The mean height of Hadza males has been estimated at 162.24 centimeters, i.e. roughly 64 inches or 5 foot 3. Since Aka Pygmy males are reported as averaging 153 centimeters, or roughly 5 feet, the Hadza don't seem all that much taller. And as we've learned, certain Bushmen groups fall into roughly the same ballpark. Did the Hadza, Pygmies and Bushmen inherit their small height from a common ancestor or is it some sort of adaptation, or even perhaps a coincidence? Only biological research can tell us for sure, so this remains an open question.

The Hadza language is correctly described as an isolate. Despite the use of clicks it has not been possible to group it with Khoisan or any other family. However, like so many other African languages, it is tonal. According to Finkel, "Genetic testing indicates that they may represent one of the primary roots of the human family tree — perhaps more than 100,000 years old," but I don't know of any research supporting that. On the contrary, the Hadza appear to be a genetic isolate. Consider the following graph, based on an analysis of autosomal microsatellite markers (Tishkoff et al 2009):

See Figure 5.1

The Hadza are easy to spot as they are represented by a bright yellow vertical band roughly one-third of the way in from the left. The fact that they are the only group represented by this color tells us how distinctive their genetic profile is. The Hadza are a musical isolate as well, as far as I've been able to determine, with a vocal style completely different from both P/B style interlocking and the call and response pattern so typical of Bantu singing. Here is an example of Hadza vocalizing, from the two CD set, *The Hadza Bushmen of Tanzania*, disk 2, track 7: *Audio Example 11: La Source de Chemchem*.

To my knowledge no one has ever done a systematic study of Hadza music, so my impressions are based exclusively on this particular set of recordings, which might not be fully representative. On this basis, it would seem that Hadza singing, like Hadza autosomal markers, is highly distinctive — very beautiful indeed, but quite different from any other type of sub-Saharan African music with which I am acquainted. For one thing, the vocalizing on these CDs is almost exclusively in "social unison," where all voices sing more or less in the same rhythm (albeit polyphonically, in a manner not unlike the parallel organum of the Medieval church) – while not unknown in sub-Saharan Africa, social unison is far less common there than call and response antiphony.

Moreover, the Hadza tend to sing in relatively free, loosely coordinated, rhythms, and the rhythmic relation between the accompanying handclaps and the voices doesn't appear to be very clearly coordinated — all of which is very unusual for Africa south of the Sahara, where rhythms and rhythmic coordination tend to be clearly defined and precise. While the existence of musical isolates is not unheard of in Africa, the unusual style of Hadza vocalizing is surprising and also puzzling, especially since they have so much else in common with Pygmies and Bushmen, whose musical style we could expect them to share.

While there is indeed something very mysterious in both the genetic and musical pictures for the Hadza, such anomalies could be explained, I believe, by a severe population bottleneck.[1] Such an event, leaving only a very small proportion of the original population to serve as a subsequent "founder group," could explain both the genetic and the musical anomalies. The highly integrated, tightly coordinated musical style of P/B could have been altered in the wake of a disaster that temporarily isolated only a small number of survivors.

It seems as though such a bottleneck could only have occurred very early on. If it occurred relatively recently, then the genetic picture for the Hadza would not look so radically different from that of all other African populations (see graph). This is my own interpretation of the genetic evidence, and I am by no means an expert, but as far as I can tell a very early bottleneck appears to be the only logical explanation for the Hadza "mystery." I'll be discussing such bottlenecks and their cultural effects in much more detail presently.

When we leave aside the genetic, linguistic and musical differences, we see a great many striking similarities with Pygmy and Bushmen culture, strongly suggesting that, bottleneck or not, a great many traditions could well be survivals from HBC. For one thing, we learn from the article that a significant number of Hadza, one-quarter, "remain true hunter-gatherers," with strong evidence that all Hadza lived solely by hunting and gathering in the not too distant past.

> Anthropologists are wary of viewing contemporary hunter-gatherers as "living fossils," says Frank Marlowe, a Florida State University professor of anthropology who has spent the past 15 years studying the Hadza. Time has not stood still for them. But they have maintained their foraging lifestyle in spite of long exposure to surrounding agriculturalist groups, and, says Marlowe, it's possible that their lives have changed very little over the ages (p. 104).

"The Hadza do not engage in warfare," "have plenty of leisure time," "live almost entirely free of possessions," "collect honey," and hunt with poison arrows, cultural characteristics shared among all three of our baseline "feeder" groups, EP, WP and Bu. Additionally, they "recognize no official leaders," favor "individual autonomy," and rarely stand on ceremony for events such as weddings, funerals and other rituals.

In this latter respect they do differ somewhat from HBC, where we would expect to find rituals similar to the *Elima* girl's initiation, or the *Molimo* festival, as practiced by the Mbuti, or the *Xhoma* male initiation ritual of the Ju/'hoansi Bushmen. Moreover, "there are no Hadza priests or shamans or medicine men." Perhaps such traditions were lost in the same bottleneck event that may have affected their genetic profile and their music.

The status of women among the Hadza appears extremely close to their status among EP, WP and Bu — and thus HBC — i.e., a state of relative equality, with very clear overtones of subservience in certain areas, as reflected in sometimes very different gender roles and limitations.

The Hadza also have "beehive" huts, very much like those of the Pygmies and Bushmen: "During the rainy season, they construct little domed shelters made of interwoven twigs and long grasses: basically, upside-down bird's nests."

See Figure 5.2

I'll be getting more deeply into the very intriguing question of Beehive huts as possible HBC survivals in an upcoming chapter.

Core HBC values such as avoidance of conflict and strong emphasis on sharing are also present among the Hadza: "Most conflicts are resolved by the feuding parties simply separating into different camps. If a hunter brings home a kill, it is shared by everyone in his camp." The Hadza also practice scarification, as is evident from a photo on p. 119 of the National Geographic article:

See Figure 5.3

Other Groups

The *Cambridge Encyclopedia of Hunters and Gatherers* contains separate articles on 53 different groups from seven world regions and to the best of my knowledge they are merely skimming the surface. Each group has its own individual history, of course, and certain distinctive qualities not shared with many of the others. Moreover, each author of each study has his or her own approach and his or her own philosophy regarding what hunter-gatherers (aka "foragers") are and how to think about them. Nevertheless, a consensus does seem to have emerged, in this volume and elsewhere, at least among those who still think the category "hunter-gatherer" has any meaning at all.

In the Introduction, "Foragers and Others," by editors Richard Lee and Richard Daly (Lee and Daly 1999:1-19), it is acknowledged that "Hunter-gatherers are a diverse group of peoples living in a wide range of conditions." Nevertheless,

> within the range of variation, certain common motifs can be identified. Hunter-gatherers are generally peoples who have lived until recently without the overarching discipline imposed by the state. They have lived in relatively small groups, *without centralized authority, standing armies, or bureaucratic systems*. Yet the evidence indicates that they have lived together surprisingly well, solving their problems among themselves largely without recourse to authority figures and *without a particular propensity for violence* (p. 1 — my emphasis).

Other commonalities noted by Lee and Daly are: relatively egalitarian ethic; mobility; flexible patterns of concentration and dispersion; communal ownership of property; "generalized reciprocity" (i.e., sharing of most resources with no expectation of return).

Another important trait shared by almost all hunter-gatherer groups is some form of Shamanism:

> Shamanism is another major practice common to the great majority of hunting and gathering peoples. The word originates in eastern Siberia, from the Evenki/Tungus word saman meaning "one who is excited or raised." Throughout the hunter-gatherer world community-based ritual specialists (usually part-time) heal the sick and provide spiritual protection. They mediate between the social/human world and the dangerous and unpredictable world of the supernatural. Shamanism is performative, mixing theatre and instrumental acts in order to approach the plane of the sacred (ibid:3-5).

Remarkably, just about everything Lee and Daly have found that all or almost all hunter-gatherers have in common are features we've identified as characteristic of HBC. Is this commonality due simply to the fact that the three groups we've been using to construct our HBC model happen themselves to be hunter-gatherers? In other words, is the long list of commonalities among so many hunter-gatherers to be explained by "hunter-gatherer-ivity"? Or, to put it in functionalist terms, is hunter-gatherer culture in general a function of hunting and gathering in particular?

I wonder how many anthropologists have realized how circular this "explanation" is. Hunters and gatherers apparently live the way they do because they hunt and gather. And they hunt and gather because that's the way they live. Significantly, neither the editors nor any of the other contributors to this very thick volume make any attempt whatsoever to explain all these remarkable similarities, as though they could simply be taken for granted.

Is there an explanation? Yes, of course. As seems clear to me, hunters and gatherers live the way they do, not because they hunt and gather (duh!), but because they are highly conservative peoples who have gone to a tremendous amount of trouble over many thousands of years to preserve their traditional way of life, based on practices and beliefs that could only have been established tens of thousands of years ago in the culture of a common ancestor. Such deeply ingrained conservatism would explain not only why they all seem to share so many cultural attributes, but also why they continue to live by hunting and gathering, wherever possible, in the face of so many forces at work in the world of today trying to "modernize" them.

Violence and Competition

The Cambridge Encyclopedia of Hunters and Gatherers covers North and South America, Africa, North Eurasia, South Asia, Southeast Asia and Australia — but not New Guinea or Island Melanesia. These areas are a problem for hunter-gatherer studies because the great majority of the many indigenous groups therein are not, strictly speaking, foragers, but usually described as "horticulturalists" — which boils down, in many cases, to hunter-gatherers who also do a bit of simple gardening.

What makes this a problem is that it isn't always so easy to distinguish the two. For example, the Encyclopedia includes a chapter on the Batak, in the Philippines, despite the fact that "they have long produced some rice by shifting cultivation, together with smaller amounts of maize, cassava and sweet potato, but cultivation is a far less important activity for them than it is for their lowland neighbors" (p. 295). I have a feeling that much the same could be said of a great many Melanesian horticulturalists as well.

In an online article, *The Hunter-Gatherer Spectrum in New Guinea* (http://climatechange.umaine.edu/Research/projects/NewGuinea.html), Paul Roscoe informs us that some New Guinean populations are — or were — hunter-gatherers after all:

> It has long been supposed that New Guinea is a land of cultivators. . . However, a close examination of the ethnographic record – in particular, of unpublished and non-English language sources – has revealed numerous references to the presence of "hunters and gatherers."

Roscoe distinguishes two principal types of New Guinea foragers, those dependent on "terrestrial and arboreal game," who "markedly resembled the classic hunter-gatherer societies typified by the Kung, Inuit, Mbuti, and many Australian Aboriginal groups. . ." and those concentrating on "aquatic resources." The former were "relatively egalitarian," with "mobility as an important conflict resolution mechanism," and a "comparatively unelaborated" ritual life." However, "Contradicting a common stereotype that war is attenuated or absent among hunters and gatherers, *fighting was endemic*." [my emphasis]. The latter typically exhibited a cultural complexity rivaling that of agriculturalists in New Guinea and they strongly resembled other aquatically adapted, hunter-gatherer societies such as the Native American communities of the Northwest Coast. . . Most of these groups also had developed highly elaborate ceremonial and visual art. Some, such as the Asmat, Karawari, Kwoma, and Purari are among the most famous of New Guinea's ritual artists.

And once again, as with the terrestrial foragers, violence is an important element in the cultural mix: "Warfare was generally intense, and most of these groups were head-hunters."

The importance of violence among New Guinea's hunter-gatherers, and in Melanesia generally, even among the simpler, more egalitarian societies, certainly does go against the stereotype, an "inconvenient truth" that must be accounted for by anyone seeking to characterize hunter-gatherers in general according to the "core values" identified in our baseline.

The contradiction is not lost on Roscoe:

> Hunter-gatherer scholarship has largely overlooked the importance of war, partly because of long-standing assumptions that warfare is a relatively recent emergence in human history and that hunter-gatherers lead a peaceful life. There is increasing evidence, however, that these assumptions are misplaced and that New Guinea's foragers may more accurately represent the hunter-gatherer past. Recent primate research finds that chimpanzees practice a form of lethal aggression against neighbors that has striking similarities to ambush in human society. This suggests that organized deadly violence may antedate the human-chimpanzee split, some 5 to 7 million years ago, and therefore may have characterized the whole of human prehistory.

Another complication posed by Melanesia, not mentioned by Roscoe, but of equal relevance, is the importance in just about every Melanesian society of the so-called "Big Man." According to Marshall Sahlins, who made an intensive study of Melanesian social structure,

> Politics is in the main personal politicking in these Melanesian societies, and the size of a leader's faction as well as the extent of his renown are normally set by *competition* with other ambitious men. . .
>
> [A Big Man] must be prepared to demonstrate that he possesses the kind of skills that command respect . . . Typically decisive is the

deployment of one's skills and efforts in a certain direction: towards *amassing goods*, most often pigs, shell monies and vegetable foods, and *distributing them* in ways which build a name for cavalier generosity, if not for compassion (Sahlins 2003:290-291).

While Melanesian social structure is still often referred to as "relatively egalitarian" or "more-or-less egalitarian," the notion of a "Big-Man" in the above sense would be pure anathema to any of the Pygmy or Bushmen groups whose cultures we've been examining. As we've learned, these cultures are more than simply "egalitarian," they perpetuate social mechanisms that actively discourage any attempt on the part of any individual to stand out from the group. While certain individuals do emerge as "natural leaders" due to certain outstanding abilities, personal ambition is strongly frowned upon, and overt competition of any kind is almost unheard of.

It's important to understand, moreover, that neither violence nor "Big-Man" politics among either hunter-gatherers or horticulturalists is confined to Melanesia, though both are particularly common in this region. In fact certain "hunter-gatherer" groups have exhibited highly competitive and violent behavior, in many parts of the world.

Does this mean that "deadly violence" in fact "characterized the whole of human prehistory," as Roscoe has alleged? Does it mean that competition is genetically ingrained into the human spirit? Only if we are willing to accept the commonly held view of "hunter-gatherers" as representative, for better (the traditionalist view) or worse (the revisionist view), of some sort of universalized essence of "Stone-Age Man." I'll be delving more deeply into this extremely important issue in the following chapter.

1. "A *population bottleneck* (or *genetic bottleneck*) is an evolutionary event in which a significant percentage of a population or species is killed or otherwise prevented from reproducing." (*Wikipedia* — http://en.wikipedia.org/wiki/Population_bottleneck)

Sidebar 3: Independent Invention, Convergence, or Survival

From Franz Boas, *Race, Language and Culture*, Macmillan: New York, 1940:

> If it is possible that analogous anatomical forms develop independently in genetically distinct lines, it is ever so much more probable that analogous cultural forms develop independently. It may be admitted that it is exceedingly difficult to give absolutely indisputable proof of the independent origin of analogous cultural data. Nevertheless, the distribution of isolated customs in regions far apart hardly admits of the argument that they were transmitted from tribe to tribe and lost in intervening territory. . . (p. 252)
>
> Some anthropologists assume that, if a number of cultural phenomena agree in regions far apart, these must be due to the presence of an exceedingly ancient substratum that has been preserved notwithstanding all the cultural changes that have occurred. This view is not admissible without proof that the phenomena in question remain stable not only for thousands of years, but even so far back that they have been carried by wandering hordes from Asia to the extreme southern end of South America. Notwithstanding the great tenacity of cultural traits, there is no proof that such extreme conservatism ever existed. (p. 253)
>
> It follows from these observations that when we find analogous single traits of culture among distant peoples, the presumption is not that there has been a common historical source, but that they have arisen independently. (p. 271)

The arguments presented above, along with many others of a similar nature by one of the fathers of modern anthropology, constitute a doctrine fundamental to the thinking of almost all social scientists today. The doctrine seems eminently reasonable. No one wants to return to the bad old days of *Kulturkreis* thinking. Hardly anyone is prepared to accept even the possibility that *any* tradition could be perpetuated unchanged over vast expanses of both space and time. And as a result, the characteristic fallback position regarding similarities of this kind, even the most striking, has become: independent invention, or the closely related notion of "convergent evolution."

It's difficult to argue the case for ancestral survival because independent invention appeals so strongly to common sense. After all, what seems more likely, the survival of the same tradition over many thousands of years among hundreds of different groups in remote parts of the world, or the independent invention of something similar in many different places, due simply to either coincidence or "convergence," based on some universal property of the human mind, or analogous thinking in the face of similar environmental challenges.

To dispel the myth of independent invention it is important to realize, first, that inventions of any kind, in any society, are very rarely independent. They are almost always variants of cultural elements already in play, or else borrowings from some neighboring group. The automobile is based on the horse and buggy, which is in turn based on the simple horse-drawn cart, which already takes us back many thousands of years. The computer is based on the electronic calculator, which is based on the adding machine, based on calculating machines developed in the early 1800's, based on 17th century prototypes by Leibnitz and Pascal, all of which are preceded by the Abacus.

Second, it's important to realize that indigenous societies value the passing on of ancestral traditions far more than they do innovation. In fact innovation is actively discouraged in such societies. I would challenge anyone reading here to find an instance of truly independent invention of *any* kind, recorded in the ethnographic or historical literature over the last 2,000 years for *any* such group. When we see change it is almost invariably based on outside influence of some sort, or else gradual modifications or improvements of cultural elements already long established. On the other hand, as I believe I have established, there is very strong evidence for the survival of a highly distinctive musical tradition (P/B) over tens of thousands of years.

Another View of Discontinuous Distribution

It might be a good idea, at this point, to review what another important anthropologist, Edward Sapir, once had to say about the "agreement" between "cultural phenomena . . . in regions far apart":

> For chronological purposes, cases of the interrupted distribution of a culture element are of particular importance. In a general way, a culture element whose area of distribution is a broken one must be considered as of older date, other things being equal, than a culture element diffused over an equivalent but continuous area. The reason for this is that in the former case we have to add to the lapse of time allowed for the diffusion of the element over its area of distribution the time taken to bring about the present isolation of the two areas, a time which may vary from a few years or a generation to a number

of centuries. . . . [T]he interrupted distribution of a culture element gives us a minimum relative date for the origin of the culture element itself. The element must have arisen prior to the event or series of events that resulted in the geographical isolation of the two areas ("Time Perspective in Aboriginal American Culture, a Study in Method." Geological Survey Memoir 90: No. 13, Anthropological Series. Ottawa: Government Printing Bureau (1916), p. 41).

It's not difficult to understand the logic behind Sapir's observation. When we see essentially the same traditions among groups that, as far as we can tell, have been isolated from one another for a very long time, and we see these isolated communities surrounded by societies with very different traditions, then there would seem only three possible explanations:

1. coincidence, based on "independent invention";

2. "convergent evolution," based on the assumption that the tradition represents an adaptation of some sort, stemming from some universal property of the human mind;

3. an early "diffusion of the element over its area of distribution," followed by "events that resulted in the geographical isolation of the . . . areas."

Since essentially the same coincidental, "independent invention" or adaptation would have had to occur in each and every case, in a great many different parts of the world, the first two possibilities seem extremely unlikely.

Scientific Method

The strongest refutation of Boas's argument has its origin in certain fundamental principles of science itself, or, more accurately, certain hermeneutic principles grounding scientific method. When considering two conflicting interpretations of any body of evidence, it can sometimes be argued that one is the default or fallback position, which can be taken for granted, while the other must shoulder the burden of proof.

For Boas, the choice is obvious: "when we find analogous single traits of culture among distant peoples, the presumption is not that there has been a common historical source, but that they have arisen independently." (See above) In other words, independent invention or convergence require no proof because we can presume ahead of time that they are the most likely alternative. And if anyone might wish to challenge that, it is *he* who must provide adequate proof.

While seemingly reasonable, this view is, in fact, inconsistent with two of the most important principles of modern science: 1. The principle of sufficient reason, as developed by Leibnitz and Kant; and 2. Occam's Razor. The first principle insists that all "truths of fact" (as opposed to "truths of logic") must have a sufficient reason for their existence.

While independent invention and/or convergence are certainly reasons, they are by no means *sufficient* reasons, because they are incapable of explaining how any particular practice in any part of the world could have come into existence. Ancestral survival on the basis of shared heritage, on the other hand, is fully sufficient to explain the existence of any trait shared among different groups, whether widely separated or contiguous.

Occam's Razor can be summarized as follows: if there is no necessary reason to do so, it is better not to assume that any particular phenomenon has a plurality of causes (in this case, independent inventions), when a simpler explanation (in this case, shared heritage) fits the evidence equally well.

The power of Occam's Razor is often overlooked. The basics are explained in a particularly clear *online discussion* by Francis Heylighen:

> [Occam's Razor] underlies all scientific modelling and theory building. It admonishes us to choose from a set of otherwise equivalent models of a given phenomenon the simplest one. . .
>
> Though the principle may seem rather trivial, it is essential for model building because of what is known as the "underdetermination of theories by data". For a given set of observations or data, there is always an infinite number of possible models explaining those same data. This is because a model normally represents an infinite number of possible cases, of which the observed cases are only a finite subset. The non-observed cases are inferred by postulating general rules covering both actual and potential observations.

An excellent example of Occam's Razor is provided by the application of Newton's principle of universal gravitation to our understanding of the planetary orbits. Strictly speaking the ancient Ptolemaic theory of planetary epicycles, based on an Earth-centered universe, could, in Newton's day, account just about as accurately for the planetary movements as Newton's theory.

Without a principle such as Occam's Razor, we might want to consider both theories as equally acceptable, since both are capable of fully accounting for the data. However, Newton's explanation, being far simpler than that of

Ptolemy, satisfied Occam's Razor, and thus became universally accepted in his day — despite the fact there was, at that time, no way of knowing for sure that the planets did not revolve around the Earth in complex epicycles after all.

Thus, according to basic scientific principles, when we reach a point that two or more theories account equally well for all the evidence, Occam's Razor more or less compels us to favor the theory offering the simplest explanation. Which does not rule out the possibility that new evidence might someday arise that might force us to reconsider.

All too often in the social sciences we find people who are unaware of Occam's Razor, or believe they can easily ignore it, assuming, as did Boas, that it's necessary to demonstrate the impossibility of every alternative before any theory can be accepted. Not true. All that should be necessary to establish a given theory is to demonstrate 1. that it fully accounts for all the currently available, relevant, evidence; and 2. that it presents a simpler explanation than any alternative which may also happen to account for the same evidence. That doesn't mean the theory is necessarily proven, i.e., true for all time. Absolute proof, contrary to popular opinion, is *not the objective of scientific inquiry*. And any theory can be overthrown on the basis of contradictory evidence.

Thus, all else being equal, when we find it necessary to choose between independent invention, convergence or shared heritage, it is only the last possibility that satisfies both the principle of sufficient reason and Occam's Razor, meaning that, contrary to Boas, the burden of proof lies with the first two alternatives, not the last. Of course it is always better to offer convincing reasons for any hypothesis and it would be a mistake if we were to fall back on either Leibnitz or Occam and claim that similar cultural practices must always be understood as archaic survivals. That is not at all my intention, and in fact there are certainly cases where independent invention seems more likely – but *only* on the basis of compelling evidence in its favor. If there is no such evidence then survival must be accepted as the most likely possibility, at least until conflicting evidence emerges.

Chapter Six: Utopia, Then and Now

> "Though to speak plainly my real sentiments, I must freely own that as long as there is any property, and while money is the standard of all other things, I cannot think that a nation can be governed either justly or happily . . . "
>
> "On the contrary," answered I, "it seems to me that men cannot live conveniently where all things are common: how can there be any plenty, where every man will excuse himself from labor? . . ."
>
> "I do not wonder," said he, "that it appears so to you, since you have no notion, or at least no right one, of such a constitution: but if you had been in Utopia with me, and had seen their laws and rules, as I did, for the space of five years, in which I lived among them . . . you would then confess that you had never seen a people so well constituted as they."
>
> St. Thomas More, *Utopia*

Demonic Males

In their book, *Demonic Males*, evolutionary biologists Richard Wrangham and Dale Peterson ask the question, "Where does human violence come from, and why?" (Wrangham and Peterson 1997) Their answer? It is imprinted in us as part of our pre-human heritage. How do they know this? From studying our "cousins," the chimpanzees, who, in the wild, "live in patrilineal, male-bonded communities," operating through "a system of intense, male-initiated territorial aggression, including lethal raiding into neighboring communities in search of vulnerable enemies to attack and kill. Out of four thousand mammals and ten million or more other animal species, this suite of behaviors is known only among chimpanzees and humans. . ."

How is it that humans are so much like chimps?

> [S]imilar evolutionary forces continue to be at work in chimpanzee and human lineages, maintaining and refining a system of intergroup hostility and personal violence that has existed since even before the ancestors of chimpanzees and humans mated for the last time in a drying forest of eastern Africa around 5 million years ago.

The message has been widely disseminated and its premise uncritically accepted in the media (though it's hardly the first of its kind — viz. Robert

Ardrey's equally influential *The Territorial Imperative*). Witness the response of Washington Post literary critic Daniel Pinchbeck, who is clearly convinced (http://www.washingtonpost.com/wp-srv/style/longterm/books/reviews/demonicmales.htm):

> Such male aggression has structured the lives of humans as well as chimpanzees for thousands of generations. Every human society has been patriarchal, with men retaining most of the dominant spots in the hierarchy and using their power to control women and annihilate their enemies.

Actually, there are matriarchal as well as patriarchal societies, but you get the point. He continues, echoing an all too familiar refrain:

> The authors regretfully dismiss the possibility of some paradisiacal society that existed in a Golden Era or on a South Seas island, whether matriarchal or truly non-hierarchical and peaceful. Yet they do not believe that this means the future is a closed book. Evolution means continual adaptation and change, and the authors hold a rational faith that "to find a better world we must look not to a romanticized and dishonest dream forever receding into the primitive past, but to a future that rests on a proper understanding of ourselves."

Wrangham and Peterson base their hopes for the future on a close cousin of the Chimp, another sort of ape, whose social behavior does indeed suggest "some paradisiacal society that existed in a Golden Era or on a South Seas island": the *Bonobo*. According to the authors, "Chimpanzees and bonobos both evolved from the same ancestor that gave rise to humans, and yet the bonobo is one of the most peaceful, unaggressive species of mammals living on the earth today."

As far as bonobos are concerned, I fully agree. However, as far as humans are concerned, we know that Wrangham and Peterson are almost certainly wrong. As evolutionary biologists, they have done their job. Their assumptions regarding chimp behavior may well be accurate. And their conclusions regarding human behavior would appear to follow quite logically from the evidence they present.

As we've learned, however, the Pygmy and Bushmen groups on whose traditions I've drawn for the construction of an ancestral baseline, are nothing like chimps. Indeed, when we examine those cultural elements shared by so many Pygmy and Bushmen groups, promoting close cooperation and free interaction, sharing, equal treatment for all, relative indifference to property rights, individual autonomy and freedom, non-violence, the independence of women and the loving indulgence of children, we approach a social structure remarkably similar to the one described in Thomas More's frequently referenced, but rarely read, *Utopia*. It looks, in fact, as though our ancestors were closer to bonobos than chimps. And if so, then maybe it isn't so easy to dismiss "the possibility of some paradisiacal society that existed in a Golden Era."

An Age of Gold?

So, would the ancestral society I've posited here (HBC) have been a Utopia? Not exactly. For one thing, Thomas More's Utopia was an agricultural society, while early homo sapiens were almost certainly hunter-gatherers. Utopia had towns, but there's no evidence of towns during the Old Stone Age. Utopia had fortifications, but there's no evidence of Old Stone Age fortifications either. Perhaps they weren't needed. Utopia was a hierarchical society, with magistrates of varying degrees of power, and also a prince, but, as seems likely, our ancestors, like today's Pygmies and Bushmen, were non-hierarchical and acephalous. Also, the Utopians, believe it or not, had slaves.

More's remarkable book notwithstanding, the word "Utopia" has come to imply some kind of ideal society — too ideal, perhaps, to actually exist. So did our ancestors live in an ideal society? A paradise? Was theirs a Golden Age? A "Utopia"? For an answer, you can read any number of books and articles on the Pygmies and Bushmen, listen to their recorded music, watch the films — and decide for yourself. You'll find opinions pro and con, and you can make up your own mind. Sadly — tragically — you may not be able to find any of these societies actually functioning in the world of today, since most have been hobbled or destroyed by forces beyond their control — from the inroads of farmers or logging camps, the social pressures exerted by missionary groups, well meaning environmentalists, valuing animals over humans, or, more recently, the forces of what is known as "market reform" or "the global economy," the same forces that are currently tearing our own world apart.

I personally find it difficult to see Pygmy or Bushmen societies as Utopias, either in the literal sense, as more primitive replicas of the community fantasized by Thomas More, or in the generic sense of an ideal society, where everyone gets along perfectly, disputes are rare, and always settled fairly and without violence. On the contrary, what we learn from those who've spent time with them in the field is that individuals can be quick to assert themselves if something bothers them, which means that disputes, especially marital disputes, are not unusual and serious violence, though rare, is not unheard of. This is only to be expected. In any society that values both group integration and individual autonomy, tensions are going to emerge, people are going to assert themselves, and there is always the possibility of violence.

What especially troubles me in this regard is the tendency by many of our intellectuals and public pundits to make exactly the sort of "romantic," idealizing statements justifiably questioned by skeptics such as Roscoe (see previous chapter), Wrangham and Peterson, and ridiculed by the "revisionist" school of contemporary anthropology. Such skepticism is understandable given the widespread tendency for laymen and even professional anthropologists to make unwarranted assumptions when writing about hunter-gatherers. A case in point is the book *After Eden*, by Kirkpatrick Sale, who decides, on the basis of very little evidence indeed, that *homo erectus* must have lived in much the same manner as contemporary hunter-gatherer groups, what he calls "immediate-return" societies. Quoting some of Colin Turnbull's more enthusiastic descriptions of the Mbuti, he concludes, on the basis of no evidence whatsoever, as follows:

> Thus the ethnographic record provides a striking picture of the coherence and concord of immediate-return societies, who are after all managing for the most part . . . to carry on traditions that in many respects date back more than a million years. Back to the Erectus, who, if we accept the premise that all immediate-return societies must look pretty much alike, can be regarded as having lived in some generally similar way. The worldview of the Mbutis: that is what I take to be the worldview of Erectus (p. 118).

Far too much of this sort of highly questionable speculation, based purely on assumptions, has been written and uncritically accepted by far too many. So much so, that it's not surprising when we find serious professionals responding with dismissive knee-jerk reactions in the opposite direction. What too often gets lost in all the posturing and rhetoric is exactly what was neglected in the first place: the evidence. As someone who prides himself on following the evidence, I find myself caught in the middle, where it's all too easy to be mis-perceived as yet another one of those hopeless "romantics," drawing extravagant conclusions on the basis of unwarranted assumptions.

As far as the evidence is concerned, it's necessary to reiterate the fact that all "immediate-return societies" do *not* look alike. A great many such societies around the world, whether strictly hunter-gatherers or nearly so (e.g., part-time swidden gardeners), can be, as we have learned, extremely violent, waging continual warfare with their neighbors and in some cases, until recently at least, engaging in head-hunting and cannibalism. While a great many such groups worldwide do tend to be egalitarian and non-hierarchical, strong leaders do emerge, in the form of so-called "big men," and what may well have begun as Pygmy/Bushmen-like customs of communal sharing have sometimes morphed into elaborate and occasionally destructive systems of extravagant gift-exchange, not too different from what we would call conspicuous consumption.

It's also important to understand that we have very few means of uncovering any aspects whatever of the non-material culture of either homo erectus or neanderthals, known to us only through a sparse and incomplete fossil and archaeological record. While, in my view, it *is* possible to extrapolate backwards into our deep past, on the basis of comparative studies of the culture and genetic makeup of living peoples, sifting the evidence and drawing inferences, there is nothing in the culture or genes of living people that can tell us anything at all regarding what amounts to a completely different species, either homo erectus or neanderthal, with essentially independent histories.

We cannot even say very much about the earliest homo sapiens, because, for all we know, they may have been very different from the Pygmies and Bushmen of today. I've been very careful to draw conclusions only where they are warranted by the evidence and reasonable inference therefrom. On such a basis I feel confident in arguing that it *is* acceptable to draw certain conclusions regarding the common ancestors of the Pygmies and Bushmen *as of the period of earliest divergence*. Prior to that cutoff, we are no longer in a position to draw meaningful inferences — though we are certainly free to speculate.

Regardless of all the many differences between More's original vision and the lifestyle of my hypothetical baseline population, we *do* in fact find some striking similarities when we, once again, pay special attention to core values. In More's *Utopia* there is no private property, and money has been eliminated as a "standard of all things." He praises the Utopians as a society "with so few laws; where virtue hath its due reward, and yet there is such an equality, that every man lives in plenty . . .," and praises Plato for advocating "a community of all things," and "setting all upon a level." In such statements, More encapsulates what could be called the core values of his Utopia, all but identical to those I've postulated for HBC. Which would, in that sense at least, have made the society of our mutual ancestors, if not a Utopia, then at least: Utopian.

A Lesson for Today

The baseline ancestral group whose culture I attempted to recreate in Chapter Four, would not have been some generic founding band of "anatomically modern" humans, but the very specific group of common ancestors who existed prior to the earliest divergence of the Pygmy and Bushmen lineages — very real people who, as suggested by the genetic evidence, were "our" ancestors as well. It is this group whose core culture appears to have been maintained among certain Pygmy and Bushmen peoples of today.

As I see it, therefore, whatever we can learn about our ancestors will necessarily be based on what we can learn about them. It's important to remember that I am not talking about "hunter-gatherers" or "indigenous peoples" in general, because, as we've learned, many such groups have very different sorts of culture, often far more violent and far less egalitarian. Too many anthropologists and cultural commentators tend to lump all these groups together, a huge mistake.

So. If we can put aside that difficult and divisive word "Utopian," and simply consider the culture of our common ancestors, as mirrored, however imperfectly, in the baseline I've concocted, we might, out of the corner of our eyes, catch a glimpse of a society that, while by no means perfect or ideal, may well have embodied at least some of those idealist "stereotypes" so many love to roll their eyes over.

For me, there are at least two aspects that stand out as especially important for us, their "sophisticated," "globalized" descendants, to note: first, the avoidance of war, vendetta, or any other type of socially sanctioned violence; second, the "setting of all upon a level," to quote More, i.e., the imperative toward social equality in terms of individual liberty, indifference to personal property, and the equal sharing of goods. The fact that so much in the common wisdom of the day so confidently contradicts this view, on the basis of completely unsubstantiated assumptions, is especially disturbing.

Here, for example is a recent interview with economist Paul Seabright (https://www.americanscientist.org/bookshelf/pub/paul-seabright), from *The American Scientist*, which begins as follows:

> Economist Paul Seabright is fascinated by human cooperation. Mistrust and violence are in our genes, he says, but abstract, symbolic thought permits us to accept one another as "honorary relatives"—a remarkable arrangement that ultimately underlies every aspect of modern civilization.

Everyone's favorite pundit, Steven Pinker, is particularly grating on this topic. In a recent essay (Pinker 2007), he ludicrously asserts that humans have, contrary to popular opinion, been getting progressively *less* violent through history:

> In the decade of Darfur and Iraq, and shortly after the century of Stalin, Hitler, and Mao, the claim that violence has been diminishing may seem somewhere between hallucinatory and obscene. Yet recent studies that seek to quantify the historical ebb and flow of violence point to exactly that conclusion. . .
>
> At the widest-angle view, one can see a whopping difference across the millennia that separate us from our pre-state ancestors. Contra leftist anthropologists who celebrate the noble savage, quantitative body-counts—such as the proportion of prehistoric skeletons with axemarks and embedded arrowheads or the proportion of men in a contemporary foraging tribe who die at the hands of other men—suggest that pre-state societies were far more violent than our own.

Once again, as with so many others, Pinker indifferently lumps all "contemporary foragers" together into one category of "inherently" violent representatives of humanity at its earliest stages. He continues, digging an even deeper hole for himself:

> At one time, these facts were widely appreciated. They were the source of notions like progress, civilization, and man's rise from savagery and barbarism. Recently, however, those ideas have come to sound corny, even dangerous. . . . The doctrine of the noble savage—the idea that humans are peaceable by nature and corrupted by modern institutions—pops up frequently in the writing of public intellectuals . . . But, now that social scientists have started to count bodies in different historical periods, they have discovered that the romantic theory gets it backward: Far from causing us to become more violent, something in modernity and its cultural institutions has made us nobler.

Aside from this being utter nonsense on its face, a perfect example of the revisionist impulse at its most ignorant and embarrassing, it also reflects what has become an all too common article of faith, that humans are inherently violent, something determined, no doubt, by their genetic makeup, as has been "proven" evidently by our close affiliation with all those violent chimps. In full, self-satisfied, Victorian mode, Pinker is determined to set us straight on the value of the "improvements" civilization has provided in our battle against our own deepest and direst instincts.

There is more. If Pinker can't convince us that violence is in our genes, maybe it's there because, after all, it's "only logical":

> . . . Hobbes got it right. Life in a state of nature is nasty, brutish, and short, not because of a primal thirst for blood but because of the inescapable logic of anarchy. Any beings with a modicum of self-interest may be tempted to invade their neighbors to steal their resources. The resulting fear of attack will tempt the neighbors to strike first in preemptive self-defense, which will in turn tempt the first group to strike against them preemptively, and so on. This danger can be defused by a policy of deterrence—don't strike first, retaliate if struck—but, to guarantee its credibility, parties must avenge all insults and settle all scores, leading to cycles of bloody vendetta.

While the above "logic" may, very sadly, hold for certain societies, past and present, in truth there is neither a "primal thirst for blood" nor an "inescapable logic of anarchy," mistrust, fear, and violent self-defense. We know this because there are peoples in the world who have lived in peace and harmony with their neighbors and one another for a very long time. And, indeed, as I have been at pains to demonstrate, there is strong evidence that their "pre-state ancestors" shared the same values.

There is no evidence whatsoever that we began as mistrustful, selfish, fearful and violent barbarians. And it is not necessary for any society to behave in such a manner in order to survive. If the evidence I've been presenting here is credible, the line from HBP to the Pygmies and Bushmen of today is as long as any in human history — and throughout the length of that line we see, in generation after generation, essentially the same picture: an image of survival through cooperation, equality, sharing, independence, mutual respect and non-violence, all the values we so cherish today, but have such a difficult time achieving.

Chapter Seven: The Migrants

For we cannot tarry here,
We must march my darlings, we must bear the brunt of danger,
We the youthful sinewy races, all the rest on us depend,
Pioneers! O pioneers!

Walt Whitman

According to the *Out of Africa* model of human history, a relatively small group of Homo Sapiens migrated across the Red Sea, possibly at its southernmost point, the *Bab el-Mandeb* ("Gate of Tears"), some 80,000 to 60,000 years ago. There would have been nothing special about this group whatsoever. They were not the first to have crossed the Red Sea to Asia — relics of a much earlier migration have been found in Israel, but that lineage seems to have died out. And there may well have been other groups to have made a similar crossing both before and after them, though none of these other lineages seems to have survived either.

As far as they were concerned the perilous journey across the bay to a shore they could barely make out on the horizon might not have been much different from other such crossings made over wide rivers as they journeyed from place to place — they were, in all likelihood, nomads. It's possible they crossed the Red Sea to escape some other people seeking to destroy or enslave them. Or maybe they simply hoped to find better opportunities for hunting, fishing, collecting shellfish and other nutrients. We'll never know.

They had their picture taken — though it wasn't developed until tens of thousands of years later:

See Figure 2.4

That's them, roughly in the middle, toward the bottom, in the violet area, under the words "Out of Africa" — the ones labeled M and N. According to this model, everyone whose ancestors lived outside of Africa is descended from this one small group, which I'll be calling HMP, or the "Hypothetical Migrant Population." I'll refer to their culture as HMC, or the "Hypothetical Migrant Culture."

A Migrant Baseline

My goal in this chapter will be the compilation of a second baseline representing the culture of this small but extremely important population. Assuming a single Out of Africa exodus, *all* non-African societies everywhere in the world ultimately derive not only from the genes, but also the culture, of these "Out of Africa" migrants.

In formulating the HBC baseline, I extrapolated from the present, on the basis of certain affinities among Pygmy and Bushmen groups, to the past of their common ancestors. Similarly, in formulating HMC, I must also extrapolate from the present to the past. In this case, however, there is no analogy to the valuable clue afforded by the unexpected conjunction of genetic and musical evidence which enabled us to focus on only three populations. We'll need to search among a great many non-African peoples for the commonalities we need, and as a result our thinking will be more speculative and our conclusions more tentative.

The precisions of the "triangulation" method must of necessity give way to a somewhat less rigorous, but nevertheless potentially fruitful, approach, based on the following principle: *Any distinctive tradition, in the form of a value system, belief system, artifact or attribute not likely to be the result of outside influence, found among a significant number of non-African indigenous groups in at least two different regions of the world, may be regarded as a potential survival from an older tradition traceable to the original Out of Africa migrants, and thus ascribable to HMC.* Naturally, the more widespread the instances of any given tradition, the more convincing the result will be.

In this context, it will be helpful to keep in mind the basic issues raised in Sidebar Three. On the basis of both the principle of sufficient reason and Occam's Razor, and contrary to a commonly held dogma of modern anthropology: all else being equal, survival of any given tradition from a common ancestor can be regarded as the default explanation, while any argument for independent development or convergence requires corroborating evidence. In other words, if there is not enough evidence to clearly support one of these positions over the other, then survival should be favored as it constitutes sufficient reason and provides by far the simplest explanation, thus satisfying Occam's Razor.

This should by no means be taken as a basis for drawing premature conclusions in the absence of sufficient evidence and analysis. Indeed literally everything presented in this book should be understood as a testable hypothesis, to be evaluated in the light of all the evidence, and by no means definitive in itself. It does, however, provide us with a useful heuristic, through which the likelihood of a hypothesis can be determined in cases where evidence is inconclusive. On this basis, it's important to understand that the argument for survival from a common ancestor should never be uncritically dismissed, as has so often happened in the past, simply because independent development or "convergence" is assumed to be the more reasonable explanation. It is not.[1]

Let's begin our HMC reconstruction by considering some of the traditions already covered in Chapter Four:

Bows and Arrows

Did the Out of Africa migrants have bows and arrows? And if so, did they use poison arrows? While the use of bows and arrows and arrow poison by HBP remains open to debate, since this technology may have been borrowed from neighboring Bantu groups (see Chapter Four), the widespread presence of bows and arrows both in and out of Africa makes it extremely likely that this technology was an important part of the material culture of HMC, from where it would have spread to the rest of the world.

While it's possible to argue, on the basis of its late appearance in the Americas, that the bow and arrow may have been independently invented there, it seems highly unlikely that it could have been independently invented everywhere it is found, as is sometimes claimed. There is nothing obvious about bows and arrows, and certainly nothing obvious about the archery skills necessary if they are to be of any use. Given what we now know about African origins, it seems logical to conclude that a technology as widely used as this must have had its beginnings on that continent and spread from there via HMC.

While the evidence for independent development in the Americas is very strong, and must be acknowledged, I see no such evidence for independent development in any other part of the world. As for the use of poison tips, on arrows, spears and darts, it seems logical to conclude that this too is very likely to have been an important part of the hunting technology of HMC, since such tips can be found among so many indigenous peoples in so many parts of the world today.

Bodily Decoration

We've already considered examples of scarification and body painting among Pygmies and Bushmen. Examples of both practices can be found in many different parts of the world:

See Figures 7.1 – 7.4

The question has always been whether or not all or most of these traditions are related and, if so, how. If scarification and body painting were already established as traditions among HBP, it seems likely that all such forms of bodily decoration stem from the same source. If so, such practices could only have been transmitted from Africa to the rest of the world via HMC.

Shamanism

Many explanations for the origin and spread of shamanism have been offered, as well as many different definitions of what it is and what sort of practices should be included as part of it. If we interpret it in the broadest possible terms, as a system of beliefs and behaviors incorporating trance, spirit possession, ritual, and ritual healing, then I think it safe to conclude that it must have originated within HBC, regardless of whether or not this ancestral group actually practiced "shamanism" in the strictest sense of the term. And if this is indeed the case, then it seems reasonable to argue that more or less the same cultural "package" could only have been transmitted to the rest of the world via HMC.

As I see it, those who insist that shamanism could only have originated where the word itself originated, among the paleo-Siberians of northern Eurasia, are still thinking in multiregional terms. Assuming it did originate in Siberia, then I see no way in which its spread throughout the rest of the world could have been accomplished, since there is no evidence of the migration of paleo-Siberians anywhere beyond the regions where they are now found.

The Sucking Cure

One of the most common techniques in the repertoire of shamans, healers, "medicine men," etc. is the method of curing the sick by literally *sucking* the sickness out of their bodies. Often it emerges in the form of a small stone, bone or "dart." As we've seen, such practices are common among EP, WP and Bu healers, and have thus been ascribed to HBC. More broadly, suction as a healing method is referenced several times in Mircea Eliade's comprehensive, though now somewhat outdated (1964), *Shamanism*. Eliade wrote the following with reference to North American Indian practice, but its similarity with Hewlett's description of Aka healing (see Chapter Four) is striking:

> Injurious objects are usually projected by sorcerers. They are pebbles, small animals, insects; the magician does not introduce them in concreto, but creates them by the power of his thoughts. They may also be sent by spirits, who sometimes themselves take up

86

residence in the patient's body. Once he has discovered the cause of the illness, the shaman extracts the magical objects by suction. (p.301).

Similar practices are reported by Eliade and many others among traditional peoples in many parts of the world. Here, for example, is a description of shamanic practices among Nepalese Buddhists:

> Both Wangchuk and Lhamo Dolkar are reputed to be able to cure both physical and complex psychosomatic or supernaturally caused complaints. Their main healing technique is sucking . . . Lhamo, who is in trance . . . when she heals, sucks any afflicted part of the body . . . . extracting in the process either a dark liquid or a dark sticky substance . . . and in the event of a more serious affliction, she may even extract stones, which are either white, brown or black
> (*Buddhist Healers in Nepal: Some Observations*, Angela Dietrich (http://himalaya.socanth.cam.ac.uk/collections/journals/contributions/pdf/CNAS_23_02_07.pdf), p. 474).

Of special interest is the following observation, also from Eliade's book:

> By suction, the shaman draws out with his teeth a small object "like a bit of black or white thread, sometimes like a nail paring." An Achomawi told De Angulo: "I don't believe those things come out of the sick man's body. The shaman always has them in his mouth before he starts the treatment. But he draws the sickness into them, he uses them to catch the poison. Otherwise how could he catch it" (*Shamanism*, p. 307).

The skepticism of the Achomawi informant makes sense. In fact there is very good evidence that the healer's performance in a great many instances — if not all — is a clever sham. I remember a story concerning a healer disturbed at his inability to produce the necessary object — until he learned the trick from an older colleague. He persisted with his investigations of the healer's "art" until he learned to produce an impressive display of blood along with the sucked out object — by biting his tongue!

If the history of religion begins with shamanism, as many now believe, then a clever bit of deceit may lie at its heart.

I've already made what I believe to be strong case for P/B style vocalizing as a pervasive and important aspect of HBC. What must be considered now is what role the style might have played in HMC. One clue, as far as Africa is concerned, is the very interesting center of P/B style to be found in a region very close to what is widely considered both a possible birthplace of "modern" humans and the staging area for the Out of Africa migration: the Omo River valley in southwest Ethiopia.

The following peoples in this region, all speakers of "Omotic" languages, vocalize at least some of the time using interlocking counterpoint, one of the most distinctive features of P/B: the Ari, Dorze, Gamo, Ghimira and Wolamo. As far as I know, the Dorze are the only ones who regularly yodel, though for them, as for just about all non-Pygmy or Bushmen groups worldwide, P/B is only one genre of many, and is performed only in the context of certain work situations or festivals. The similarity to Pygmy and Bushmen vocal style is striking: *Audio Example 12:Dorze Maskal Song*. (From *Ethiopia:Polyphony of the Dorze*, recorded by Bernard Lortat-Jacob.)

Judging from the widespread distribution of certain features of this very distinctive style, especially in certain key regions along the southern Out of Africa route along the Indian Ocean coast and beyond, it's difficult for me to believe that a very similar musical practice would not have played an important role in HMC. Indeed, aspects of P/B vocal style appear to have survived as a kind of "African signature" among indigenous groups in Southeast Asia, Southern China, Taiwan, the Philippines, Indonesia, New Guinea, Island Melanesia, and also among certain Siberian, Inuit and Amerindian groups, as well as among certain peasant communities in various regions of Europe, although such practices would appear to have a very different meaning for these peoples than it has for African Pygmies and Bushmen.

For one thing, the style usually tends to be more or less "watered down," lacking the complexity, subtlety, spontaneity and creative freedom so characteristic of almost all Pygmy and Bushmen music. The counterpoint is often more limited in scope, the degree of improvisation restricted, or in many cases non-existent. Performances tend to be planned in advance and often rehearsed, with a fixed rather than open-ended number of parts.

The social context in which this particular type of music is performed also tends to be far more restricted. In a great many cases, as for example, among the Dorze, the style is reserved for special occasions, often associated with some of the most important rituals, as though this music were consciously associated with the oldest and most powerful ancestral traditions. In other cases, we find it, as in the "throat singing" hocket of certain Paleosiberian and Inuit groups, characterized as a game, though as Nattiez (1999) has demonstrated, this "game" has decidedly shamanic roots.

It's important to understand that such limitations do *not* apply among African Pygmies and Bushmen. While certain repertoires are reserved for special ceremonies, such as the girl's *elima* or the *molimo* ceremony among the Mbuti, or the Eland or *Xhoma* rituals among the Ju/'hoansi Bushmen, the style as a whole is a characteristic, spontaneously expressed, aspect of everyday life, as it very likely was for HBC. Whether the same applies to P/B as practiced by HMC is not completely clear, especially since we find "watered down" and contextually restricted forms of P/B among many African groups as well.

Musical Instruments

Of special interest in our assessment of HMC are the many hocketed, polyphonic wind ensembles, of pipes, whistles, trumpets, horns or flutes, to be found among certain groups in Africa, organized in a manner very similar to the interlocking of parts so characteristic of P/B vocalizing. Typically, each instrument has a single note to play, or in some cases, a repeated phrase, which interweaves with all the other parts to produce a *resultant* melody, rhythm or polyphonic texture.

The Mbuti perform with hocketed ensembles of single-note pipes called *Luma*, tuned and kept for them by their Bantu "masters": *Audio Example 13: Mbuti Pipers*. (From *On The Edge Of The Ituri Forest*, recorded by Hugh Tracey.) The BaAka use the easily portable *mobeke* pipe, described as "a small whistle made from the stem of a papaw plant," for the same purpose. Among the Ba'Benzele Pygmies similar pipes are called *hindewhu*. In all cases, the pipes participate as equal partners with voices in hocketed/interlocked P/B style performances. Although today's Bushmen don't appear to have ensembles of this sort, hocketed panpipe ensembles are *reported* to have been an important aspect of the culture of their close relatives, the Khoi-Khoi (Hottentot) cattle herders.

Such ensembles, of pipes, panpipes, horns and trumpets are common in Africa. But very similar ensembles are also found outside of Africa among many of the same indigenous or "folk" populations that vocalize in some version of P/B style — a distribution pattern almost impossible to explain unless the tradition had been disseminated from Africa via HMC. The vocal and instrumental forms of P/B are so close stylistically and structurally that the latter most likely developed from the former, very early on. To give you an idea of how similar some of these widespread traditions can be, let's compare some audio clips: *Audio Example 14:Ouldeme Pipes* (from *Cameroon:Flutes of the Mandara Mountains*, recorded by Nathalie Fernando et Fabrice Marandola); *Audio Example Fifteen: Russian Pipers from Plekhovo Village* (recorded by *Olga Velitchkina*); *Audio Example 16: Panpipes of Buma*, Solomon Islands, (from Saydisc, *Spirit of Melanesia*).

Hocketed percussion, possibly a development from the very complex polyrhythmic interactions of P/B handclapping, is also an important tradition in many parts of Africa, with important echoes, once again, among indigenous populations along the "Out of Africa" route. Another instrument of great interest, with a very similar multi-regional distribution, is the slit drum, which is also, like stamping tubes, often played in hocketed/interlocked ensembles. Once again, it would seem as though the distribution of this very important instrument, often elaborately carved and with great ritual significance in certain cultures, can be explained only if it were part of a tradition disseminated via HMC.

Core Values

HMC would appear to have maintained many if not all of the most important core values of HBC: egalitarianism, relative gender-equality, cooperation, conflict avoidance, individual autonomy, and the sharing of vital resources, with strong sanctions against competition and violence. Since all of the above are characteristic of so many other hunting and gathering peoples worldwide, it seems likely that these values were inherited from HBC via HMC.

We mustn't forget, however, that not all indigenous peoples value non-violence, and indeed many are quite warlike, so we will need at some point to account for this very fundamental cultural shift. On the basis of a recent study correlating genetic and ethnographic evidence, Eduardo Moreno concludes that the Out of Africa migrants must have had a violent and warlike culture (Moreno 2011). Moreno's paper is the only one I've come across to date that deals with such issues from the perspective afforded by the "Out of Africa" model. Significantly, he is not an anthropologist, but a geneticist, and his paper has been published in a biological, not anthropological, journal.

Moreno begins in a spirit very much like mine, by reminding us that "the culture of the tribe(s) that left Africa to populate the rest of the world is likely to have dramatically shaped the subsequent cultures of History, because all non-Africans would have inherited those traditions as a primordial cultural background." He continues as follows, asking more or less the same questions I've been asking: "What did that ancestral tribe that migrated out of Africa look like? What of their culture and religion? Were they peaceful or belligerent? Those are questions of utmost importance because the cultural biases of such a tiny clan are likely to have influenced all non-African cultures."

Moreno associates a lack of violence with essentially the same groups I've singled out, those populations, such as the Pygmies and Bushmen, whose ancestry occupies the deepest clades of the mitochondrial tree (specifically L0, L1 and L2). I'm not sure I agree with his contention that the "Out of Africa" migrants (represented by L3) must have been warlike, but he makes a strong case, based on thinking very close to my own in style, which I find gratifying. Where his analysis differs from mine is in the emphasis he places not only on violent and warlike behavior, but also on the importance of certain other types of behavior that could be construed as consistent with a warlike culture, namely competitive sports and games such as wrestling and ritual combat.

This is an important aspect of his argument, because there are in fact many indigenous groups, particularly hunter-gatherers, which apparently share the Pygmy-Bushmen ethos of nonviolence and have no history of warlike behavior, head-hunting, etc. According to Moreno, however, several of these groups apparently engage in competitive games that might signal a warlike past. I must admit, he's uncovered a possibly important clue that I've overlooked. His sampling of hunter-gatherer groups with violent histories and warlike games is relatively small, however, and any exceptions would have to be accounted for — especially since it's much easier to understand how a peaceful population could be goaded into violence than vice versa.

Moreno may well be on the right track, but as I see it, future research along such lines will have to be very precise regarding the nature of the games and rivalries that could be associated with a violent ethos, and his sampling will need to be more complete. Given the many reports of pacifist behavior and values among so many foraging groups outside of Africa, it does seem to me that HMP may well have inherited the pacifist traditions and values of HBC, despite Moreno's very interesting argument to the contrary. Clearly additional investigation of this issue is needed. Regardless, Moreno has made an important contribution, opening the door to what could be a very fruitful line of research.

A Second Baseline

As with the list presented in Chapter Four, *Table One*, below, encapsulates all the evidence I've been able to come up with so far regarding the culture of the Out of Africa migrants. In this case, however, more than simply a list is required, because it's necessary to present not only the possible roots of any given tradition in the ancestral culture (HBC) but also to assess its distribution, insofar as possible, in both Africa and the rest of the world:

Table One – Worldwide Distribution of Cultural Elements Possibly Associated with the Out of Africa migrants (HMC)

	HBC	Distribution in Africa	Distribution Outside Africa	HMC	Comments
Hunting & Gathering	Yes	Present but sparse.	Present among certain indigenous peoples in South Asia, Southeast Asia, Siberia, N. Japan, Australia, Melanesia, the Americas. Absent in Europe and Polynesia.	Yes	
Honey Gathering	Yes	Present.	Ubiquitous among Hunter-Gatherers whenever available.	Yes	
Horticulture	No	Present.	Currently common as a secondary source of food for many indigenous groups, including groups usually regarded as hunter-gatherers.	No (?)	Presence in HMC unlikely, assuming HMP were nomadic

	HBC	Distribution in Africa	Distribution Outside Africa	HMC	Comments
Small bands	Yes	Among hunter-gatherers only.	Common among hunter-gatherer groups.	Yes	HMP was probably a single small band.
Nomadic	Yes	Among hunter-gatherers and pastoralists	Common among hunter-gatherers and some pastoralists.	Yes (?)	HMP were most likely nomadic, but not necessarily.
Kinship: informal, "universal"	Probably	Rare.	Very rare.	?	
Economics: communal	Yes	Among hunter-gatherers only.	Common among hunter-gatherers, rare elsewhere.	Yes	
Political Structure: acephalous	Yes	Among hunter-gatherers only.	Common among hunter-gatherers.	Yes	
Beehive huts	Yes	Common among Pygmies, Bushmen and Hadza. Variants common among other African groups, such as the Swazi and Zulu.	Sparse but very widespread; found mostly among hunter-gatherers.	Yes	For more on beehive huts, see the following chapter.
Spears	Yes	Very common.	Very common worldwide.	Yes	
Bows and arrows	Most likely	Very common.	Very common worldwide.	Yes	
Poison spear and/or arrow tips	Most likely	Present mostly among hunter-gatherers, but also some farming groups.	Widespread among many hunter-gatherer groups.	Yes	

	HBC	Distribution in Africa	Distribution Outside Africa	HMC	Comments
Wooden tools	Yes	Common.	Common.	Yes	
Stone tools	Yes	Now rare.	Now rare. Replaced almost everywhere by metal tools.	Yes	
Tone Language	Yes	Widespread.	Widespread in Southeast Asia and East Asia. Common in the Punjab region of India and Pakistan. Not uncommon in Melanesia and the Americas. Rare elsewhere.	Yes	

	HBC	Distribution in Africa	Distribution Outside Africa	HMC	Comments
Music: vocal interlock	Yes	Common among Pygmy and Bushmen groups. Also found among certain other African groups, either associated with Pygmies or Bushmen or currently living in refuge areas. Especially common among certain farming groups in the highlands of southwest Ethiopia. Found also among the Mikea foragers of Madagascar.	Relatively rare, but widely distributed among indigenous peoples in various refuge areas of Southeast Asia, Indonesia, Taiwan, Siberia, Melanesia, Europe, the Caucasus and Central and South America, almost always in refuge areas. Very rare or absent in South Asia, West Asia, Central Asia, Northeast Asia, Australia, North America (aside from California) and Polynesia.	Yes	The Pygmies and Bushmen of Africa, and possibly the Mikea of Madagascar, appear to be the only people in the world who sing in this manner spontaneously and on an everyday basis. Among other peoples, in Africa and elsewhere, this style of singing is usually reserved for special occasions, e.g. rituals, harvest celebrations, etc.

	HBC	Distribution in Africa	Distribution Outside Africa	HMC	Comments
Music: yodel	Yes	Common among almost all Pygmy and Bushmen groups, though not found among the Bedzan Pygmies. Much less common elsewhere in Africa.	Often found among indigenous peoples, and, more rarely, among some European peasant groups, where it is usually associated with vocal interlock (see above). Also found in the Caucasus, and in certain herding songs of Europe (especially Switzerland) and the USA (e.g., cowboy songs).	Yes	

	HBC	Distribution in Africa	Distribution Outside Africa	HMC	Comments
Music: hocketing pipe, panpipe, flute, trumpet or horn ensembles	Very likely	Relatively rare but widespread. Pipe or whistle ensembles found among both western and eastern Pygmy groups, but not currently among Bushmen groups.	Rare but widespread among indigenous groups in Southeast Asia, Indonesia, Melanesia, Europe, Central and South America, almost always in refuge areas. Absent in Taiwan, Siberia, South Asia, Australia, Polynesia and North America, with the possible exception of Northwest Coast.	Yes	While pipe ensembles are not currently found among Bushmen, they were widely reported among the closely related "Hotten-tots," suggesting that some Bushmen groups may have used them in the past.

	HBC	Distribution in Africa	Distribution Outside Africa	HMC	Comments
Music: hocketing percussion ensembles (stamping tubes, drums, gongs, xylophones, etc.)	No	Very common.	Commonly found among indigenous groups in SE Asia, Indonesia, Melanesia, Polynesia and South America. Rare in Europe, with the exception of an unusual type of Basque stamping tube tradition	Pro-bably	
Music: slit drums	No	Not uncommon.	Commonly found among indigenous groups in Southeast Asia, Indonesia, Melanesia, Polynesia, and the Americas. Absent in Europe, Central and NE Asia, Taiwan, Siberia, South Asia (?), and Australia.	Pro-bably	
Music: membrano-phones (drums with skin heads)	No	Very common, especially among Bantu groups.	Commonly found among a great many different societies worldwide. Not found in Australia.	Pro-bably	

	HBC	Distribution in Africa	Distribution Outside Africa	HMC	Comments
Music: Songs originating in dreams or trance.	Yes	Not uncommon. Associated with shamanism.	Not uncommon among indigenous peoples. Associated with shamanism.	Yes	
Wood carving, especially masks.	No	Common.	Commonly found along the southeastern-most range of the Out of African trail, e.g., southeast Asia, Melanesia, Polynesia, and also the Americas, especially among NorthWest Coast and South American Indians.	Yes	
Rock Art	No	Associated with Bushmen groups of the past. Not found among contemporary groups.	No longer practiced, but many examples have been found, from every continent.	Yes	Since we see no evidence of rock art among any Pygmy group, we are unable to include it as part of HBC.

	HBC	Distribution in Africa	Distribution Outside Africa	HMC	Comments
Shamanism	Possibly	Common.	Common among indigenous groups worldwide.	Yes	
Possession and trance	Yes	Common.	Common among many indigenous groups worldwide.	Yes	
Extraction of harmful objects by suction	Yes	Common.	Common among many indigenous groups worldwide.	Yes	
Scarification	Yes	Common	Common among many indigenous groups worldwide.	Yes	
Core values 1: egalitarian-ism, cooperation, individual-ism, sharing of vital resources.	Yes	Found almost exclusively among hunter-gatherers.	Common among many hunter-gatherer and horticultural societies worldwide. Rare elsewhere. Thought by Marija Gimbutas to have been characteristic of "Old European" culture.	Yes	

	HBC	Distribution in Africa	Distribution Outside Africa	HMC	Comments
Core values 2: non-violence, conflict avoidance.	Yes	Found almost exclusively among hunter-gatherers.	Found among some, but not all, hunter-gatherers and horticulturalists. Many such groups engage in endemic warfare, blood feuds, headhunting, cannibalism, etc. Possibly characteristic of "Old European" culture.	?	More research is needed to determine whether HMP were or were not violent and warlike. See discussion of Moreno 2011, above.
Gender Relations: relative equality, based on male-female complemen-tarity.	Yes	Found almost exclusively among hunter-gatherers.	Found almost exclusively among certain hunter-gatherer groups, but not all. Rare elsewhere.	Yes (?)	

	HBC	Distribution in Africa	Distribution Outside Africa	HMC	Comments
Behavior: mostly cooperative, unaggressive and peaceful; however, sometimes contentious, sexist and/or violent in spite of relative gender equality and strong social sanctions against violent behavior.	Yes	Characteristic of most hunter-gatherer groups.	Characteristic of certain hunter-gatherer groups, but not all.	Pro-bably	

Table 1 should be understood as a tentative first step. Clearly much more research will be needed before any of these hypotheses can be definitively evaluated. Many of these issues will be examined in more detail in upcoming chapters, as we follow the descendants of HMP in their wanderings through many different regions of the world.

_ _

1. Granted, this approach will seem counter-intuitive to most anthropologists. The notion that so-called "universals," such as music, language, religion, etc., or simple commonalities, such as the widely distributed use of certain tools or dwellings or artistic or musical styles, etc., are best explained through some mysterious process of convergence, due to certain innate properties of the human mind or the natural environment, was long taken for granted, because it was the only explanation consistent with the multiregional view that dominated anthropological thinking for many years. If modern humans and their culture had originated in very different corners of the world, based on the traditions of various far flung archaic hominids, such as Neanderthals or Homo Erectus, such an interpretation would make sense. Hardly anyone accepts that model anymore, as it has

been completely contradicted by the genetic evidence. But old habits die hard.

From the standpoint of the Out of Africa model, based on the notion that all modern humans share a relatively recent ancestry, it seems much more reasonable to infer that the many cultural commonalities we see worldwide most likely stem from the same common inheritance. As should go without saying, all such hypotheses on either side of the fence, regardless of Occam's Razor or any other principle, scientific or otherwise, must be regarded as provisional until decisive evidence one way or the other becomes available.

Chapter Eight: Beehive Huts in Depth

Could the Out of Africa migrants (HMP) have inherited beehive huts from the ancestral group (HBP), and passed on that same tradition to at least some of their many descendants? I'd like, at this point, to focus our attention on this particular question because a comparative analysis of beehive huts from many different parts of the world can serve as a model for how one might go about evaluating the distribution of any cultural element. And, thanks to the Internet, we have at our disposal a rich store of photographic evidence to consider and evaluate.

There are many types of "beehive" hut in various parts of the world — and the question is: are they related or is their shape simply a coincidence. When the designs and methods of construction are extremely similar, and they are found among hunter-gatherers or horticulturalists with many traditions in common with HBC, then it would be difficult, I think, to deny common ancestry. When found in more "advanced" societies, in more elaborate forms, or built from different construction materials, then the relationship is not so clear — further research is certainly indicated, because the shape itself may have been passed on traditionally, even if other aspects of construction have changed.

Here's a painting of some beehive huts, very much like the Pygmy, Bushmen and Hadza huts we've already seen:

See Figure 8.1

Only these are from Australia. Australia might seem extremely remote, certainly very far from Africa. Nevertheless: it is exactly the same distance from HBC as are the Pygmies and Bushmen as far as time is concerned. It's generally accepted that humans migrated all over the world from Africa, so does it really make a difference how far they wandered, so long as they were intent on maintaining their traditions? And if there is anything we know about indigenous peoples, it is their absolute fixation on their ancestors and the traditions associated with them.

Getting back to Africa, here are beehive huts from the Dorze people, of Southwest Ethiopia:

See Figures 8.2 and 8.3

The Dorze are not hunter-gatherers, and in fact have a culture considerably more complex than that of the Pygmies or Bushmen. As we heard in the previous chapter, their music, nevertheless, has many striking points in common with P/B style, including rather elaborate interlocking counterpoint, and yodel as well. Unlike Pygmy or Bushmen huts, these are definitely built to last. Was there some evolutionary process that began with HBC, or are these huts a completely independent invention? Would it be possible to find a string of huts in various places leading up to the Dorze type that might represent different "stages" in their evolution? Would it matter if we could find such intermediary "stages"? I'm not sure. One thing I do know, however: if the geneticists are on the right track, then the Dorze, like every other people now living in our world, are descended from HBP. If their ancestors had beehive huts, then why would it be surprising to find beehive huts among them now?

Similar speculations arise regarding more permanent dwellings by other, more "advanced" African groups, such as the Zulu and Swazi:

See Figures 8.4 and 8.5

The very similar Swazi and Zulu huts depicted above are clearly more elaborate than the huts we've seen from Pygmy, Bushmen and Hadza sources. But when we compare them with a more traditional type of Zulu hut, it appears as though the more complex design could have evolved from the simpler:

See Figure 8.6

The following "beehive" hut is from a completely different part of the world, and made of stone rather than wood and leaves:

See Figure 8.7

It's beehive shape might well be a coincidence. Or it might have evolved from an earlier type, also found in the British Isles, but much closer to traditional African designs:

See Figure 8.8

Compare the above with these huts, from New Guinea:

See Figure 8.9

I'm wondering how the stone hut was constructed. If a wooden framework, similar to the framework of the traditional African huts, were constructed first, it would have been easy to position the stones against the wood, which could be easily removed once the stone structure was complete. Without such a superstructure it's difficult to conceive how the upper stones would have remained in place, especially since mortar was not used. In this way it might be possible to imagine a single line of evolution from the wood and grass huts pictured above to the stone ones. On the other hand, if some other method of placing the stones had been used, then the connection wouldn't be so clear.

The same thinking could be applied to these mud huts, from the Near East:

See Figures 8.10 and 8.11

How were they constructed? If built over a wooden framework similar to that of the traditional African huts, that would suggest a possible connection with HBC. If not, then one would have to consider independent invention.

Is the igloo a derivation from the beehive hut?

See Figure 8.12

Not all Igloos are made of ice. This one is covered with skins and probably had a wooden frame:

See Figure 8.13

Did the ice Igloo evolve from a hut like this one? If so, could it too be traceable to HBC? Skins are a natural substitute for leaves or grass in an environment without much vegetation. And when there's no wood around to build a framework, then ice might be the only recourse. Nevertheless, the Igloo is definitely one of the more brilliant inventions of the human mind, no question. It's also an excellent example of cultural adaptation to environmental conditions. But where there is adaptation, there must also be something already on hand that's been adapted.

The remarkable similarities between the framework of the Wigglesworth Observatory

See Figure 8.14

and that of a traditional beehive hut

See Figure 8.15

are truly fascinating. As should be obvious, an historical connection between them is highly unlikely. However, a comparison between the two can be instructive when assessing whether common origin or independent invention is most likely. The first lesson to be learned is that looks can be deceiving — two designs can be strikingly similar and yet historically unrelated. For one thing, the observatory, unlike the Australian hut, is not a dwelling. For another, it is not at all typical for the culture in which it is a part, where almost all buildings are rectangular in shape.

Moreover, it was designed to serve a very specific, very specialized function, characteristic of the technological orientation of its culture, which has no equivalent in the culture of the Australian aborigines or indeed any hunting and gathering people. Finally, there is no historical record of any connection between the design of an observatory and the design of a dwelling, nor any record of any intermediate types between the two ever having existed.

When we turn to a comparison between Hadza huts and those of Bushmen the situation is radically different. Here too, we find a strong similarity:

See Figures 8.16 and 8.17

But in this case the circumstances are also similar, in fact just about identical. In both cases we are dealing with dwellings; they are typical for both groups; they are both typically constructed by females; and they serve identical functions, despite the fact that they were constructed in totally different environments. Moreover, the two groups share a very similar hunter-gatherer lifestyle, along with a very similar, essentially egalitarian, value system. And since the Hadza also live in Africa, suggesting at least the possibility of an historical association at some point in the past, it might not be all that difficult to persuade even the most dedicated anthropological "splitter" that there just might be a connection of some sort between them.

Next, let's consider a cluster of huts from a totally different part of the world:

See Figure 8.18

In this case, all the above similarities apply except for one. These huts are not from Africa, but Australia. Because of the vast distance between the two continents, no possible historical connection can be inferred — unless we are willing to consider common origin, i.e., survival from an ancestral culture common to the ancestry of both groups, prior to a divergence that could only have taken place tens of thousands of years ago.

If, on the other hand, we want to assume that some Australian ancestor independently invented the beehive hut at some point in Australian history, we need to ask ourselves what sort of dwellings might have preceded it, and what their motivation would have been to change to some new design despite their otherwise strictly traditional lifestyle, and why that new design would just happen to resemble a beehive hut.

Also, we would need to ask why so many other groups in so many other parts of the world, and in so many different environments, would make a similar change from a traditionally established dwelling, to "converge" on essentially that same type of beehive design, each with reasons stemming from a different cause, with the similarities to all the other designs purely due to coincidence. (Remember that beehive huts are found in a great many different environments, so convergent evolution due to environmental adaptation won't hold much water.)

Is it Really That Simple?

While it might seem as though a design as "simple" as the beehive hut could have been invented many times in the past, as a convenient means for hunter-gatherers to put together a handy, temporary dwelling, beehive huts are by no means all that simple, and in fact a considerable amount of careful planning and effort goes into their construction.

I propose a thought experiment along the following lines. Hire several teams made up of people from many different backgrounds and cultures, with the sole proviso that none come from cultures where beehive huts are found. Drop each into a different environment where beehive huts are known to have been commonly used in the past. Inform them that they are to live in this environment for at least a week and instruct them to build temporary shelters for themselves, solely from materials normally available to hunter-gatherers, that will hold up decently during that period.

If even a single instance of anything close to a beehive hut is produced I would be extremely surprised. What one would expect to see would be various types of lean-to shelters, or teepees, or crude rectangular designs of various sorts. The closest thing to a beehive hut that such a group might come up with might look something like this, for example:

See Figure 8.19

Here we have a photo of a crude teepee-like framework, covered by skins. A shelter of this kind would be far simpler to design and construct than a beehive hut and yet serve its purpose equally well, I would think.

How to Build a Beehive Hut

Why would anyone interested only in cobbling together something simple and practical, with minimal effort, want to go to the extra trouble of building a shelter that required all the following steps?

Instructions for constructing a beehive hut (from "Home, Home on the Ridge," based on the native American culture of Poverty Point, Louisiana http://www.crt.state.la.us/archaeology/ppexpeditions/homehandout.html):

Materials:
Eight willow branches, each 10 feet tall, for the uprights
About eight willow branches for the crosspieces
Bark from the willow branches or string
Lots of palmetto leaves
Indoor hut: a large piece of cardboard for the base, cardboard corner scraps to secure the framework, hot glue gun, and exacto knife
Outdoor hut: post hole digger or a digging stick to dig holes for the framework

Directions:
1. Use a string and a pencil as a large compass. Draw a circle on either the cardboard (inside) or the dirt (outside). The diameter of the hut can be as big as you like. Experiment with the different diameters because a larger diameter will result in a shorter hut. All of your willow poles will need to be the same length.
2. Divide your circle into eight equal parts by marking halves, fourths, and eighths.
3. Dig eight holes for your upright poles along the circumference of the circle.
Outside: Use a digging stick just like the Poverty Point people may have done or use a post hole digger to make your holes.
Inside: Hot glue a cardboard corner square scrap along the diameter of the circle where you want the "hole." Ask an adult to use an exacto knife to "dig" the hole by cutting into the scrap piece of cardboard.
4. Build the upright section of your hut by placing two willow branches in the holes on opposite sides of the circle.

Outside: Stomp dirt back into the hole around the pole.

Inside: Squirt hot glue in the hole before you place the branch in it.

5. Bend the two opposing branches so that they form an arch. Overlap the branches and tie them together at the top with a strip of willow bark or string. Continue with steps 4 and 5 until you have connected all four pairs. Tie the pairs together at the top of the house.

6. Add horizontal crosspieces around the sides of the hut by tying branches to your uprights. The distance between the crosspieces will be determined by the size of your palmetto leaves. The palmetto leaves should overlap each other, so the distance between the layers of crosspieces should be slightly less than the measurement of the palmetto leaves from the stem to the tip. This will probably be about one foot.

7. Leave room between two of the uprights for a door into your hut.

8. Tie a palmetto leaf to the bottom crosspiece. Use the end spikes on the palmetto as string by tearing them all the way to the stem (if they break off, just use the next spike). Put both palmetto spikes over the crosspiece and then bring them back to the front of the palmetto leaf. Tie the spikes together in a square knot (right over left, then left over right on top of the palmetto leaf).

9. Continue tying palmetto leaves on the crosspieces, overlapping them so the rain won't get in your house. Each palmetto leaf acts like a little umbrella. When you get all around the bottom level of the house, begin tying leaves on the next level up, making sure that the top leaves overlap the ones on the lower level. Continue adding levels of crosspieces and palmetto leaves until you get to the top!

10. Leave a smoke hole at the top of your house, but DO NOT build a fire in your hut! Remember that the real huts were 12 to 14 feet in diameter.

(For drawing of hut framework, see Figure 8.20)

I rest my case.

Chapter Nine: The Migration

I want at this point to move from the migrants to the great migration they are thought to have initiated, sometime between 80,000 and 60,000 years ago, with a short but probably quite hazardous trip from the Horn of Africa to what is now Yemen. According to the preponderance of the archaeological and genetic evidence, they and their descendants subsequently made their way slowly (or possibly rapidly) across the continent of Asia, following a "southern route," along the Indian Ocean coast.

In his pathbreaking book, *The Real Eve*, Stephen Oppenheimer, one of the most thorough explicators and synthesizers of the "Out of Africa" model, summarizes the mitochondrial (mtDNA) evidence as follows:

> [O]nly one small twig (Out-of-Africa Eve) of one branch, out of the dozen major African maternal clans available, survived after leaving the continent to colonize the rest of the world. From this small group evolved all modern human populations outside Africa.... I cannot overemphasize the importance of the simple and singular fact that only one African line accounts for all non Africans. (The Real Eve:64)

To clarify (or confuse, as the case may be), here's a family portrait of homo sapiens, from the female (mtDNA) point of view, as seen by population geneticists (phylogenetic tree designed by "Maju," for his blog *Leherensuge* — http://leherensuge.blogspot.com/2009/04/mtdna-tree-version-11.html):

See Figure 9.1

That's mitochondrial Eve, at the upper left, followed by her two daughters, L0 and L1. The "twig" Oppenheimer calls "Out-of-Africa Eve" branched off from one of the major haplogroups, L3, and subsequently divided into two more twigs, which eventually grew into very thick branches indeed: M and N. As Maju's tree indicates, literally all non-African populations belong to either the M or the N lineage.

On his website, *The Journey of Mankind* (2004a), Oppenheimer traces the Out of Africa route in red, starting roughly 85,000 years ago, from the horn of Africa across the Red Sea, northeast along the coast of the Arabian desert, then southeast along the coast of India, and from there following the coastline of the Indian Ocean eastward all the way through Indonesia, at that time part of the Asian mainland, and then northward, up the Pacific coast to what is now southern China.

See Figure 9.2

Following the Trail

Oppenheimer estimates the entire trip, starting with the initial crossing of the original band from the Horn of Africa to Yemen and thence from the Arabian coast all the way to Indonesia, might have taken no more than 10,000 years (Oppenheimer 2004b:70-71). How does he know all this? Through evidence gleaned from indigenous peoples still living along the same pathway:

> If all non-Africans share one ancestral origin [i.e. Africa]...all their trails should lead back to one point in space and time; and all the colonies, left behind en route, should hold genetic and even physical keys to who went that way. This is the case.... Along the coastline of the Indian Ocean we still find small colonies of aboriginal peoples who may be descended locally from those first beachcombers.... (156)

Let's attempt as best we can to recreate the original "beachcomber" journey. Apparently the migrants, having made their way across the Bab el Mendab and the coast of the Arabian Peninusla, continued eastward to the Indus Delta and from there some may have proceeded up that river while the rest continued along the coast of what are now Pakistan, India and Bangla Desh. Sri Lanka would, at that time, have been part of the mainland, so they would have passed through that region as well. The question is whether or not they left colonies in place as they traveled or simply bypassed South Asia altogether, gradually progressing eastward as a mobile unit. Everything depends on how we interpret the genetic, archaeological and ethnographic evidence.

One possibility is a so-called "wave of advance," with each generation taking root in a particular spot and subsequent generations moving on only when feeling increased pressure as the region becomes saturated. This would produce not so much isolated colonies as an ever growing population continually expanding in all possible directions. If this had been the case, then we would expect to find evidence that the Out of Africa migrants expanded into all inhabitable regions of South Asia before continuing east along the coast — the migration would not in fact have been a coastal migration at all, but a progressive saturation of the South Asiatic peninsula, leaving numerous archaeological sites north of the coastal regions, dating from the same, very early period; and the genetic haplotypes found throughout central and northern Asia today would be far older than any found further along the coast.

However corroborating evidence for such a "wave of advance," from either archaeology or genetics, is nowhere to be found. In fact some of the oldest evidence of the migration is located well beyond India, in Southeast Asia, New Guinea and Australia. Such a pattern strongly suggests that the migrants must, as Oppenheimer argues, have had a coastal culture, constraining them, largely, to the ocean front as they progressed. So if there was a "wave of advance" it would most likely have been confined to the coast.

What seems most logical is a relatively rapid migration, with the migrants moving along the seacoast by boat or raft, leaving various colonies behind as they went, eventually progressing beyond South Asia to Southeast Asia, and what is now Indonesia, as well as many other places in that same general area, including Sahul. This would have left the Out of Africa immigrants strewn out in various colonies along the Indian Ocean coast, all the way from the western border of Pakistan to Indonesia, the Philippines, southern China, and also New Guinea and Australia.

A Straightforward Scenario

If the migrating populations simply marched or sailed across the full length of the Asiatic beach, leaving colonies as they went, it stands to reason that all these colonies would have been pretty similar in a great many ways. Since I went to so much trouble to characterize HMC, I could save myself further effort by characterizing the culture of their migratory descendants in essentially the same terms. Why not? If they were direct descendents of HBP and HMP, why wouldn't they be maintaining the same traditions? And there is some evidence that would tend to support such an idea.

For example, I have before me a paper titled "The Muduga and Kurumba of Kerala, South India and the Social Organization of Hunting and Gathering" (Tharakan 2007). Both groups are characterized as hunter-gatherers, though they also practice "non-intensive" agriculture. They "hunted and gathered in rain forests" but also, like so many African Pygmy groups, "frequently interacting with outsiders."

> Gathering in the forest is of great importance both as a means of obtaining food and also as a source of raw materials. Major plant foods include tubers, edible roots, mushrooms, leaves, berries, nuts, seeds and seasonal fruits (Table 2). A considerable portion of the diet

comes from roots, tubers, yams and green leaves (p. 9). . . Gathering and collecting is done both by men and women, although it is mainly a women's activity. . .

Collection of honey is done only by men who are highly skilled in activities such as climbing big trees, driving away the bees, and also tracing the bees and locating the honey comb in the thick forest (p. 10). . . Hunting is mostly a male activity where groups of men, both agnates and affines, gather together and proceed into the forest in search of game for one or two days (p. 11).

So far this sounds very much like the African hunter-gatherer norm. There are differences as well. The Muduga and Kurumba now hunt mainly with rifles and traditionally hunted with traps rather than bows and arrows, a tradition which was, apparently, lost at some point. They do hunt with dogs, however, as do African Pygmies.

As far as core values are concerned,

game is shared equally among all those who participate in the hunt and if the game is sizable a share is given to all other households in the hamlet. Apart from the normal share, the inner meat (i.e., heart and liver) and a thigh go to the person who shot the animal. . .

Sharing and food exchange among the Muduga/Kurumba is a highly institutionalized daily activity. It is necessary that those who obtain game share with those who did not. The Muduga/ Kurumba believe that even small game should be shared among all members of the hamlet so as to avoid the craving (daham) they feel for meat. However, small game is often shared only among the members of the hunting party and their close kin. Large game animals are always widely shared (pp. 12-13).

All of the above is strikingly similar to what we find among African Pygmies and Bushmen, though in the case of the Mbuti, the best cuts go to the owner of the arrow rather than the one who did the shooting.

As far as kinship is concerned, we find a flexibility quite similar to what we've seen for both Pygmies and Bushmen: "Though they are patrilineal by descent, the system shows bilateral tendencies of a flexible and loosely structured system (p. 15)." Also, as with the Pygmies and Bushmen, we see no signs of warlike or competitive tendencies, but on the contrary, a willingness to peacefully share with others, even from other groups:

Among the Muduga/Kurumba it is the corporate group, the clan, which owns the land and has primary rights over its plant and animal resources. However, people from other groups and hamlets are never restricted from hunting and gathering in the clan's territory.

Though there are significant differences as well, the most important being their clan structure and their long-term involvement with swidden agriculture, these Indian tribals do in fact seem quite close, in a great many ways, to African Pygmies and Bushmen, and thus to their HBP and HMP ancestors. And as I hope everyone reading here understands, such strong affinities should no longer simply be attributed to "hunter-gatherer-ivity." Here we have very strong cultural evidence, consistent with the genetic evidence, of a historical continuity between the Out of Africa migrants and at least some of the many tribal peoples of India.

The picture of a continuous migration path from Africa through South Asia is reinforced by additional cultural information gleaned from the *Cambridge Encyclopedia of Hunters and Gatherers*, on seven Indian tribal groups, the Andamanese Islanders (Jarawa and Onge), the Birhor, Chenchu, Nayaka, Paliyan, Hill Pandaram and the Veddahs of Sri Lanka. The picture for most of these groups is roughly similar, with gathering and hunting (often with bows and arrows) supplemented with some form of swidden agriculture in all but the Andaman groups, who completely lack farming traditions. The term "egalitarian" is used in almost all instances to characterize their political and economic situation and most (though not all) of these groups are described as generally non-violent and informally communal, with no permanent leaders.

The Gap

The picture I have drawn thus far, of a relatively straightforward west-east progression, seems reasonably logical and relatively unproblematic. But there are some serious discrepancies that cannot be ignored — it does not completely fit all the evidence. Oppenheimer offers a hint when he notes that

[c]uriously, some of the best, if not the only archaeological evidence...comes not from India, South Arabia or Africa, but from the later parts of the trail—the Malay Peninsula, New Guinea, and Australia (ibid.:156, 159).

Oppenheimer's observation is particularly apt in view of a curious and disturbing gap in the genetic evidence, due to

> the paradox of the Indian genetic picture, in which the genetic trail of the beachcombers can be detected, but the bulk of Indian subgroups...are unique to the subcontinent, especially among the tribes of the south-east. This is what we would expect for a recovery from a great disaster (*The Real Eve*, p. 193).

What sort of disaster could have taken place, and how could we possibly determine what it was and when it occurred? Oppenheimer finds a very interesting and possibly very important clue in "the greatest natural calamity to befall any humans, ever," the eruption, c. 70,000-74,000 years ago, of Mount Toba, in Sumatra. The explosion was so vast it left a plume of ash over the entirety of India for approximately five years, what Oppenheimer has called a "nuclear winter," in which almost every living thing in that area would have been wiped out (Oppenheimer 2004b:82). This is one of the very few events in prehistory that can be precisely dated and measured, since "a metres-thick ash layer is found throughout the region."

Additional genetic evidence for such a gap is provided by an apparent discrepancy in the distribution of mtDNA haplogroups M and N (which he nicknames "Manju" and "Nasreen"):

> In West Eurasia there is only Nasreen; in most of East Eurasia there are even mixtures of Nasreen and Manju, but on the east coast of India there is nearly all Manju. The latter is consistent with near local extinction following the Toba explosion with recovery only of Manju on the east coast.

Oppenheimer next proceeds to a consideration of the most important of Nasreen's "daughters," haplogroup R, which he dubs Rohani:

> What is perhaps most interesting about the unique Indian flowerings of the Manju and Rohani clans is a hint that they represent a local recovery from the Toba disaster . . . A devastated India could have been recolonized from the west by Rohani types and from the east more by Manju types (183).

Turning to evidence from the male line, as found in the Y chromosome, he finds a yawning gap in the distribution of the Y haplogroup referred to as YAP (which he calls "Abel"):

116

A puzzling aspect of the Abel trail is the big gap in his distribution between West Eurasia and the Far East and, notably, *his complete absence from India*. That he was on the beachcombing trail is evident from the presence of Asian YAP in the Andaman Islands, Cambodia and Japan (my emphasis — p. 188).

For Oppenheimer this disconcerting gap can best be explained

by the devastating effect of the Toba blast on the Indian subcontinent, as suggested by the geology and the maternal genetic story. . . Toba could have created a genetic bottleneck in India, which was followed by a predominant local recovery of the Seth line [haplogroup S] at the expense of his two beachcombing brothers Cain [haplogroup C] and Abel. (189-190)

The notion of a major genetic bottleneck in South Asia, occurring after an initial "beachcomber" colonization of the entirety of the Indian Ocean coast, is potentially very significant. For geneticists, a "bottleneck" represents a sudden population loss, due either to migration or some sort of disastrous event, which severely reduces the genetic diversity of the original population. This usually leads to a "founder effect" through which a new lineage, with a very different genetic profile, is born.

While Oppenheimer's evidence could be considered somewhat out-of-date (his book appeared in 2003), results consistent with the mtDNA discrepancy he highlighted can be seen in a more recently published paper, "Phylogeographic distribution of mitochondrial DNA macrohaplogroup M in India" (Maji, Krithika and Vasulu 2009), where we see a map of haplogroup M distribution very similar to the one displayed on p. 181 of Oppenheimer's book:

See Figure 9.3

Of the 13 different mainland tribal groups represented in the leftmost map, 10 are located in the Eastern and Southern portions of India and only 3 elsewhere, consistent with the distribution reported by Oppenheimer, and reflecting, for him, the effects of a devastating ancient event, centered to the East and South of the Indian subcontinent.

Still more genetic research reinforces Oppenheimer's surprising finding. A recently published article, "Correcting for Purifying Selection: An

Improved Human Mitochondrial Molecular Clock" (Soares et al. 2009) notes a genetic inconsistency between South and East Asia:

> In the context of the southern-coastal-route model, it should be noted that although the distribution of haplogroup M has . . . been used to support the southern route model, the age of haplogroup M in India, at 49.4 (39.0; 60.2) kya, is significantly lower than in East Asia, at 60.6 (47.3; 74.3) kya . . . At face value, this could suggest an origin of haplogroup M in East Asia and a later migration back into South Asia, suggesting that it may have been a "pre-M" lineage that initially crossed South Asia. . . Southeast Asia may [therefore] be the point of origin of haplogroup M . . . Alternatively, *if M dispersed with N and R through South Asia, M may have been caught up in a subsequent bottleneck and founder effect so that its age signals the time of re-expansion rather than first arrival* (p. 752 — my emphasis).

Additional evidence for the same gap comes from an unusually thorough and critical study by Richard Cordaux et al, Mitochondrial DNA analysis reveals diverse histories of tribal populations from India, 2003. While it is sometimes assumed that the tribal peoples of India are directly descended from the initial wave of Out of Africa migrants, Cordaux et al found little sign of that:

> Our analyses of mtDNA variation in tribal populations of India indicate that groups in different geographic regions have different demographic histories. In general, southern tribes have reduced mtDNA diversity and mismatch distributions strongly indicative of recent bottlenecks. The distinctiveness of southern groups is also emphasized by the MDS analyses and AMOVA. However, *it is difficult to distinguish from these data between old and severe bottlenecks or more recent and less severe bottlenecks* (my emphasis).

The picture they found is, in fact, more consistent with a gap:

> three typical east-Asian mtDNA haplogroups (A, B and F) are absent or virtually absent from non-northeast India . . . Furthermore, the fourth typical east Asian mtDNA haplogroup M has a different structure in India as compared to other Asian areas. This suggests that, although they show close affinities, the east Asian and Indian mtDNA gene pools are fairly distinct. *This result is consistent with the*

suggestion that the east Asian and Indian mtDNA pools have been separated from each other for about 30 000 years (262 — my emphasis).

The genetic discrepancy is paralleled by morphological and linguistic distinctions, as noted by Oppenheimer:

> In Nepal, Burma and Eastern India we come across the first Mongoloid East Asian faces. These populations generally speak East Asian languages, contrasting strongly with their neighbors who mostly speak Indo-Aryan or Dravidian languages (pp. 181-182).

While such a gap might at first seem to be a stumbling block in our understanding of the earliest migrations of modern humans out of Africa, it is also, as I see it, a potentially important clue, which could explain certain other discrepancies, some of which are so obvious as to have been taken for granted by the great majority of investigators.

A Musical "Signature"

What struck me with tremendous force while reading this portion of Oppenheimer's book for the first time, was the truly remarkable correspondence with the musical evidence. There is in fact a surprising gap in the musical picture, which conforms very closely indeed to the gap identified in so much of the genetic, ethnographic and archaeological evidence. To understand the meaning of this gap, we must first make ourselves aware of certain striking affinities among musical traditions in many different parts of the world.

As we learned in Chapter One, one of the most distinctive aspects of Pygmy/Bushmen style (P/B) is the interlocking or interweaving of parts. In many cases the interwoven effect is produced by a practice known as "hocket," where one part is completed by another part, with the effect of a phrase or melody tossed back and forth between two, or sometimes several, interlocking and often overlapping voices or instruments, to produce an integrated "resultant" texture. Similarly interlocking, contrapuntal and/or hocketed traditions, often featuring yodeling as well, have been found among indigenous peoples located along portions of the "Out of Africa" trail, along a path stretching from Southeast Asia, Taiwan, and the Philippines, down to Indonesia and beyond, to New Guinea and many of the smaller islands of Melanesia.

Here, for example is a recording from Bosavi, in the New Guinea highlands, with many of the same features we'd expect to find in a Pygmy or

119

Bushmen performance: *Audio Example 17:Bosavi Yodeling* (From *Bosavi: Rainforest Music of Papua New Guinea*, cd2, track 1, recorded by Steven Feld.) Compare with the Bushmen "Giraffe Medicine Song" we heard in Chapter One: *Audio Example Eight:Giraffe Medicine Song*. Here's another example of yodeled interlock, this time from Guadalcanal, in the Solomon Islands: *Audio Example 18: Women's Song* (from the CD set *Voices of the World*, recorded and edited by Gilles Leothaud, Bernard Lortat-Jacob and Hugo Zemp).

Closely related types of instrumental hocket, similar to that of the pipe, flute, whistle, horn and percussion ensembles of Africa, have also been found in roughly the same regions, among indigenous peoples of New Guinea, the Solomon Islands, Indonesia (Flores, Bali, Java, among others), the Philippines, Vietnam, and certain other enclaves in Southeast Asia, and China. We find somewhat similar practices, both instrumental and vocal, in certain villages in Russia and other parts of Europe, both East and West, and also the Andes and other regions of Central and South America. In some cases we hear vocal-instrumental interactions of a very similar type.

Particularly telling is the distribution of the panpipe, an instrument known today through the performance of virtuoso soloists, but, among indigenous peoples, played almost exclusively in hocket, by ensembles of two or more performers. In many cases, each plays a single note on a single pipe; in other cases, a group of two or more pipes are bundled, either bound or unbound, into sets of multiple pipes, played by a single individual. While, strictly speaking, only the bundled pipes are referred to as "panpipes," both practices are closely related.

Hocketing ensembles of pipes or panpipes are currently found among so called "aboriginals," "tribals," or "peasants," of Southeast Asia, Indonesia, Melanesia, Central and South America, Africa, and Europe; archaeological records place panpipes in Polynesia, though the performing tradition seems to have died out there.

Since found in so many different parts of the world, so apparently unrelated to one another geographically, historically, or culturally, the distribution of the panpipe, and the distinctive method of ensemble hocketing associated with it, has been especially difficult to understand. In the light of the new genetic findings, however, all such ensembles seem likely to be of African origin, archaic survivals widely spread among indigenous peoples in many corners of the world, as part of a process of dissemination stemming from the original "Out of Africa" migrants (HMC).

Essentially the same explanation would account for the distribution of many other closely related types of wind ensemble, consisting of either trumpets, horns, and flutes, or certain types of hocketing percussion, organized along very similar lines, as commonly found in Southeast Asia,

Indonesia, the Philippines and Melanesia, e.g., stamping tubes, slit drums, and gong ensembles, including aspects of Balinese and Javanese gamelan performance.

The independent invention of certain instruments in so many different places, unlikely as it seems, might be regarded as a remote possibility. But the strong association with hocketing just about everywhere we find them makes such an explanation far more difficult to accept. And it works both ways. If we might want to regard the presence of hocketing as an independent invention, we have to ask why it is so often associated with particular instruments, such as pipes, panpipes, horns, stamping tubes, gong ensembles, etc. — not to mention very distinctive forms of vocalizing, such as yodeling and so many of the other features associated with P/B. One might argue that a particular type of instrument or a particular type of musical interaction could be independently invented. But for both to be independently invented in tandem, in so many different places, seems quite a stretch.

There is one more turn of the screw. Throughout Southeast Asia, Indonesia, China, New Guinea, island Melanesia, and South America as well, the various instruments associated with hocket, especially panpipe ensembles, but also slit drums, and, in Indonesia, gongs and gamelans, are regularly divided into male-female pairs. The strong association with this type of symbolism in so many disparate places would seem to make independent invention especially unlikely.

Some Examples

Here's a sampling of instrumental hocket/interlock performance both in and out of Africa, as described above, beginning with some very distinctive hocketed interactions between pipes and voices:

Audio Example 19: Voice with Hindewhu, BaBenzele Pygmies (from *Anthology Of World Music: Africa - Ba-Benzele Pygmies*, recorded by Simha Arom);

Audio Example 20: Hocket with Voice and Pipe, Huli people, highland New Guinea (recorded by Artur Simon).

In this example, first heard in Chapter Seven, we hear multiple voices and pipes woven together: *Audio Example 14:Ouldeme Pipes* (from *Cameroon:Flutes of the Mandara Mountains*, recorded by Nathalie Fernando et Fabrice Marandola).

121

Pipes and voices are interwoven in a similar manner in the following video, as filmed in the Russian village of Plekhovo, by Olga Velitchkina: *Video Example One: Russian Pipers*.

For comparison, let's listen again to some Mbuti Pygmy pipers, hocketing in a manner similar to both of the above, though without singing (also from Chapter Seven): *Audio Example 13:Mbuti Pipers*.

Next, a hocketing panpipe ensemble from the *Ede*, a "Montagnard" group of Vietnam: *Audio Example 21: Ede Panpipes* (from *Anthology of Ede Music, Musique du Monde*).

Another hocketing panpipe ensemble, in a somewhat different style, this time from the Are'are people of the Solomon Islands: *Audio Example 22:Are'are pipers* (from *Solomon Islands:The Sound of Bamboo*, recorded by Buaoka & Sekine).

Now for the most spectacular leap, all the way to Central America. Compare the panpipes we've been hearing with this hocketed duet from the Cuna Indians of Panama: *Audio Example 23:Cuna Pipes* (*Primitive Music of the World*, Folkways).

Similarly organized hocketing trumpet ensembles are not uncommon in Africa. Here's one from the Banda Linda people: *Audio Example 24:Banda Linda Trumpets* (from *Centrafrique: Trompes Banda Linda*, recorded by Simha Arom).

Trumpet ensembles can also be found in Melanesia, South America and Europe. Compare the preceding with these *Ragai* trumpets from, of all places, Lithuania: *Audio Example 25: Tytytitit*.

As I hear it, the remarkable distribution, among so many indigenous peoples, of all these highly distinctive musical elements — vocal interlock, counterpoint, hocket, yodel, panpipes, hocketing wind and percussion ensembles, etc. — all of a type apparently originating in Africa and strongly associated with Pygmy/Bushmen style (P/B), can be regarded as a kind of "African signature." Wherever this particular constellation is found, we may well be hearing echoes of the ancestral culture, as filtered by HMC.

A Musical Gap

Surprisingly, however, the "African signature" is almost completely absent from both South Asia and the Near and Middle East, yet reappears in Southeast Asia and many other points farther east and south. Indeed, hardly any evidence of hocket, interlock, counterpoint, yodel, or anything else resembling P/B, can be found anywhere along the portion of the "southern migration route" now known as the Middle East, Pakistan and India. And, as with the vocal traditions, there is no sign of P/B related instrumental ensembles, of pipes, panpipes, flutes, trumpets, or percussion.

Both the strong evidence we find of the "African signature" in the music of so many indigenous groups to the east and southeast of India, and its almost total absence throughout the extent of West and South Asia, fit surprisingly well with essentially the same gap noted by Oppenheimer, as revealed by the genetic evidence.

A Cantometric Table

The situation is clearly encapsulated in the following table, drawn from the Cantometric database, showing the distribution of sung contrapuntal polyphony in the samples from Asia, Island Southeast Asia, Melanesia and Australia:

Area Name	Area Sample	Culture	Culture Sample	% Counterpoint in Culture Sample
CENTRAL ASIA	107	BALKAR	1	100%
		TATAR	10	20%
HIMALAYAS	43	SIKKIM	3	33%
N.E. ASIA	119	— –-	-	0%
S.E. ASIA	126	EDE	4	50%
		JINGPO	1	100%
		LUA	11	27%
		PWO KARENS	10	20%
		TEMIAR	17	24%
		JAHAI	15	33%
		JAKUN	12	25%
SOUTH CHINA	229	NAXI	1	100%
		LOLO	2	50%
		MIAO	7	29%
		AMIS	30	40%
		BUNUN	13	60%
		SAZEK	5	23%
EAST INDONESIA	41	ATA KROWE	4	50%
		LAMAOJAN	3	67%
		MANGGARAI	5	20%
		TIMOR	10	40%
		WOGO	3	33%
WEST INDONESIA	197	DYAK	3	33%
		HANUNOO	10	20%
		JAVANESE	18	17%
		MINANGKABAU	14	7%
		MURUT	12	8%
		NIAS	7	43%
MELANESIA	212	AJIE	11	27%
		'ARE 'ARE	13	69%
		BAEGA	4	50%
		BUIN	4	50%
		BUKA	5	20%
		BUNLAP	4	25%
		CHOISEUL	10	40%
		DOBUANS	13	15%
		FATALEKA	5	40%
		GUADALCANAL	7	100%

		HAHON	2	50%
		HALIA	1	100%
		KANAK	2	100%
		MAKOLKOL	1	100%
		NASIOI	2	50%
		PIVA	1	100%
		SAVO	7	86%
		TIMPUTZ	1	100%
		TORAU	1	100%
		USIAI	15	7%
		UVOL	2	50%
		VELLA LAVELLA	3	33%
		W.NAKANAI	11	18%
NEW GUINEA	308	ABELAM	13	8%
		BALIEM	3	33%
		BIAMI	11	9%
		BISORIO	1	100%
		BUZI	10	20%
		DANI	14	36%
		EIPO	14	57%
		GIZRA	7	43%
		HAMTAI	2	50%
		KALULI	15	60%
		KOVAI	13	15%
		KUNIMAIPA	6	17%
		MAOPA	12	8%
		MONI	1	100%
		MOTU	12	17%
		OK	5	60%
		TOARIPI	2	50%
		YALI	7	14%
TRIBAL INDIA	165	HILL SAORA	13	8%
VIL. INDIA NORTH	108	GONDOGRAM	11	9%
VIL. INDIA SOUTH	25	———————–	-	0%
NEAR EAST	103	———————–	-	0%
MIDDLE EAST	45	———————–	-	0%
AUSTRALIA	43	———————–	-	0%

Table 9.1 Contrapuntal Polyphony in Asia and the Pacific

Note the dramatic differences in the representation of this very distinctive musical feature, with so many instances among indigenous groups in Southeast Asia, South China, Indonesia, Island Melanesia and New Guinea, and yet only a single instance among the entire 165 song sample for Tribal India, one other for the entirety of Village India, and no instances whatsoever for Northeast Asia (including Han China), the Near East, Middle East and aboriginal Australia.

Since contrapuntal polyphony is a highly distinctive feature of Pygmy/Bushmen style, along with hocket/ interlock, yodel, etc., and clear echoes of this style can be found among indigenous peoples in so many different parts of the world, it's not difficult to conclude that some form of

P/B must have been carried by the beachcombers to southern and southeastern Asia as part of a tradition already established among HMP, and from there to enclaves of traditional culture in Oceania, Europe and the Americas.

If that were the case, and we accept the theory of a steady progression of the migrant lineage through southern Asia from west to east, then we are once again forced, but this time on the basis of the musical evidence, to conclude that something drastic must have happened at a very early stage of their journey which caused them to lose this tradition, since there is no trace of it anywhere in West or South Asia. Such a sudden loss shouldn't, in itself, be surprising and in fact many such abrupt cultural shifts are known to have occurred in human history.

What is surprising is the sudden reappearance of strikingly similar practices in so many indigenous enclaves of Southeast Asia and beyond. The notion that an important tradition can suddenly be lost at a certain point in history and then, thousands of miles and God knows how many years later, be revived out of thin air, is, to say the least, difficult to reconcile with the Out of Africa model, in which all roads tend to lead backward to a single source. Interestingly enough, we find a very similar pattern reflected in yet another important cultural realm: language.

The Linguistic Evidence

Since we have no way of knowing what the original Pygmy language might have been, or if Pygmies ever had a fully formed (i.e., fully syntactic) language of their own, it has not seemed possible to formulate a meaningful hypothesis regarding the language spoken by either HBP or HMP. While many have speculated that Khoisan (the click language of the Bushmen) could represent the earliest language, there is no evidence that Pygmies ever used clicks and for that matter no reason to believe clicks were used by either HMP or any of its Asiatic, European, Oceanic or American descendants, since clicks are absent from just about all world languages outside of south and east Africa.

However, another significant, possibly highly diagnostic, aspect of language has rarely if ever been given its due. Almost every single language in SubSaharan Africa is, with very few exceptions, a tone language, i.e., a language in which differences of meaning are determined by differences in pitch. Thus, if homo sapiens originated in Africa, as is now generally believed, the first language is very likely to have been tonal, which tells us that if HBP had language at all, it would have been tonal, and the language of HMP would almost certainly have been tonal. Even if HBP didn't have a fully formed, fully syntactic language (as I suspect they may not have), then whatever vocabulary they had would most likely have contained tonally differentiated phonemes.

The extremely interesting and suggestive tone language evidence has never been fully appreciated, however, because a very puzzling gap can be seen in its worldwide distribution:

See Figure 9.4

Note the absolute saturation of tone languages (blue discs) in Africa; their near saturation in Southeast Asia and also Melanesia; and their almost total absence in exactly the same region where comparable gaps in the genetic and musical evidence have been found: South Asia and the Middle East. This map is taken from a remarkable website, The World Atlas of Language Structures Online (WALS), consisting of 141 maps of distinctive linguistic features, and as far as I've been able to determine from studying the contents of this site, it's very unusual for any one region to be so completely dominated by a single linguistic trait. Thus the chances of this highly structured distribution being a coincidence have to be pretty close to nil.

If modern humans originated in Africa, then what this map tells us is that the earliest languages, including the language spoken by the Out of Africa migrants (HMP), were almost certainly tonal, and if the Out of Africa migration had been straightforward, with no complicating factors, then we would have no reason to assume that all the languages of the surviving indigenous peoples along this route would not also be tonal.

The idea that language may originally have had pitch as an important phonemic and/or morphemic differentiator is, in fact, consistent with a commonly held theory that music and language may well have shared the same roots and, at least initially, developed together. If the cultivation of tonal awareness were an important aspect of both speech and music from the start, then the ubiquity of tone language in Africa is no longer a mystery. But what could have happened when HMP left Africa for points East?

When we turn our attention to the southern route, from the Bab el Mendab to the Arabian peninsula and beyond, tone languages all but completely disappear — until we reach Southeast Asia. And once again, as with the musical evidence, we are faced with the conundrum of an important cultural tradition that suddenly vanishes, only to reappear many years later, in a completely different part of the world. Tone languages reappear, in fact, at the exact same point that our P/B-related "African signature" reappears.

Which leaves us with the third possibility: an early diffusion of both P/B and tonal language, as two different aspects of HMC, across a truly vast expanse, followed by some sort of event that would have resulted, ultimately, in the fragmentation and isolation of the cultures that maintained the original traditions, a process that would no doubt have had other consequences as well, both cultural and "racial," and would almost certainly have left its mark on the genetic record. Since the gap I've been pointing to is so enormous, and since it is centered on a crucial region of the "southern route," it is here that we must look for clues as to the nature of the event that produced the gap, an event that may well have been a turning point in human history. Which returns us to Stephen Oppenheimer and his "Toba" theory.

Chapter Ten: The Bottleneck

A catastrophic disaster centered somewhere in South Asia may well have produced one or more major population bottlenecks, which could have had important consequences for the future of the human race. As we've learned, Stephen Oppenheimer has a particular event in mind, the gigantic explosion of Mt. Toba, ca. 74,000 years ago. Let's take a closer look at this hypothesis. Here, according to Oppenheimer's *Journey of Man* website (http://www.bradshawfoundation.com/journey/), is how the *homo sapiens* world would have looked circa 75,000 years ago, prior to the Toba eruption:

See Figure 9.2

Here's how he thinks things looked just 1000 years later, ca 74,000 years ago. The grey puff you see is the fallout from the explosion of Mount Toba – the red dot is where Toba is located, in northwest Sumatra:

See Figure 10.1

One of the many things that makes Toba potentially useful as evidence is that we have a pretty good idea when it erupted and the extent of the damage it would have caused, thanks to the considerable amount of volcanic ash it dumped, which can be identified and dated. The remnants of Toba ash were found largely to the west and north of the volcano, thus the prevailing winds must have been northwest at the time.

Oppenheimer's *The Real Eve* was published in 2003. A paper from the following year (Metspalu et al. 2004) provides striking support for some of the same discontinuities noted by Oppenheimer, confirming, among other things, the strange bias in the distribution of the M haplogroups (see previous chapter): "Our results indicate that the frequency distribution of haplogroup M varies across different Indian regions by a significant cline towards the south and the east . . ."

The very interesting distributions of some of the most important M sub-haplogroups are mapped in their Figure 1:

See Figure 10.2

Note especially the distributions of M6, M6b and M2b, all found, for the most part, in the east and south, where Oppenheimer noted the prevalence of haplogroup M. There is an equally interesting presence of M6 and M6b in the northernmost reaches of the Indus valley. The pattern is clear from the map at the upper left, where the heaviest distribution of M6 is found in two different places, not only the south and east of India, but also far to the northwest, in the Punjab-Kashmir region shared with Pakistan.

There are two things about this region that make it especially interesting: its location places it at a greater distance from Toba than any other part of South Asia, and it is the only region between Africa and East Asia where tone languages are commonly found. This would have been a likely spot where a branch of the Out of Africa migrants, who could have broken from the main group to travel north along the banks of the Indus, might have been able to survive the effects of Toba with their African traditions more or less intact. If tone language was part of their HMC inheritance, then that could explain the prevalence of tone language in this area today.

The maps presented in Figure 11 of the same paper are especially significant:

See Figure 10.3

From the caption:

> *The segregation of West Eurasian, East Eurasian and South Asian mtDNA pools.* Partial map of Eurasia illustrating the spatial frequency distribution of mtDNA haplogroups native to West Eurasia (panel A), South Asia (panel B) and East Eurasia (panel C)... [1]

The three so-called "isofrequency" maps, based on some of the oldest known Asiatic lineages, some estimated to date from over 70,000 years ago, paint a remarkable picture of human history in this part of the world, from possibly only a few thousand years after the Out of Africa migration began, to the present, with the most significant later migrations presented as clines.

They remind me of another map that some of you may recognize, produced by a satellite known as the *Cosmic Background Explorer* (COBE):

See Figure 10.4

Here we see an image produced by truly ancient (ca 14 billions years old) microwave signals, emanating from every corner of the universe, based on events thought to have taken place ca 380,000 years after the Big Bang. The maps of Figure 10.3 are strangely analogous in that they too give an idea of the distant past by mapping evidence available in the present. Instead of the echo of ancient microwave signals still detectable in space after billions of years, we have the echo of ancient mutations, still detectable in our DNA after thousands of years. But the pictures are very different, in the first case relatively uniform, in the other radically disjunct. In fact the genetic maps are described as "The *segregation* of West Eurasian, East Eurasian and South Asian mtDNA pools."

If the Out of Africa migration was a smooth progression along the "southern route," from the Horn of Africa to Southeast Asia and beyond, then this should be reflected in the genetic markers as a steady west-east cline. Unless the traces of the original migration, like those of the Big Bang, were obliterated by what happened at a later time. What happened during the course of the Big Bang, according to a theory now widely accepted, was "cosmic inflation." What happened during the course of the great migration is unknown — but it must have been something big, because it had a huge effect.

Here's how the authors explain the strange discontinuities so clearly illustrated in their maps:

> We found that haplogroup M frequency drops abruptly from about 60% in India to about 5% in Iran, marking the western border of the haplogroup M distribution. A similarly sharp border cuts the distribution of Indian-specific mtDNA haplogroups to the east and to the north of the subcontinent. We therefore propose that the initial mtDNA pool established upon the peopling of South Asia has not been replaced but has rather been *reshaped in situ by major demographic episodes in the past* and garnished by relatively minor events of gene flow both from the West and the East during more recent chapters of the demographic history in the region (my emphasis).

There is a significant difference between the discontinuity dividing the Middle East and the South Asian Peninsula and that between the Peninsula and its neighbors to the east and north. The ancient haplogroup M is hardly found at all to the west of Pakistan, while it is found in abundance in India, Southeast Asia and East Asia generally. Since the mainland of the Arabian Peninsula and neighboring Iran would have been uninhabitable desert at the time, we can safely assume either that no colonies were left in these regions during the Great Migration (GM) or that whatever colonies might have been left never survived. Thus the discontinuity so evident in Maps A and B can be attributed to the presence of a natural barrier. What we see in Map A must therefore be the result of migrations dating from a much later period.

The very strange discontinuity illustrated in Maps B and C cannot be so easily accounted for. In this case, the same ancient root, haplogroup M, underlies the genetic picture for both regions; representing, no doubt, a faint

130

echo of the original east-west migration (and in all likelihood confirming the southern route). But the M's found in India are not the same as the M's found to the east, southeast and north. Which is why Map B has a different color than Map C — based on the fact that a very different set of haplogroups, M included, are "native to" each region.

How can this be? Unlike the region to the west of Pakistan, there is no natural barrier that might hinder the colonization of territories bordering on, or beyond, India's eastern boundary. The authors wisely explain "that the initial mtDNA pool established upon the peopling of South Asia," i.e., the great migration following the Out of Africa exodus, "has not been replaced." This is evident by the pervasiveness of certain ancient haplogroups, not only M but also N and R, in India. But their attempt to explain the discontinuities that so clearly overlay and obscure the traces of this early migration, on the basis of an mtDNA pool "reshaped in situ by major demographic episodes in the past," while reasonable, is inadequate.

First of all, the clear demarcation we see between India and its closest neighbor to the east, Myanmar, is unlikely to have been produced by a series of different, unrelated, events or migrations. It's hard to believe it could have been produced by more than one. And clearly it was not produced by a migration, since a migration would have resulted in continuity, not discontinuity. So it could only have been produced by a disruptive event of major proportions.

To facilitate comparison, I've blown up Oppenheimer's map, representing the fallout from the Toba explosion, and placed it just above Map C, from Figure 10.3 (see above). You'll recall that the red dot on the upper map represents the location of Toba, in northwest Sumatra. The northernmost tip of Sumatra can just barely be seen at the bottom of the lower map.

See Figures 10.5 and 10.6

The match between the ash cloud and the negative space formed by the haplogroup distribution (in shades of orange) is remarkable. Note that the outer edges of the Toba cloud perfectly match the distribution cline to its northeast. Since there are no significant natural borders along the coastal route, and no other readily apparent explanation for the genetic segregation of the two areas, it's certainly tempting to attribute the pattern we see in the lower map to the event represented in the upper.

Toba would not only explain the discontinuity between India and points east, so evident on the genetic maps, but also the gap I've been stressing, involving cultural practices found in both Africa and greater Southeast Asia, but almost completely absent from the Middle East, Pakistan and India.

African-related cultural survivals can indeed be found in exactly those areas to the east and northeast of Toba that would have been upwind from the eruption and thus relatively unaffected.

The Toba event might also explain the strange distribution of both M and N-related haplogroups in South Asia. As Oppenheimer noted, and Metspalu et al confirmed, there is a distinct northwest to southeast cline in the distribution of M, with most instances by far to be found along the eastern and southern coasts. N-derived haplogroups, on the other hand, are relatively rare in this region, though common in the west and northwest of India — and also farther east, beyond the border with Myanmar.

Oppenheimer associates this puzzling distribution with the Toba event, suggesting that the prolonged ash cloud could have devastated all or most of India, especially both M and N related populations in the east and south, closest to the volcano. He hypothesizes that this area could then have been repopulated by M dominated groups immigrating from the east, who might then have spread, in a cline, to the rest of the subcontinent, while N-related groups to the west could have repopulated India from that region. This could have left India populated by more recent M and N hapolotypes than those found farther east, a pattern noted by both Cordaux et al and Soares et al, as reported above.

What makes the Toba hypothesis particularly convincing is the fact that it seems to fit our gap so well. As we've seen, the plume of ash perfectly covers a large portion of the gap. And the regions to the northeast, east and south, which would have been upwind from the direction of the plume, would have been largely, though not completely, spared. Which fits beautifully with the distribution of the African musical signature, both vocal and instrumental, scattered among so many indigenous peoples of Southeast Asia, southern China, Indonesia, Taiwan, the Philippines, and Melanesia. Those largely spared could have managed to preserve a significant part of their African traditions, while those caught in the gap could have lost most or at least some of them – assuming they or their descendants survived at all.

The Archaeological Evidence

There is no controversy regarding the eruption of Toba itself. It definitely happened, it was huge, and can be dated to within a few thousand years. Everything else is controversial and there is a lot of misinformation and confusion out there. The first person to associate it with human evolution was archaeologist Stanley Ambrose and it is his interpretation that's usually quoted. According to Ambrose, modern humans were all living in Africa when Toba exploded, but the explosion was so huge that it had a dramatic effect on their development, even at so great a distance. For Ambrose, the trauma of Toba was a major factor in prompting humans to become more "advanced," a development that in his view led directly to the Out of Africa adventure.

Ambrose was also the first to suggest that Toba could have been responsible for human differentiation, producing the various "races" and other signs of major biological and cultural diversity. However, if all humans were confined to Africa when Toba hit, as Ambrose assumes, it's impossible to see how any differences produced by that event could have evolved into the worldwide distinctions so evident today, of which Africa is a relatively homogeneous part. Toba can explain the large-scale differentiation patterns we now see only if humans had already left Africa and had occupied most or all of the south Asiatic coast by the time it erupted. However, Ambrose, for reasons that continue to puzzle me, insists that this is not possible and that all the archaeological evidence points to an African exodus *after* the Toba eruption, not before (personal communication).

It was only Stephen Oppenheimer who saw the necessity of the Out of Africa migration preceding the Toba event, because otherwise it could not have had the necessary effect. And in this sense it's possible to turn things around, so that instead of timing the great migration on the basis of (shaky and incomplete) archaeological assumptions, we can use the timing of the Toba eruption itself to much more precisely estimate the date of the fateful exodus, which, if Oppenheimer is right, would have to have preceded it by at least a thousand years or so.

Currently, most archaeologists and geneticists seem to agree, based on certain fossil finds in Australia, as well as estimates of genetic "coalescence," that the most likely date for the great migration is somewhere between 60,000 and 50,000 years ago, thousands of years *after* Toba. And on that basis, Toba has been discounted as a factor in human evolution. For many, the last nail in the coffin was provided by archaeologist Michael Petraglia, who, after years of digging and probing, found some very interesting stone tools both below and above Toba ash (*Middle Paleolithic Assemblages from the Indian Subcontinent Before and After the Toba Super-Eruption*, Petraglia et al, 2007).

In a blog post entitled "At Last, the death of the Toba bottleneck" (http://johnhawks.net/weblog/reviews/archaeology/middle/petraglia_toba_in dia_continuity_2007.html) paleoanthropologist and long time Toba skeptic John Hawks gleefully reported the findings thus: "This week's paper by Petraglia and colleagues (2007) appears to have sunk the Toba bottleneck entirely. Very simply, they found a Toba ash horizon in India, and found very similar archaeology both below and above the eruption." Petraglia's results were widely reported in the media in much the same terms, as though the mere fact that more or less the same type of tools were found above as below the ash meant that the effects of the Toba eruption could be discounted.

What was all but ignored in such reports was a far more significant finding:

> these pre- and post-Toba industries suggest closer affinities to African Middle Stone Age traditions (such as Howieson's Poort) than to contemporaneous Eurasian Middle Paleolithic ones that are typically based on discoidal and Levallois techniques. . . *This interpretation would be consistent with a southern route of dispersal of modern humans from the Horn of Africa;* the latter, however, will remain speculative until other Middle Paleolithic sites in the Indian subcontinent and Arabian Peninsula are excavated and dated (my emphasis).

In other words, what Petraglia found that went almost unnoticed at first was *evidence that the Out of Africa migrants may have been in southern India at the time of the Toba eruption after all*. This was a finding of major importance, the first archaeological evidence consistent with the presence of modern humans in Asia at such an early date, but it got lost in all the hoopla surrounding the apparent debunking of the Toba "myth."

Petraglia went out of his way to clarify the meaning of his results in a subsequent interview (*Modern Humans Lived in India Earlier Than Thought, Study Finds*, by Chris Dolmetsch, Bloomberg http://www.bloomberg.com/apps/news?pid=newsarchive&sid=apBnqDezjd DE&refer=india):

> "This is some of the earliest evidence for the spread of modern humans out of Africa towards Australia," Petraglia said in a telephone interview from New York.
>
> The study says the relics, made of limestone, quartzite, chert and other minerals, are likely from a variety of stone tools from the Indian Middle Paleolithic era that lasted from about 150,000 to 38,000 B.C.
>
> Yet the characteristics of the artifacts are more typical of the African Middle Stone Age that ended about 40,000 years ago than they are of younger artifacts found elsewhere in Europe and Asia, the study says. *That finding suggests that modern humans had migrated out of Africa and were already in southern India when the Toba Tuff eruption blanketed the region in ash.* [my emphasis]

"It will be very much debated," Petraglia said. "There are people that are wedded to their theories and won't like it at all, and there are others who will welcome our study because this part of the world is very understudied."

Oh and by the way, the artifacts in question were found "under a 2.5 meter (8.4-foot) thick ash deposit . . ." It's hard to see how the effects of an accumulation of over 8 feet of ash on human survival can be discounted.

In another interview, from the National Geographic (http://news.nationalgeographic.com/news/2007/07/070705-india-volcano.html), Petraglia makes this clear:

> "The fact that we have this ash is just icing on the cake, because it tells us that if it's modern humans, then they were able to persist through a major eruptive event," he said. "But they would have had a very, very difficult time."

What Petraglia's findings suggest is that the Toba blast was not sufficient to have had much of an effect on Africa, as Ambrose has argued, or Europe either — but it would certainly have had a very significant effect on any modern humans living in South Asia shortly after the out of Africa excursion, and could for that reason have had lasting consequences for subsequent human history.

Climatological Evidence

Additional evidence on Toba has surfaced recently, in the form of two climatological studies. In the first (Robock et al. 2009), the authors conducted
> six additional climate model simulations with two different climate models, . . . in two different versions, to investigate additional mechanisms that may have enhanced and extended the forcing and response from such a large supervolcanic eruption.

While "none of the runs initiates glaciation" and, in all cases, their simulations revealed that "the climate recovers over a few decades", nevertheless,

> the "volcanic winter" following a supervolcano eruption of the size of Toba today would have devastating consequences for humanity and global ecosystems. *These simulations support the theory that the Toba eruption indeed may have contributed to a genetic bottleneck.* (my emphasis)

A *second study,* conducted by Stanley Ambrose and Martin Williams, was recently (Nov. 2009) reported in *Science News*:

> Ambrose and his colleagues pursued two lines of research: They analyzed pollen from a marine core in the Bay of Bengal that included a layer of ash from the Toba eruption, and they looked at carbon isotope ratios in fossil soil carbonates taken from directly above and below the Toba ash in three locations in central India.

The investigators concluded that there was

> "incontrovertible evidence" that the volcanic super-eruption of Toba on the island of Sumatra about 73,000 years ago deforested much of central India, some 3,000 miles from the epicenter . . . The bright ash reflected sunlight off the landscape, and volcanic sulfur aerosols impeded solar radiation for six years, initiating an "Instant Ice Age" that — according to evidence in ice cores taken in Greenland — lasted about 1,800 years.

When we combine such reports of Toba-induced devastation with Petraglia's findings, strongly suggesting the presence of modern humans in South Asia at the time, the possibility of major population bottlenecks downwind from the volcano seems strong indeed. While stone artifacts were found both above and below the Toba ash, indicating that at least some humans survived, we can assume that any survivors would have been struggling very hard in an environment radically different from the one that first greeted them. And while the presence of the artifacts suggests that they survived the immediate effects of the disaster, this does not mean they were able to survive its long-term effects.

As both the archaeological and genetic evidence suggests, much of the Indian subcontinent, especially the east coast, directly in the path of the volcanic plume, could have been depopulated, only to be repopulated at a later time from the East, as Oppenheimer suggests, by people who would also have been affected by the disaster, but to a lesser extent. It is these Toba survivors who would most likely have experienced severe population loss, resulting in bottlenecks, both genetic *and* cultural. Populations even farther to the east and southeast, and also farther to the north (assuming there *were* any at that time) would also have suffered, but to a much lesser extent, and would thus show fewer signs of genetic, morphological and cultural change. This does indeed seem to be the case, though the situation is obscured by the considerable movement of various peoples into and out of this region for many thousands of years since.

It's possibly for this reason that, as Oppenheimer noted, "some of the best, if not the only archaeological evidence for dating the beachcomber's trek along the coast of the Indian Ocean, comes not from India, South Arabia, or Africa, but from the later parts of the trail — the Malay Peninsula, New Guinea, and Australia" (*The Real Eve*, 159), those areas least affected by the volcanic fallout.

The Toba Effect

The possible effects of a Toba-induced bottleneck on modern humans ca 74,000 years ago, were succinctly summarized by Michael Petraglia's collaborator, Sacha Jones:

> This bottleneck would have greatly reduced modern human diversity as well as population size. With climatic amelioration, population explosion out of this bottleneck would have occurred, either ~ 70 ka, at the end of a hypercold millennium . . . or ~10ka later with the transition from OIS (Oxygen Isotope Stage) 4 to warmer OIS 3. Post Toba populations would have reduced in size such that founder effects, genetic drift and local adaptations occurred, *resulting in rapid population differentiation* (Ambrose 1998). *In this way the Toba eruption of ~74 ka would have shaped the diversity that is seen in modern human populations today* ("The Toba Supervolcanic Eruption," in *The evolution and history of human populations in South Asia*, ed. Petraglia and Allchin, 2007, p. 177 — my emphasis).

In the aftermath of a disaster such as the Toba eruption, many groups in the path of the huge, thick ash cloud would not have survived. For those who did, life would have drastically changed. For one thing many if not most, if not almost all, of their population may have been killed outright, simply suffocated in a sea of ash. Some might have been in a position to retreat to the depths of certain caves, where the worst effects of the ash cloud might not have penetrated. When emerging, they would have been faced with a world largely depleted of both vegetation and wildlife.

To get a sense of what life would have been like in an environment suddenly deprived of almost all the usual sources of food, water and communal support, we can consider the fate of the group Colin Turnbull, in his book *The Mountain People*, called the "Ik." Ik society was, at that time, undergoing severe stress due to external conditions they could not control, and the stress had very definite and very dire effects on a people who had become increasingly desperate with hunger and other forms of deprivation, to the point that their cultural values were disappearing into a mode of existence based, as one might expect, on the philosophy of "every man for himself" or "dog eat dog."

While the Ik may be seen as victims of a characteristically modern, "post-colonial" situation, the radical changes recorded by Turnbull can give us an insight into what could have happened at certain times in the past, when a particular population is suddenly placed under tremendous stress to the point that the most basic cultural norms begin to break down. Of special significance for us is the relative scarcity of musical references in the book. Whenever singing is mentioned, it is almost always solo singing, not surprising in an atmosphere where social cohesion is breaking down and "every man for himself" has become the norm.

The only group singing noted by Turnbull among the Ik is the singing of Christian hymns, and that takes place only when a group is expecting a consignment of food from some missionaries (who never show up). He has nothing to say about what their music might have been like in the past, but if the Ik were a typical African tribe, we can be almost 100% sure that group singing — and dancing — would have been a common, if not everyday event. In the context described in the book, however, occasions for such activities, either for pleasure or for traditional ritual purposes, no longer exist.

As Petraglia's findings suggest, there appear to have been Toba survivors, though they would certainly have been only a small fraction of the population directly in the path of the disaster. It's also possible that the artifacts he discovered were from survivors in a neighboring area, where the fallout wasn't quite as heavy, who moved into this area at a later time. In any case, anyone trying to survive in the post-Toba environment would have been faced with extraordinary difficulties, paralleling in some ways the hardships faced by the Ik.

And, as with the Ik, it's not difficult to imagine such a disaster leading to a population dying out completely. But what if it doesn't die out? What if there are survivors who manage to begin anew at some point, what will they be teaching their children? What aspects of their old culture are likely to survive, what are likely to be lost and what new elements are likely to be introduced? Under such dire circumstances it's difficult to imagine that a highly interactive, group-oriented musical tradition such as P/B could have survived. And it's not difficult to imagine how it could have been replaced by something much simpler, as was apparently the case among the Ik.

And other traditions reflecting the African origins of the migrants may also have been lost. If the most gifted and experienced wood carvers had been killed, then the African wood carving traditions might have died with them. If the leading shamans died, then the most elaborate rituals might have died with them. It's important to realize that once a tradition is lost, to the point that there is no longer anyone to hand it down to the younger generation, then it is gone forever.

It's not difficult to see, moreover, how some of the original core values, inherited from HBP, might also be lost. What does it mean to share meat when the only meat available might be from mice or rats, hardly enough to feed one person, let alone an entire group? Egalitarian values might also go by the boards in a situation where the strong can only survive at the expense of the weak. And the weak survive only if protected by someone stronger — and more aggressive. Once such a situation is established, it's very easy to see how it could become a self-perpetuating tradition.

Instead of an egalitarian ethic, steeped in non-violence, a new system of values, based on the survival of the strongest, most assertive and most competitive individuals, and their subservient followers, could emerge. Once such a tradition is established, it would be almost impossible to go back to the old way of doing things and even of thinking. Even if things might improve over time, to the point that the society is no longer stressed, and no longer dependent on strong, aggressive leaders, it might not matter, because traditions tend to perpetuate themselves long after they have lost their original purpose and even their meaning.

Genetically it's not simply a matter of a "population bottleneck" forming among relatively neutral mitochondrial or Y chromosome genes, but the favoring, if only by chance, of certain genotypes and phenotypes (so called "racial" characteristics). All societies contain a certain amount of morphological variation, but when almost everyone is struck down by a disaster, or chooses to leave in search of better conditions elsewhere, then the genetic and morphological characteristics of the survivors become the new norm, which could be quite different from the old one.

For example, if only a few members of a particular migrant colony happened to have what we would now consider "Mongoloid" features, and that group happened, by sheer chance, to survive, while most of the others died or migrated elsewhere, then such a development could lead to the establishment of a new "race," with "Mongoloid" features exclusively. Thus, it's not difficult to see how an event such as Toba could have been the trigger for certain very fundamental changes, cultural, genetic and morphological, which could explain the highly structured differences we now see among different populations in different parts of the world.

We see, in East Asia, people who've been described as having "mongoloid" features, and a highly distinctive, extraordinarily sophisticated culture, unlike any other on earth. In Central Asia, we see very different people, mostly horse nomads. Northern Asia is dominated by so-called Paleosiberian people, mostly reindeer herders, who span the entirety of the circum-polar world, from the Lapplanders of Europe all the way to the Inuit of North America. In Europe we find, again, people who are unique, both physically and culturally unlike any others anywhere in the world (though there are some intriguing morphological links with, for example, the Ainu of Japan).

Among native Americans we find people who, again, have been described as "mongoloid," possibly because they are descended from the same ancestral group that gave rise to both the East Asians and Paleosiberians. But North American Indian culture is very different from that of East Asia or Paleosiberia — and equally unique. In southeast Asia, Indonesia, the Philippines, Melanesia, Australia, etc. we find a more complex mix of people with morphologies often characterized as either more or less "negroid," or mongoloid, or some mix thereof.

Which is why I find the notion of a major bottleneck very early on, due to Toba or perhaps some other serious event, so compelling. Because it would seem as though only such an event — at such an early stage — could have had the sort of major impact needed to produce the large-scale patterns of difference we now see. In my view, it is only when we pay attention to such large scale distributions of certain traits, characteristics, traditions, etc. that we can find useful clues with the potential for recreating historical events that might otherwise seem totally beyond our reach.

It is, admittedly, not always easy to consistently reconcile all the details of the various genetic, social and cultural distributions in this vast region, not to mention the many different interpretations of such evidence. But the explanatory power of this event is potentially so strong that further research is certainly justified. Toba can no longer be on the back burner, it must come to the forefront of our attention.

---

1. Though tribal populations constituted roughly 50% of the 2572 total sample for India (4600 samples for Asia overall were analyzed, and considerably more added for Figure 11), they are, very unfortunately, not represented on the isofrequency maps (A, B and C), for reasons explained as follows in the "methods" section:

> In relatively small and isolated groups (e.g. tribal groups) random genetic drift might seriously affect the haplogroup frequencies, which may become uninformative when a whole region

(e.g. state) is considered . . . Therefore, the tribal data were excluded from the haplogroup isofrequency maps calculation. When illustrating the spread of mtDNA haplogroups native to West Eurasia, East Eurasia and India (Figure 11, panel D) we present these data as pie diagrams. The respective sample size and origin are indicated adjacent to the diagrams. (p. 22)

The effect of the tribal data on maps A, B and C may, to some extent, be inferred from the pie charts in map D. And, indeed, the picture presented in D, of a major division between South (mostly green and blue) and Southeast Asia (mostly orange), is consistent with what we see in the maps above.

Chapter Eleven: The Later Migrations

Regardless of whether or not the Toba eruption can be safely regarded as the cause of the gap I've been making so much of, it does seem likely that some sort of disastrous event, centered in roughly the same region, must have taken place at some point after the completion of the "southern route" migration, because the gap is real, and must be accounted for. Before proceeding to discuss the aftereffects of such an event, let's review the (hypothetical) sequence of events leading up to, and including, it:

1.   The development of HBC (the Hypothetical Baseline Culture of our most recent common ancestors) from traditions inherited from the oldest human ancestors, based in turn on the behavioral patterns and traditions of their pre-human primate ancestors.

2.   The development of HMC (the Hypothetical Migrant Culture of the Out of Africa émigrés) from HBC, as modified by events subsequent to the divergence of the proto-Pygmy and proto-Bushmen populations from the ancestral group.

3.   The spread of HMC in colonies scattered throughout the Indian Ocean coast, from the western border of what is now Pakistan, through southern India, and onward to Southeast Asia, Island Southeast Asia, and the Sahul (New Guinea and Australia, joined at the time by a land bridge).

4.   The occurrence of a large-scale disaster of some sort, centered in South Asia, that would have precipitated major changes in the population patterns, genetic markers, social structure and culture of all colonies along the coast of South Asia; but would, for the most part, have spared those to the east of India. In the areas most affected, those colonies that survived would have been seriously decimated, producing what geneticists refer to as "population bottlenecks."

This event could have been a major volcanic eruption, such as the explosion of Mt. Toba, ca 74,000 ya – the prevailing northwesterly winds would have carried vast amounts of Toba ash into the heart of the South Asian Peninsula while sparing most points due north, east and south of the eruption site (in northern Sumatra); however, a major Tsunami, centered somewhere southeast of India could possibly have had much the same effect – the southern route implies a maritime culture, focused on sea-based resources, and thus especially vulnerable to an event of this sort; or possibly a major flood – weather patterns affecting the Indian Ocean area are dominated by the monsoon cycle, which can produce very heavy flooding during the summer months; or a prolonged drought – the same monsoon cycle can produce several successive months of little to no precipitation, and an anomalously weak monsoon season could leave the entire area seriously devoid of water.

We are now in a position to take our story beyond the disastrous event, whatever its cause, to consider the all important subsequent migrations leading to the demographic and cultural patterns we see today. We can begin by taking another look at the fascinating "isofrequency maps" introduced in the previous chapter:

See Figure 10.2

Maps B and C especially tell a remarkable story. Given the Toba scenario we've been exploring, it seems clear that the resulting bottlenecks would have led to fundamental changes, away from the typically African characteristics of HMP and HMC, toward those more typical of what we now see among most (though not all) of the various "racial" and large-scale "ethnic" subdivisions of Asia, Europe, the Americas, etc. However, since India would have borne the brunt of the disaster, it might seem likely that a repopulated India would have been the principal staging ground for the migrations that would have spread the newly altered genetic/cultural lineages to the four corners of the world. But maps B and C tell a different story. According to map B, India has remained relatively isolated, while the scenario implied in map C suggests a massive migration rooted east of India, and spreading both north and northwest from there, with the Himalayas as a significant barrier, channeling the migrants away from India and in the direction of Central Asia and, ultimately, Europe.

Another map, Figure 5 from the same paper, is explicitly devoted to the migration pathways, but from a somewhat broader perspective:

See Figure 11.1

From the caption:

> *Peopling of Eurasia.* Map of Eurasia and northeastern Africa depicting the peopling of Eurasia as inferred from the extant mtDNA phylogeny. . . [T]he initial split between West and East Eurasian mtDNAs is postulated between the Indus Valley and Southwest Asia. Spheres depict expansion zones where, after the initial (coastal) peopling of the continent, local branches of the mtDNA tree (haplogroups given in the spheres) arose (ca. 40,000 – 60,000 ybp), and from where they were further carried into the interior of the

143

continent (thinner black arrows). Admixture between the expansion zones has been surprisingly limited ever since.

Though it's extremely difficult to account for every aspect of the genetic picture in terms consistent with a Toba-like hypothesis (or any other hypothesis), I'd like to propose the following, necessarily provisional, post-disaster scenario:

1. ca 74,000 ya: Population bottleneck or bottlenecks produced by the disaster, with varying degrees of intensity depending on how close each population is to the center of the disruptive event. The effect of each bottleneck will be different, depending on completely unpredictable circumstances associated with each group affected. In each case, either the group or its lineage does not survive at all, or, if it does survive, its character, both physical and cultural, will be determined contingently by the unique qualities of each new founder group and the environment in which it finds itself.

2. ca 73,000 - 70,000 ya: We can't be sure how many such bottlenecks would have occurred. It's even conceivable that only one group might have survived in the general area, either in India itself or to the east. Or possibly there were many groups with at least a few survivors each, and thus many different founder effects. It's also very difficult if not impossible, at least at this time, to correlate such founder effects with the genetic evidence. A major disaster may well have produced one or many population bottlenecks by destroying human life en masse, but we have no reason to assume it would have produced even a single mutation. So it might be a mistake to read a separate founder effect into each different branch of M, N, or R.

Following Oppenheimer, I will at this point explore the possibility he raises, that the Toba eruption would have completely destroyed all humans caught within range of the thickest fallout, which means that the tribal populations we now see in India originated either west or east of the subcontinent, from where various scenarios of repopulation would have occurred. If the pocket we identified in the northwest Punjab-Kashmir region survived, then west India might have been repopulated from there. As for repopulation from the east, any groups living just east of India during the Toba blast would almost certainly have suffered serious bottlenecks and may well have lost at least some of their original African traditions.

This could explain the absence of significant P/B characteristics in their music, especially since P/B is a highly group-oriented practice and the major loss of life coupled with scarcity of food and other resources might well have seriously eroded the social fabric — as documented by Turnbull for the Ik (see previous chapter). It could also have affected many other traditions since many if not all the old rituals might have been suspended during a period when survival may have depended, literally, on the behavior of the strongest, most violent and most ruthless, rather than the most cooperative, peace loving and selfless, which may have been the traditional HMC ethic.

So the gap we now see centered in India, might well represent a displacement of a gap that really began farther east — and was transmitted to India over time by neighboring groups east of the border that eventually migrated there. It's important to remember that a great many groups now living in East and Southeast Asia appear to have also lost many of the same African traditions, probably as a result of the same disastrous event, so it would be a mistake to locate the gap only in South Asia.

As we've seen, survivals of old HMC traditions, especially the musical ones, can be found today largely among marginalized groups living in isolated refuge areas in a vast region stretching from the Malay Peninsula to Indonesia, the Philippines and Melanesia, and also northward among certain tribal groups of South China and Taiwan. Since we see so many HBC and HMC traditions (and often African morphology as well) among such groups, it's not difficult to conclude that they must originally have been located far enough to the east or south to suffer least from the effects of the disaster and thus manage to hold on to most (though clearly not all) of their original traditions.

3.   ca 70,000 - 40,000 ya. According to the genetic evidence, the population of south Asia seems to have undergone a major expansion at some point after the bottleneck event. However, as the maps suggest, the region seems to have been relatively self-contained during most of the paleolithic and neolithic as well, with many groups migrating into the region but relatively few migrating out.

4.   ca. 60,000 - 20,000 ya. The genetic maps reproduced above reveal population clines emanating in all directions, but mainly from southeast Asia to the north and northwest. It seems likely that there were major migrations into central Asia, east Asia, northeast Asia and probably also north to Siberia at various points during this very long period. And since many of the peoples now inhabiting these regions have varying degrees of so-called "mongoloid" features, it's possible to speculate that such features may have originated with a single, relatively small, post-bottleneck founder group based somewhere to the east of what is now Bangladesh. During this same period and for some time afterward, it seems likely that a considerable amount of mixing, both "racial" and cultural, was taking place in greater southeast Asia, including the Malay Peninsula, Indonesia, the Philippines, South China and portions of Melanesia and Micronesia. The complexity of this region is reflected in the truly bewildering variety of musical styles

therein. Of all the regions of the world, this may well be the most difficult to characterize.

Alternatives

So what has been learned from our explorations so far, and what other options might we consider as we attempt to relate various possibilities to the evidence? And I suppose the answer would be that one's conclusions will depend, to some extent, on the sort of problems that come to mind. If one sees no problem with a straightforward functionalist/diffusionist explanation for the cultural, morphological and genetic similarities and differences we now see in the world around us, and are content to accept independent invention as the best explanation for all the many widespread but isolated similarities not easily attributable to cultural diffusion, then there is no problem with the most straightforward Out of Africa scenario: a small group of humans migrated from Africa to Asia; their descendants expanded along the southern coast of that continent, settling at first in India, where they quickly expanded throughout all of South Asia, with some continuing on to Southeast Asia and eventually migrating from there to East Asia, Siberia and Central Asia, with one or more of the Western colonies branching out to Europe at some point.

The many differences we now see in the world around us would therefore be due to the various adaptations people made to the different environments in which they found themselves; and the similarities would be due to the ways in which certain cultural elements diffused over time from one group to another — or else to the workings of "convergent evolution," where, by virtue of some inborn, universal process that can't really be explained, different groups in different places find themselves evolving in a similar direction.

This is one way of thinking about the Out of Africa model, and about anthropology generally, and if one is not overly critical it might seem the most likely and/or reasonable scenario. Whatever problems it might encounter can be attributed to our lack of detailed information regarding exactly how certain features get diffused from one group to another to facilitate change, or how certain practices can be explained as "cost-effective" adaptations to environmental pressures, or how various encounters and interactions among various neighboring groups can produce, via some sort of genetic and/or cultural "drift," large geographical regions that differ from one another, morphologically, genetically and culturally. This all fits quite nicely with anthropology as currently practiced, where almost all the effort is concentrated on sifting through the myriad details required to explain all the

146

many mini-problems that will invariably emerge from such a vaguely defined model.

However, this very "reasonable" approach to human evolution breaks down when we attempt to deal with certain problems that become evident only when we do something very few anthropologists of today seem willing to do: carefully and critically examine the patterns that emerge when we consider the large-scale distribution of cultural practices worldwide.

The current mainstream approach is a bit like the old Ptolemaic theory of the universe, where the Earth was at the center and all the heavenly bodies revolved around it according to "epicycles" that could only be determined through painstaking and detailed observation and calculation, not at all unlike the laborious efforts of all the armies of anthropologists, archaeologists, paleontologists, etc. seeking to make sense of the human world by either counting and classifying every single stone, bone and shard or interviewing every "native" in sight.

The Asiatic Mainstream

What convinced me that there is something very wrong with this near-sighted view was my discovery, thanks to Alan Lomax, of the remarkably consistent large-scale patterns we become aware of as we systematically study the various musical practices of traditional cultures on a worldwide basis. And once that door is opened, a magnificent socio-cultural vista becomes discernible, rich with many other possibilities — and problems. (For a review of the worldwide musical evidence, based on a hypothetical phylogenetic tree and a set of coordinated maps, see *Appendix B: A Phylogenetic Tree of Musical Style*.)

As far as Asia is concerned, almost the entire continent is now dominated by either solo singing or group singing in unison, in a manner radically different from just about anything we find in Subsaharan Africa today (aside from societies heavily influenced by Islam). I'm speaking of a particular, highly distinctive style and its various substyles, all very different from P/B or any other typically African music. "Elaborate style," as Alan Lomax called it, is a type of vocalizing characterized by intricate tonal embellishments; highly verbal; tending toward long, complex phrases and through-composed forms, often built around various combinations of "mosaic" elements; narrow intervals; frequent use of microtones and other types of vocal nuance; improvisation; tense, constricted vocal timbre; precise enunciation of consonants.

Such performances are often accompanied by instruments playing in unison or with variants of the same melodic line in a manner technically

147

called "heterophony." This is a style of music-making commonly found throughout Asia, from the Middle East (including North Africa) to Pakistan and India, to East Asia, Southeast Asia, Island Southeast Asia, and, in a somewhat less extreme form, Central Asia as well.

The contrast with Sub-Saharan Africa isn't universal, and there are in fact certain types of repetitive singing based on short phrases tossed back and forth in call and response style — but almost always with tense voices and in unison, as polyphony of any kind is rare. This type of vocalizing is quite different from the relaxed, open-throated, highly group-oriented, often elaborately interwoven part singing associated with what I've been calling the "African Signature."

Asian mainstream instrumental music is not as easily characterized, and somewhat more varied, but is also dominated by heterophony and also tends toward complex, highly elaborated microtonal structures, often performed in a virtuosic, highly nuanced manner. When polyphony appears it is almost always produced by a drone part rather than independent lines, even in large ensembles. Again, this type of performance is radically different from what is typical for Africa, where embellishment, microtones and nuance are rare. (As always, there are exceptions, but in most cases they are associated with Islamic influence.)

Some Examples

A more or less typical example of tense-voiced, embellished leader-chorus interchange from the Near East, an Arabic love song from Lebanon: *Audio Example 26:Lebanese Love Song* (from *Arabic and Druse Music,* Smithsonian Folkways).

Compare with this somewhat similar example from the province of Assam, in India: *Audio Example 27: Toka Bihu* (from *Bihu,* Smithsonian Folkways).

Some examples of very similar types of tense-voiced solo vocalizing, with unison or heterophonic instrumental accompaniment, from widely separated regions of Asia:

Laos: *Audio Example 28:LoveSong* (*Music of Southeast Asia,* Smithsonian Folkways FW 04423, track 207).

Korea: *Audio Example 29: Chang Poo Ta Ryong* (*Folk and Classical Music of Korea,* Smithsonian Folkways FW04424, track 1).

India: *Audio Example 30: FemaleVocal* (*Music of the Orient,* Smithsonian Folkways 04157, track 305).

Japan: *Audio Example 31: Ima nu Kazekumo* (*Folk Music of the Amami Islands,* Smithsonian Folkways 04448).

Uzbekistan: *Audio Example 32: Uchun Dur* (*The Silk Road: A Musical Caravan,*
Smithsonian Folkways 40438, track 6).
Mongolia: *Audio Example 33: The River Herlen* (*The Silk Road: A Musical Caravan,* Smithsonian Folkways 40438, track 18).
China (Yi People, Yunnan Province): *Audio Example 34: Qingge-Love Song* (*Baishibai:Songs of the minority nationalities of Yunnan,* PAN 2038, track 26).
Turkey: *Audio Example 35:I Should Die* (*Bazaar Istanbul: Music of Turkey,* Arc Music).

Questions

Can we account for the wide distribution of such a distinctive style family on the basis of a gradual process of transition from P/B or any other typically African type of music making? Or is this is a style that could only have emerged as the result of some sudden, and indeed radical, change at a very early phase of the Out of Africa migration? Given the wide distribution of the style, not only among the "high cultures" of Asia and North Africa, but also in so much of the same region's "folk" and even indigenous music as well, combined with the almost total absence of any form of vocal polyphony anywhere in the whole of Asia [1] (with the exception of the many widely scattered, marginalized and isolated groups I've already mentioned), the latter possibility seems far more likely. If it weren't rooted in so early a stage of human history, then it's hard to see how its effects could have been so all-encompassing, over such a vast region. Which returns us once again to the Toba question and the possibility of a history making "bottleneck" event. (For a more detailed analysis of the origins and diffusion of this style, see *Appendix B.* In terms of my "phylogenetic" nomenclature, "Elaborate Style" is classified as B2a1, and is rooted in the more fundamental post-bottleneck "haplogroup" B2.)

There are, as one might expect, complicating circumstances that cast something of a cloud over such issues, especially since we know of so many migrations, invasions, conquests, far-flung trading arrangements, religious crusades, etc., from the Neolithic to the Middle Ages and beyond, that carried so many cultural elements with them and had such widespread influence. While these relatively recent developments certainly had consequences of great importance, it's difficult for me to imagine how they could have had so complete and total an impact as to literally obliterate all trace of the African Signature, and indeed almost all trace of polyphonic singing and instrumental performance in so many remote corners of such a vast continent.

1. An important exception is Asiatic Russia, which does indeed have some remarkable polyphonic vocal traditions, though Russian folk polyphony seems more closely related to similar traditions in Europe and also Georgia (which is itself on the cusp between Europe and Asia) than to anything elsewhere in Asia.

Chapter Twelve: Passage to Europe

The picture for present day Europe is especially problematic due to an extraordinarily complicated history, in which all sorts of peoples from a great many places have fought time and again over the same turf for thousands of years, and almost all traces of tribal affiliation have vanished. The pre-historic picture is complicated, moreover, by an Ice Age, from *c.* 20,000-16,000 years ago, that covered vast areas of northern Europe with huge glaciers, forcing many populations to refuge areas farther south, where they remained for thousands of years before repopulating the northern latitudes. With the beginnings of the Neolithic there may well have been additional major population movements, as farmers from the Near East are thought to have migrated into Europe in large numbers.

Subsequently, there have been many large and small scale migrations, incursions, invasions, wars, revolutions, etc. that altered the social and cultural landscape of Europe in a multitude of ways. Moreover, during the last few centuries, various city-states, fiefdoms, duchies, kingdoms, etc. coalesced into modern nations, within which many previously distinct ethnic groups have ultimately lost both their independence and their identity.

While such events have certainly obscured much of the past, thanks to the work of archaeologists, linguists and, more recently, population geneticists, we are learning more and more about the early history of this vast region. Moreover, as I hope to demonstrate, there is much to be learned from a careful review of musical traditions which, in many cases, appear to have survived more or less intact over many thousands of years.

The Immigrants

According to Stephen Oppenheimer (2003:129-30), the original "Out of Africa" migrants would not have been able to make their way toward Europe "until after 50,000 years ago, when a moist, warm phase greened the Arabian Desert sufficiently to open the Fertile Crescent." Following both archaeological and genetic evidence he sees the homeland of these early Europeans in South Asia over 50,000 years ago, with a first wave of immigration, associated with the so-called "Aurignacian" culture, carrying the mitochondrial haplogroup U5 (an offshoot from superhaplogroup N), now common throughout Europe. He associates a second wave, from northwest India and Kashmir, dating from *c.* 33,500 years ago, with the somewhat later, "Gravettian," culture and a different mitochondrial haplogroup, HV, along with two Y [male line] chromosome markers, R and I, which he calls "Ruslan" and "Inos." Oppenheimer cites a recent study indicating that "the earliest roots of HV are found in South Asia...[and] the Trans-Caucasus was the site of her first West Eurasian blooming" (*ibid.*:145).

Another version of more or less the same genetic picture is encapsulated in the leftmost portion of the migration map we consulted in the previous chapter (Metspalu et al. 2004, fig. 5):

See Chapter Eleven, Figure 11.1

Since M is not found in Europe, we can concentrate on haplogroup N and its offshoots, R and U, which appear in the leftmost loop, along with X, TJ and HV. Of the two arrows leading into Europe both appear to be rooted in the same Trans-Caucasus region noted by Oppenheimer.

"Caucasoid" Origins

Nicholas Wade, in his book *Before the Dawn: Recovering the Lost History of Our Ancestors* (2006), notes that "[t]he first modern humans were an African species that had suddenly expanded its range," and continues, speculating as follows:

> For many millennia people would presumably all have had dark skin . . . It seems likely that the first modern humans who reached Europe 45,000 years ago would also have retained black skin and other African features. . . . [Thus] early Europeans, including the great artists of the Chauvet cave in France, may have retained dark skin and other badges of their African origin for many thousands of years (p. 95).

If Wade is correct, then what we now understand as typically "Caucasoid" morphology would have evolved in Europe, with white skin presumably an adaptation to a colder climate than that of Africa or South Asia. But white skin is only one feature of Caucasoid morphology; the original definition of the "Caucasian race" was based on the study of skull types, not skin color. And typically Caucasoid skull types are found not only in Europe, but among the dark skinned native peoples of southern India, known as "Dravidians."

Which raises an interesting question: did the typically "Caucasoid" physiognomy originate in Europe, as the result of a complex process of adaptation that would, aside from skin color, be extremely difficult to explain, followed by a dispersal throughout the entirety of a continent already inhabited by peoples with an African morphology, a process which is also very difficult to understand? Or could it have originated in South Asia, long before the colonization of Europe, as a consequence of the same disastrous event that may have also produced, among a different "founder group," people with a proto-Mongoloid morphology?[1]

The origin of proto-Caucasoids in South Asia at such an early date might also explain the presence of certain Caucasoid features among Paleosiberians, as well as the remarkably Caucasoid appearance of the Ainu, the indigenes of northern Japan, clearly unrelated to Europeans in any way other than appearance. As I see it, dispersal throughout Europe of a population already bearing Caucasoid features when they first entered that continent makes a lot more sense than a gradual process of morphological change magically converging on a single type over thousands of years. But this is, of course, an extremely complex issue that may never be resolved.

Georgia

If the Trans-Caucasus were indeed a major staging ground for early humans into Europe, there is reason to believe their musical practices might be alive and well in the region to this day. The Republic of Georgia is home to what are probably the richest and most complex traditions of oral vocal polyphony outside of Africa. According to Joseph Jordania, a leading authority on Georgian music (and polyphonic singing in general), "unlike many countries in Europe, where the tradition of polyphonic singing is represented only in some of the regions, the whole of Georgia is one big group of closely related polyphonic traditions" (Jordania 2006:75). However, significant differences within this region become apparent when he contrasts the pedal drone, free rhythms, metric variety and ornamented melisma of the East, with the contrapuntal polyphony, strict rhythms, duple meter, unornamented melodies and yodel of the West. The musical split is paralleled by important historical differences, as West Georgia can be associated with the older, more traditional culture of "Old Europe," prior to later migrations from the east:

> [T]hese migrations and major cultural and population changes during the 3rd-2nd millennia involved only the territory of East Georgia, while the territory of western Georgia, situated on the other side of the Likhi mountains . . . remained virtually unaffected (ibid.: 219).

Significantly, the characteristics Jordania associates with the more conservative culture of western Georgia are all typical of P/B style as well, while many other features of P/B, such as hocket, part crossing, ostinato, continuous flow, improvisation, disjunct melody, meaningless vocables, open-throated voices, precise tonal and rhythmic blend, use of the same intervals both melodically and harmonically, and free use of secundal dissonance, are also characteristic, if not omnipresent, aspects of certain types of west Georgian polyphony.

Here is a remarkable example of Georgian choral polyphony that resembles P/B style in many respects. Listen especially for the yodeling, the many repetitions of short motives, the continuous, "run-on" flow, and the rapid, hocketed exchange between interlocking groups: *Audio Example 36:Garuli Naduri* (from *Georgian Voices*, the Rustavi Choir).

Is this a style that must necessarily have evolved from monophony to polyphony, simplicity to complexity, according to traditional notions of evolutionary "development"? Or was the complexity there from the beginning, a legacy from our African ancestors and their HV, Inos, and Ruslan descendents?

The Archaeological Evidence

According to Oppenheimer, European Russia seems to have first been colonized "high up the river Don, at Kostenki, due north of the Caucasus" (*ibid*.:147). This important Paleolithic site on the Don River, near Voronezh, dating between 30,000 and 40,000 years ago, is the subject of a web site (Hitchcock 2009) containing many very interesting illustrations and discussions. Among photos of "mammoth bone dwellings" and "Venus" figurines resembling the well known Venus of Willendorf, we find drawings of two "pipes made from long, hollow bird bones" which "may have been musical instruments or animal lures" (see photo K, reproduced from Sklenar 1985):

See Figure 12.1

Another website by the same author is devoted to a closely related archaeological site, Mezhirich. Here we find an extremely interesting reconstruction of a mammoth-bone hut, designed in a manner that closely resembles some of the beehive huts we examined in Chapter Eight (http://www.donsmaps.com/mammothcamp.html):

See Figure 12.2

Note the resemblance between the curved bones joined over the entryway and the manner in which bent saplings are joined in a typical Pygmy or Bushmen hut.

According to *Encyclopédie des instruments de musique* (Buchner 1980), "The oldest Pan pipes found in Europe come from the eastern part of the continent: a neolithic necropolis (2000 BC) in southern Ukraine and a site in the region of Saratov. Each was made of seven or eight hollow bird bones" (Buchner 1980:20). (Buchner's research predates discovery of the Kostenki site. Birdbone panpipes have also been found in a tomb dating from the eleventh century BC, in Luyi, Henan Province, China (Bishop 2005)).

Folkorist Rūta Žarskienė has studied "multi-pipe whistles" from northeastern Lithuania, the Komi Republic, Briansk in southwestern Russia, and the Kaluga and Kursk regions near Moscow:

> It seems that the most striking principle, uniting Lithuanian, Komi and Russian instruments, is that the untied whistles are used only in groups and are played only collectively... The number of ...whistles [used is similar] (Lithuanian—five to eight, Komi—four to six, Russian—four to eleven). The distribution of the Lithuanian multi-pipe whistles especially while performing sung polyphonic songs, could be relevant with [the distribution] of Russian instruments into so-called "pairs". (Žarskienė 2003)

In a related article, Žarskienė examines the association of many of these instruments with bird names and the onomatopoetic imitation of birdcalls. Noting the wide area of dissemination of this practice, she suggests that such bird associations could possibly date back "to very ancient times," and, presumably, the "earliest emotional attitude of mankind." (Žarskienė 2000).

Lithuanian multi-pipe ensembles are frequently associated with one of the oldest vocal traditions in that country, the *sutartine* (pronounced su-tar-ti-nay). *Sutartines* are sung and/or played canonically in two or three interlocking parts, often emphasizing intervals of a second—a practice resembling aspects of P/B style, where imitative passages, similar to rounds or canons are not uncommon: *Audio Example 37:Sutartine-Tureja Liepa* (from Valiulytė 1998).

Sets of trumpets or horns called *ragai* were "common in northeast Lithuania for performing *sutartines*.... Each...had its own name, individual rhythms based on one or two notes and onomatopoetic words to remember these" (Sadie 1984, iii:188-89). A photo of five Lithuanian *ragai* players (*ibid.*:189) bears a striking resemblance to photos of certain hocket-based trumpet ensembles in Africa:

See Figures 12.3 and 12.4)

We've already heard an example of Ragai music in Chapter Nine:*Audio Example 25: Tytytitit.*

Research similar to that of Žarskienė was carried out by Olga Velitchkina, in the village of Plekhovo, in the Kursk region of European Russia, not far from the Ukrainian border (Velichkina 1996). The following video was presented in Chapter Nine, but let's take another look: *Video Example One: Russian Pipers.* Can you hear the performers "hooting" along with their pipes? Velitchkina presents a transcription of a pipe duet from this repertoire, clearly demonstrating how intricately the vocal and instrumental parts interweave. I'll include it here for the benefit of those who can read music:

See Figure 12.5

As Velitchkina notes, the transcription is a bit misleading, as the performers never sing and play at exactly the same time. A more detailed transcription would make the basis in hocketing even more evident. Another remarkable point of similarity between this tradition and P/B is the cyclic organization of these pieces into distinct periods. Moreover, as Velitchina's analysis makes clear, variation from one period to the next is an important element in this style, as it is in P/B. Many other points of similarity with P/B are evident from both the recordings and her analysis.

Velitchkina makes the point that "[o]n first listening, this music seems closer to African forms (for example, to the Ba-Benzele Pygmy music) than to any European folk instrument traditions." Here is an example of Ba-Benzele hocketed vocalizing with pipes, for comparison: *Audio Example 38: Song After Returning from a Hunt* (from *Anthology Of World Music: Africa - Ba-Benzele Pygmies*, recorded by Simha Arom). Here's an even closer example, from the Ouldeme people of the Mandara Mountain region of Cameroon. The "hooting" voices of the singers are clearly audible: *Audio Example 39:Zavan* (from *Cameroon:Flutes of the Mandara Mountains*, recorded by Nathalie Fernando et Fabrice Marandola). To me, the resemblance with the Russian pipers is uncanny.

To summarize, we see a clear pattern in certain remote areas of the Caucasus and Eastern Europe consistent with survival, well into the

Twentieth Century, of essentially the same "African Signature" we've already noted in remote enclaves of southeast Asia, Indonesia, Melanesia, etc. Specifically:

- The elaborately contrapuntal, interlocked, hocketed and yodeled vocal polyphony of west Georgia.
- Long-term traditions of very similar types of communal panpipe playing, with unbound pipes, and associations with birds, found scattered throughout Lithuania, the Ukraine, and Russia, many in the same general area where remains of important Paleolithic settlements have been discovered (for example, Avdeevo near Kursk and Mezin, Gagarino, and Mezhirich in the Ukraine).
- In one Russian settlement, Kostenki, hollowed pipes made of bird bone were found, which appear to have had either a musical, signaling, or hunting function, very possibly all three.
- In Lithuania, a vocal tradition, the *sutartine*, organized in a manner somewhat like P/B canonic/echoic style, in association with a tradition of hocketed trumpet and horn ensembles reminiscent of very similar practices in Africa.
- And finally, thanks to the remarkable research of Olga Velitchkina, we've learned of a Russian panpipe tradition remarkably close, in her words, to that of the Ba-Benzele Pygmies.

While the Ice Age caused most of northern Europe to be abandoned and then resettled only thousands of years later, certain regions in this area were never abandoned. "It is in the Ukraine and further north up the rivers Dneipr and Don into the Russian plain...where we find the best record of continuous human occupation—even expansion—in Eastern Europe during the Big Freeze" (Oppenheimer 2004b:250).

The West

Lest we assume P/B-related traditions are limited to Eastern Europe, let us briefly review some candidates farther to the west. Fortunately, some excellent examples of rarely heard Swiss alpine polyphony have been recorded, initially by the pioneering Romanian ethnomusicologist, Constantine Brailoiu and, more recently, by Hugo Zemp.

Listen, for example, to this recording of a group of yodeling cattle herders from the Appenzell region: *Audio Example 40:Swiss Cattle Herders* (from *Voices of the World*: disc 1, track 35). Here we have a somewhat different mix of distinctive features: a more sustained, lyrical, sound; an emphasis, as is typical for Central and Western Europe, on intervals of the 3rd and 6th; interlocking parts; *stimmtauch* (part crossing); disjunct melody; continuous flow; meaningless vocables; lack of embellishment; open throated voices; smooth vocal blend; and most notably, yodel.

Moving farther to the west, all the way to the coastal Algarve region of Portugal, a traditional song sung by fishermen as they pull up their nets, *Audio Example 41:Leva-Leva* (from *Anthology of Portuguese Music*, Smithsonian Folkways 4538, Vol. 2, track 1), is characterized by hocket; repetition; disjunct intervals; continuous flow; meaningless vocables; lack of embellishment or melisma; relaxed voices; and precise rhythms. Interestingly, this performance can be characterized as contrapuntal, but not polyphonic, as the rapidly exchanged hocketed phrases never coincide. Similar forms of tightly coordinated non-polyphonic interchange can be heard among Pygmy and Bushmen groups as well.

While polyphonic singing is extremely rare among the most traditional British folk musicians of our day, this was not always the case. Consider the testimony of the 13th Century archdeacon Giraldus Cambrensis (Gerald of Wales), who wrote as follows of some remarkable singing he observed among Welsh country folk:

> As to their musical euphony, they do not sing uniformly as is done elsewhere, but diversely with many rhythms and tunes, so that in a crowd of singers such as is the custom among these people, *you will hear as many different songs and differentiations of the voices as you see heads*, and hear the organic melody coming together in one consonance with the smooth sweetness of B flat. . . And what is more remarkable, children scarcely beyond infancy, when their wails have barely turned into songs observe the same musical performance (as quoted in Burstyn 1983: 135-136 – my emphasis).

Gerald's words could easily be a description of African Pygmy or Bushmen group vocalizing, where everyone present, including small children, typically joins in with his or her own independent part.

The Written Traditions

Gerald's comments may shed light on the origins of one of the most remarkable and mysterious of all medieval compositions, the well known round, "Sumer is Icumen In." In the words of musicologist Shai Burstyn, canonic singing, harmonically reducible to a stationary triad, is prevalent in non-European cultures. Some medieval European examples exhibit related traits. Rounds may be found in contemporary European folk polyphony, such as the East Lithuanian *sutartine*. It is therefore arbitrary to argue the unique historical position of *Sumer* on the ground of the fortuitous hard fact that it is the only such composition we possess. Since Gerald specifically defines Welsh and Northumbrian polyphonic singing as indigenous, attempts to elucidate his meaning must assume an oral tradition and should also consider the possibility of improvisation (ibid.:140).

Some of the most remarkable similarities with P/B can indeed be found in certain practices characteristic of early Medieval notated polyphony, such as the *rota, caccia* and hocket, all of which might well have roots in so-called "popular polyphony" (see especially Burstyn 1983 and Bukofzer 1940). The origins and meaning of the Medieval hocket would seem especially mysterious, unless the practice represented an attempt to incorporate certain traditional practices of the peasantry into the mainstream liturgical repertory. This isn't very different from the explanation offered by Burstyn with regard to the *Sumer* canon, which also, as he argues, is likely to have roots in polyphonic traditions already popular in the back streets and countryside.

While it is possible to trace the step by step evolution of mainstream medieval polyphony as a progressive elaboration of monophonic plain chant, "aberrant" forms such as the *rota, caccia,* and hocket seem to have emerged suddenly and out of whole cloth, suggesting that they are adaptations of long standing traditions already in place. This would, as well, explain the continual complaints on the part of so many church leaders, as though hocketing represented the encroachment of an alien and uncouth "popular" element into the sanctum of serious church worship.

There is some confusion about the nature of hocket, which has led to the belief that it is simply a matter of each voice or instrument contributing only one or two notes to a resultant melody or texture. While that is sometimes the case, more complex types of interlocking hocket are also common, as illustrated in the excerpts presented below (from Sanders 1974: 247):

See Figure 12.6

A comparison between the first excerpt, from a 12th Century *Conductus* by Perotinus, and the hocketed interplay between voices 2 and 3 in the

159

transcription of *Ju'/hoansi* Bushmen vocal polyphony presented in *Appendix A* See Figure A2), reveals some very interesting similarities indeed:

See Figure 12.7

Note especially the "fanfare"-like motives, the tightly interlocking counterpoint, the close imitation of one part by the other, the conflation of polyphony and heterophony, and the tendency for the parts to overlap at the unison or octave:

Of special interest for several reasons is the concluding section of an anonymous three voice motet from the Montpellier Codex, dating from 13th Century France, as transcribed by N. Nakamura (Amor Potest 2004):

See Figure 12.8

There is very little trace of the trained composer in this work, with its many blatant voice leading "errors," obsessive repetition of brief motives, and continuous "run-on" phrasing, with no cadences whatsoever during the entire last section until the very end. *Audio Example 42: Amor Potest*, concluding section (from *Music of the Gothic Era*: disc 1, track 8). The last two characteristics are especially interesting as they invoke not only the varied repetition and continuous vocalizing so typical of P/B, but also certain aspects of the practice of Leoninus and Perotinus, the leading liturgical composers of 12th and 13th century Europe. Note also the tendency, found throughout this repertoire, to present hocketed segments without meaningful text, again remarkably close to Pygmy/Bushmen norms.

So common was this practice in Medieval music that some scholars have assumed most hockets must have been intended for instruments alone. Additional features of at least some of these hocketed examples that can be associated with distinctive features of P/B, as presented above, are: part crossing; ostinato; canonic or echoic effects; strict rhythm; disjunct melody; lack of embellishment; a tendency to conflate polyphony and heterophony; the occasional presence of secundal dissonance. In the light of everything discussed thus far, it is difficult to see *Amor Potest* as other than a transcription or adaptation of some sort of oral "folk" polyphony, roughly along the same lines as Burstyn's view of the *Sumer* canon, only this time with the vernacular text completely replaced by a more acceptable one, in Latin.

Admittedly, any attempt to speculate regarding a possible connection between the musical practices of African hunter/gatherers and the Medieval churches and monasteries of western Europe may seem far fetched in the

160

extreme. Indeed, until recently, there was no reason to associate African and European traditions of any kind. Almost all historians and archaeologists were in agreement that African and European prehistories were completely unrelated, with Europeans in all likelihood descended from earlier, archaic humans from the same continent. Thanks, however, to remarkable developments centered in the field of population genetics, our picture of world prehistory has changed, so abruptly and so radically that many in the social sciences remain either unaware or in a state of confused disbelief regarding the most recent findings and the profound implications they bring with them.

---

1. It's important to understand that by invoking terms such as "Caucasoid" and "Mongoloid" I am *not* referring to "racial" differences, but morphological ones. In my view, "race" per se has no scientific meaning (partly because no one really knows how to define that term as anything other than a social construct) but there is certainly a science of comparative morphology, a far less ambitious, and more clearly circumscribed, mode of anthropological research, which, because of its questionable history, is often confused with "racial science."

Chapter Thirteen: Europe, Old And New

The significance of archaic survivals in remote refuge areas was brought home to me with unusual force when reading Joseph Jordania's book, *Who Asked the First Question* (Jordania 2006). In his very thorough and convincing consideration of European vocal traditions, Jordania demonstrates that societies where polyphonic vocalizing comes more or less naturally, as part of long established oral traditions, tend to be found in "refuge" areas, such as mountainous regions, islands, forests, etc. — and this appears to be a continent-wide phenomenon, extending to the British Isles as well. Surrounding these isolated pockets, oral traditions of a different kind prevail, characterized by solo singing and/or group vocalizing in unison and octaves. Both types are clearly "old," but the striking difference in their distribution — the one continuous and "mainstream," the other discontinuous and marginal — could be an important clue, not only to their relative age as distinct musical practices, but to our understanding of European pre-history generally.

Following the lead of archaeologist Marija Gimbutas (1994), Jordania associates the polyphonic traditions with what she called "Old Europe," an archaic culture either absorbed or displaced by a migration from western and/or central Asia, dating from roughly 4,000 BC, of a more aggressive, and ultimately far more successful, "proto Indo-European" culture (see below), bringing with it a very different musical style. While certain of Gimbutas' theories, such as her "civilization of the Goddess" idea, have been regarded with justified skepticism, the considerable body of musical evidence offered by Jordania tends to support her notion of a once ubiquitous but now marginalized "Old European" culture of great antiquity, fragments of which have survived in various refuge areas throughout the continent well into the Twentieth Century.

As illustrated by the many transcriptions in Jordania's book, "Old European" polyphonic singing is highly varied, ranging from interlocking counterpoints and hockets stylistically close to P/B (see previous chapter), to various types of drone polyphony, parallel harmonies, or combinations of any two or three of the above. In some places, the harmonies are "smooth," in a manner familiar to modern ears, but in other places, such as the highland regions of Bulgaria, Serbia, Macedonia, etc., harsh dissonances are favored. While many of these traditions do not carry the "African signature" precisely as I've defined it, the tightly blended polyphonic choral practices found among so many of these groups have many typically "African" characteristics. Whether they represent derivations from musical styles introduced to Europe via the Out of Africa migration, or are the result of completely independent processes must remain, for now, an open question.

Here are some examples of so-called "Old European" polyphony:

From the mountains of Liguria, in northern Italy: *Audio Example 43: Tralallero* (from *Italian Treasury: Folk Music & Song of Italy,* Rounder Records, recorded by Alan Lomax).

From Basque country, in the Pyrenees mountains of northern Spain: *Audio Example 44 : Koadrila Batsen Gara* (from *The Spanish Recordings: Basque Country,* recorded by Alan Lomax, track 6).

From the Pirin mountains of southwest Bulgaria: *Audio Example 45 :Vetar Vee* (from *Bulgarian Village and Folk Music,* recorded by Ethel Raim and Martin Koenig)

From the forests of Belarus (formerly Byelorussia): *Audio Example 46:Belarus Folksong* (from *Folk Music of the USSR,* Smithsonian Folkways 4535, compiled by Henry Cowell).

Perhaps the most astonishing example of an "Old European" survival is a traditional Basque instrument called the *Xalaparta,* as demonstrated here, via youtube — *Video Example Two, Ttukunak.*

The Xalaparta is closely related to an instrumental ensemble almost certainly of African origin and widely found among many indigenous groups as part of the "African Signature": stamping tubes. It may also be related to the xylophone, though that connection is more remote. Both traditions were in all likelihood a part of Out-of-Africa migrant culture (HMC), maintained through their epic migrations to Asia, Indonesia, Melanesia and, of course, Europe.

To illustrate, here's a youtube video of stamping tubes from Ghana: *Video Example Three: Traditional Bamboo Orchestra in Mesomagor.*

The following youtube video, by ethnomusicologist Hugo Zemp, illustrates how stamping tubes are prepared and performed among the 'Are 'are people of the Solomon Islands, in Melanesia. *Video Example Four: 'Are 'are Stamping Tubes.* Different types of group interaction can be seen if you skip to about 6 and a half minutes in. [This video is no longer available via youtube.]

A Romanian monastic tradition known as *toaca,* appears stylistically related to both Txalaparta and stamping tube performance, though in this case wooden hammers are used. On this youtube video we see as many as four nuns performing a complexly interactive hocket. *Video Example Five: Toaca.*

The European Mainstream

The most typical vocal styles of "mainstream" European folksong, once commonly heard in lowland farms, villages, and small towns throughout the continent, tend to be monophonic, highly word-oriented lyric songs or ballads, in strophic (i.e., verse) form, often with a refrain. According to the terminology adopted by Alan Lomax, the polyphonic vocal traditions of the remote highland areas are considered "Old European," while the monophonic, strophic "folk songs" of the lowland villages and towns are "Modern European."

A few examples of "Modern European" strophic song:

England: *Audio Example 47:Lord Lovell* (from *An English Folk Music Anthology*, Smithsonian Folkways).
. Hungary: *Audio Example 48: Come on Girls to the Spinning House* (from *Folk Music of Hungary*, Smithsonian Folkways, collected under the supervision of Bela Bartok).
Lithuania: *Audio Example 49: Riding Across a Forest of Green* (from *Lithuanian Folk Songs in the United States*, Smithsonian Folkways).
Italy: *Audio Example 50: Stornello Baresi* (from Italian *Folk Songs and Dances*, Smithsonian Folkways).

If Old European polyphonic singing is rooted in archaic traditions either stemming from, or closely related to, the culture of the earliest African colonists, then what could be the source of these much simpler monophonic songs and ballads? For clues, we will need to delve farther into the fascinating theories of Marija Gimbutas.

The "Kurgan" Invasion

According to Gimbutas' model, Indo-European language and culture developed in the "Dnieper/Volga" region in the "earlier half of the 4th Millennium BC" and spread from there in many directions, both to the east and west, facilitated by Kurgan mastery of horsemanship. A Wikipedia article on the *Kurgan Hyphothesis* includes the following "Map of Indo-European migrations from ca. 4000 to 1000 BC according to the Kurgan model" (http://en.wikipedia.org/wiki/Kurgan_hypothesis#_note-Oxford):

See Figure 13.1

From this map we can get an idea of what Gimbutas is talking about when she associates the Indo-European migration (or, if you prefer, invasion) into Europe with the destruction and ultimate marginalization of "Old European" culture. Note the yellow area in the map, between the Caspian and Black Seas, representing a mountainous area, roughly where Georgia is located, that was left unconquered by the aggressive and warlike Indo-Europeans.

"Matristic" vs. "Patriarchal

In an online interview with David Jay Brown & Rebecca McCLen Novick, Gimbutas spoke of her childhood in Lithuania, a country which, at the time, was, as she says, "still fifty percent pagan" [this interview is no longer avaible on the Internet]:

> In some areas, up to the nineteenth and twentieth century, there were still beliefs alive in Goddesses and all kinds of beings. So in my childhood I was exposed to many things which were almost prehistoric, I would say. And when I studied archaeology, it was easier for me to grasp what these sculptures mean than for an archaeologist born in New York, who doesn't know anything about the countryside life in Europe.

Such observations, coupled with many years of archaeological research, led her to develop a fascinating hypothesis associating the destruction of Old European civilization with the migration into Europe of "proto-Indo-European people" from southern Russia. The "Kurgans" were violent horse-mounted conquerors, who introduced their "patriarchal" social structure, with the result that European culture became "hybridized."

According to Gimbutas, Old European culture, prior to the invasion of the Kurgans was "matristic." From the interview:

> "I call it matristic, not matriarchal, because matriarchal always arouses ideas of dominance and is compared with the patriarchy. But it was a balanced society, it was not that women were really so powerful that they usurped everything that was masculine. Men were in their rightful position, they were doing their own work, they had their duties and they also had their own power. This is reflected in their symbols where you find not only goddesses but also, Gods. . ."

While the Old Europeans were nonviolent and had no weapons other than weapons for hunting, the Kurgans had military weapons and also horses, which gave them a powerful military advantage. When they invaded, the indigenous inhabitants retreated high into the hills, "sometimes in places which had very difficult access."

"There was evidence of immigration and escape from these violent happenings and a lot of confusion, a lot of shifts of population. People started to flee to places like islands and forests and hilly areas."

Whether there was literally a "cult of the Goddess" or "civilization of the Goddess," as Gimbutas claimed, is less important, as I see it, than her theories regarding an essentially "matristic," egalitarian and pacifist "Old European" culture, prior to the transformation of Europe by the Indo-Europeans. The Old Europe she describes seems quite close in many ways to the "Utopian" culture of the African Pygmies and Bushmen, as commonly described in so much of the literature. (See Chapters Three, Four and Six.)

To help us understand how "African" Old Europe may have been, let's compare two sets of images, the first an example of Paleolithic rock art from southeastern Spain, as presented by Gimbutas in *Civilization of the Goddess* (p. 187), the second a selection of four unrelated rock art images from Southern Africa, usually associated with the Bushmen culture of anywhere from several hundreds to several thousands of years ago:

See Figures 13.2 and 13.3

The Ancient Roots of "Modern European" Song

If the exuberant folk polyphony that so deeply impressed both Lomax and Jordania can be associated with "Old Europe," can we associate the more thoughtful and poetic monophonic folk songs of "Modern Europe" with the culture of Kurgan invaders and their Indo-European languages? In search of an answer, let's turn to the musical traditions of the Central Asian horse nomads, where highly poetic, monophonic, strophic songs are typical, and polyphonic vocalizing is conspicuous by its absence.

An excellent example of Central Asian strophic song at its most rhapsodic is provided in the soundtrack of yet another youtube video, from Kyrgyzstan, which will also give you an idea of how important horses are in this culture: *Video Example Six: Kyrgyz Song* (*http://www.youtube.com/watch?v=FrETbBI1kOU&feature=related*).

Equally impressive singing, and playing, is found among the neighboring Kazaks: *Audio Example 51: Kanapya*. Note how effectively the *dombra* rhythms evoke the sound of horse's hoofs.

Compare the above with this northern Albanian ballad: *Audio Example 52: Zenel Kadrija*.

While there appears to be a clear connection between the Kazak performance and the one from Albania, the connection between Central Asian strophic song and that of the more straightforward, simple, and unaccompanied strophic "folk songs" of mainstream Europe (cf. Audio Examples 47-50) isn't quite so clear. In both cases, we find a musical syntax based on clearly delineated phrases, tailored to fit carefully contrived poetic lines, with the music repeating almost note for note with each successive verse. But the Central Asian examples are often much longer, more rhapsodic and rhythmically flexible, and also, of course, usually accompanied by plucked string instruments such as the dombra, of a sort that we don't find in western Europe until the Middle Ages.

In my phylogenetic map of music style (see *Appendix B*), I labeled both types of strophic song B2a2, as opposed to another important solo style labeled B2a1, the "Elaborate Style" discussed in Chapter Eleven. According to this model, both styles derive from B2, the "Breathless Style" of the Paleosiberians and Saami, rooted in the "bottleneck event" discussed in Chapter Ten. B2a1 and B2a2 differ from Breathless Style in that phrasing has become an important feature, while Breathless Style is characterized by musical "run-on sentences," interrupted by arbitrary gasps for air. It's possible that the Central Asiatic strophic song represents an intermediate evolutionary phase between B2a1 and B2a2 rather than a simple branching from B2. It isn't as highly embellished or as "through-composed" as "elaborate" style, but it does share in some of its rhapsodic freedom, and the relation between the instrument(s) and the voice (unison or heterophony) is similar as well.

Is the European strophic song related to the strophic songs of Central Asian horse nomads via the mutual influence of the "Kurgan" horse nomads postulated by Gimbutas? Or does it have some other source, possibly as an independent outgrowth from Breathless Style? Could it be an amalgam of both? Or a completely new "independent invention"? Can we see it as part of a "modern" tradition that supplanted "Old Europe" after a "Kurgan invasion" and the introduction of Indo-European languages? Or is it a survival of a much older cultural strain, associated with the earliest development of farming and herding in Europe. In any case, this is a style that seems to have pervaded the vocal performances of most farms and villages through the length and breadth of Europe for many thousands of years.

The Role of Women

When Alan Lomax collected folk music in Spain and Italy during the 1950's, he was struck by certain differences in singing style between north and south in both countries that appeared related to the role of women. Specifically, where women played a more important and active role in the society and had a certain amount of sexual freedom, as in the north, voices tended to be more open, relaxed and "well blended," and there was a tendency to sing in groups, often polyphonically. Where women played a subordinate role, and their sexuality was strictly controlled, as in the south, voices tended to be constricted and tense, solo singing was more common, and group singing usually in harsh unison. Since Lomax was something of a Freudian — and a disciple of Margaret Mead — it's not difficult to see how he could have associated sexual tension with vocal tension, male-female harmony with musical harmony.

Since this was one of the principal "epiphanies" that led him to focus on the stylistic aspects of music, the testing of this hypothesis became one of the earliest goals of Cantometrics. Drawing upon the "Ethnographic Atlas," a database compiled by ethnologist George Murdock, containing, among other things, data pertaining to the role of women in a number of different societies, Lomax found correlations that did, indeed, appear to confirm his initial hypothesis.

Of particular interest is a graph appearing on p. 167 of *Folk Song Style and Culture*, with "productive complementarity" as the horizontal axis, and mean percentage of polyphonic singing as the vertical. The graph progressively rises from left to right, indicating a growing tendency, worldwide, for polyphonic vocalizing as the participation of women in food producing activities, according to Murdock's ratings, increases (M and N indicate male domination for such tasks, D and E rough equality of males and females and F and G almost exclusively female participation):

See Figure 13.4

Interestingly, there is hardly any difference between female polyphony (scored line) and polyphony generally (solid line), indicating that the

168

differences between "men's songs" and "women's songs" (an issue that has received much attention over the last 25 years or so) may matter less than differences in the way women are treated in the society as a whole.

While many of the relationships Lomax found between song style and social structure remain either problematic or difficult to assess, his correlations between male-female "complementarity" and aspects of song style such as polyphony, tonal blend and vocal tension have always seemed more convincing. While it's not clear whether such a correlation can be regarded as truly universal, it does seem to hold for large portions of Africa, Europe and Asia.

Lomax's notion of *complementarity* seems quite close to Gimbutas' idea of the *matristic* — a "balanced society" where women and men live and work together on a more or less equal basis. Lomax described this type of society as follows:

> [W]here women take a leading recognized part in the central activity of a society, such as supplying the main source of food, they assume, at least in this respect, a complementary, or more or less equal, interactive relationship with men. . . People tend to sing in wide voices in societies where women are most secure in their productive and sexual roles and where, therefore, they are freest to relate fully to the males (pp. 199-200).

While Lomax often writes as though he sees a cause and effect relationship between sexual and vocal tension, complementarity and polyphony, etc., he also associates polyphonic vocalizing and wide, relaxed voices with the same "Old Europe" that Gimbutas associated with the earlier, matristic societies that dominated all of Europe prior to the advent of the Indo-Europeans. Which raises a fascinating question: are we dealing with a patently Freudian situation, where tensions between men and women, both sexual and political, tend to promote behavioral tension, as expressed by tightly constricted throats and harshly blended monophonic group performance? — or do the differences, both sexual and musical, reflect a contrast between two types of culture, the *matristic, complementary,* "polyphonic" culture of Africa and Old Europe vs. the patriarchal, repressive, violent, monophonic culture of Indo-European invaders?

Is there some sort of universal cause and effect relation at work between the role of women in society and certain aspects of musical style? More specifically, is there a cause and effect relation, as Lomax claimed, between male-female *complementarity* and polyphonic vocalizing, relaxed voices, and "good" tonal blend? Or are the correlations he found due to historical processes at work in a specific time and place — in this case neolithic Europe

— affecting *both* the treatment of women *and* many other aspects of culture, as Gimbutas' theories suggest?

Universalist claims of this sort can be tested by determining whether or not the correlations still hold in a completely different socio-historical context. Consider, for example, native North America. Here we have both hunter-gatherers and agriculturalists, simple tribal cultures and advanced civilizations. We also have patrilineal societies, where women are clearly subordinate, and matrilineal societies, where women have considerable influence and freedom.

Yet throughout the length and breadth of this vast area, we find only the barest trace of polyphonic vocalizing, mostly in very limited areas, such as pockets in the Northwest Coast and, in northern California, among the Hupa, who are patrilineal. The music of just about every other native American tribe north of Mexico, whether matrilineal or patrilineal, aggressive and warlike, or relatively quiet and passive, is dominated by unison singing and moderately tense voices, with little to no trace of polyphony. Evidently, the correlation Lomax found between complementarity and polyphony cannot, therefore, be regarded as universal, as it doesn't seem to apply in North America.

As for the other musical characteristics Lomax associated with complementarity — relaxed voices and "good" tonal blend — the picture is not so clear. The Navaho and many Pueblo groups are matrilineal — and have indeed been characterized as "Apollonian" (as opposed to "Dionysian") cultures. Their voices do in fact tend to be more relaxed than is typical for native Americans in the north — and Pueblo singing is noted for its smooth vocal blend. The Apache, however, close relatives of the Navaho, and also matrilineal, tend to have a more strident, tense and harshly blended style of vocalizing. Since it's not clear whether or not the Apache pattern could be a response to relatively recent historical events, additional research would be necessary before a firm conclusion could be reached.

Returning to our consideration of Europe, we are probably safe in concluding that Old European polyphonic vocalizing, associated by Lomax with the role of women, was most likely the product of historically contingent, rather than universally necessary, forces — as implied by both Gimbutas and Jordania. There would seem to be no hard and fast rule causing humans to sing in harmony wherever women are treated as equals, though this very interesting issue is still open to further investigation.

Nevertheless, as Gimbutas would surely point out, the Old European pattern does suggest that gender-balance, acephalous, egalitarian political systems, group integration, cooperation, and sharing, along with an overall lack of competiveness and aggression, do seem to go hand in hand with musical practices expressing harmoniousness, social integration and simple pleasure. It does seem reasonable, therefore, to associate smoothly blended, relaxed voices, singing spontaneously together in harmony, with the sort of harmonious culture one might expect when both women and men are socially integrated on a free and equal basis, with minimal opportunities for sexual rivalry and tension to arise. In other words, while the correlations Lomax discovered do not necessarily point to cause and effect relationships, they strongly suggest that the various aspects of any culture can best be evaluated as parts of an integrated whole.

Chapter Fourteen: Mysteries of Sahul

At the time of the Out-of-Africa migrations, water levels in the oceans were much lower than they are today, and as a result many of the islands of Island Southeast Asia were linked with the Malaysian mainland to form a single peninsula, called Sunda; and Australia and New Guinea were also linked to form a single continent, *Sahul*:

See Figure 14.1

As you can see from the map, the low water levels meant that island hopping from Sunda to Sahul would not have been too much of a challenge — especially since, as is now suspected, the Out of Africa migrants had already been doing much of their traveling by boat. Since some of the earliest archaeological evidence of modern human habitation comes from Australia, and since some of the arguably "oldest" populations (based on both their genetic and cultural makeup) now live in New Guinea and Australia, it stands to reason that Sahul must have been part of the Out-of-Africa migration.

But there is a problem. If Sahul were populated by Out of Africa migrants when both New Guinea and Australia were joined into a single landmass, and both regions had remained relatively isolated from then to now, as appears to be the case, we would expect the populations now living in both places to be quite similar, both morphologically and culturally. And we would assume they'd be closely related genetically as well. This, however, is *not* the case.

Melanesia overall, including both New Guinea and the closely related group of islands to its east, known as "Island Melanesia," is highly differentiated culturally, whereas Australia is much more homogeneous, with almost all aborigines having distinctively "Australoid" features and sharing many traditions in common. Possibly because of the prolonged isolation of each group from its neighbors, due partly to geography, partly to endemic warfare, there are far more different languages and language families in New Guinea than anywhere else on Earth, while Australia is dominated by a single language family, called Pama-Nyungan, with all the others crowded into a relatively small area in the north, the region closest to New Guinea. The unusual distribution pattern for language families in Australia is visible in the following map (from the Wikipedia article, *Indigenous Australian Languages*

http://en.wikipedia.org/wiki/Indigenous_Australian_languages):

See Figure 14.2

The huge yellow region is where Pama-Nyungan languages are spoken, while the much smaller, multi-colored region to the north contains just about every other language family on the continent.

The African Signature

The musical picture for New Guinea and Island Melanesia is complex, with several different vocal styles and many different types of instruments. In several cases, we find P/B-related vocal styles, and also instances of instrumental hocket, especially with wind ensembles of pipes, panpipes, trumpets and flutes (see Chapter Nine, Audio Examples 17-22). In other cases we hear unison singing, and in still others, relatively simple part singing similar to that of Western Polynesia. The picture for Australian aboriginal music, on the other hand, is completely different, exhibiting a remarkably high degree of homogeneity and lacking any trace of an African signature.

Among the most compelling instances of the "African Signature" in New Guinea is Audio Example 17, already presented in Chapter Nine — P/B style yodeled/interlock, as recorded by Steven Feld in the Southern Highlands of New Guinea: *Audio Example 17:Bosavi Yodeling* (from *Bosavi: Rainforest Music of Papua New Guinea*).

A somewhat different type of yodeled interlock can be heard among the Abau people of the Upper Sepik River highlands: *Audio Example 53: Healing Song* (from *Songs & Dances from Papua New Guinea*, track 5, recorded by John Thornley).

Here is an example of relatively straightforward "shouted hocket," with yodeling, from the Huli people of the Southern Highlands: *Audio Example 54: Huli Yodeling* (from *Emap FM – Music from Oceania*).

A very similar type of shouted hocket can be heard in this recording of another highland group, the Dani: *Audio Example 55: Dani* (from *Emap FM – Music from Oceania*).

Among the Aka Pygmies of Africa a very similar type of hocketed interchange, called "esime," functions as an interlude between more complex songs (Kisliuk 1998:41): *Audio Example 56: Aka esime* (from *Musical Anthology of the Aka Pygmies, recorded by Simha Arom*). Relatively simple hocketed performances of this type are classified as "haplogroup" A1 in the Phylogenetic Tree provided in *Appendix B*.

173

Highland vs. Lowland

There are two large language families in New Guinea and Island Melanesia: Austronesian and "Papuan." The former is generally regarded as much more recent than the latter, as it is associated with groups thought to have originated somewhere in southern China or Southeast Asia that expanded during the last 4,000 years or so, first to Melanesia and then to Polynesia. Most of these newer populations settled along the northern and eastern coast of New Guinea, and on many other Melanesian islands. "Papuan" is the name given to the languages of those who were presumably already living in Melanesia when the Austronesians arrived. The so-called "Papuan" languages are actually a large group of unrelated language families — along with several languages regarded as unaffiliated "isolates" — spoken by people living, for the most part, in the interior highlands.

Geneticists Alan J. Redd and Mark Stoneking found two mitochondrial DNA clusters among Papua New Guinea highlanders with "coalescent time estimates of ~80,000 and 122,000 years ago, suggesting ancient isolation and genetic drift." There are indications that "84% of the sample of PNG highlander mtDNA belong to these two clusters" ("Peopling of the Sahul: mtDNA Variation in Aboriginal Australian and Papua New Guinean Populations," *American Journal of Human Genetics*, 65, 1999, p. 808). This is only one of several such assessments, ethnological, linguistic and genetic, that associate the ancestry of the New Guinea highlanders with the original "Out of Africa" lineage, while most Austronesian speakers of the coastal and lowland areas are considered relatively recent arrivals from the north.

To determine whether the highland-lowland dichotomy could predict the African Signature, a Cantometric search for one of the most distinctive features of P/B, vocal interlock, was conducted for the entirety of the New Guinea sample, with the following results:

Culture Name	Language Family	Location	#
BALIEM	Papuan	Highlands of Irian Jaya — Baliem Valley	1
BIAMI	Papuan	Southern Highlands	2
BISORIO	Papuan	Highlands — East Sepik Province	1
DANI	Papuan	Highlands of Irian Jaya — Baliem Valley	5
EIPO	Papuan	Highlands of Irian Jaya — Baliem Valley	10
HAMTAI	Papuan	Highlands — Gulf Province	1
HULI	Papuan	Southern Highlands	2
KOVAI	Papuan	Umboi Isl., Morobe Province, Northeast Coast	1
MONI	Papuan	Highlands	1
OK	Papuan	Highlands of West Papua — near Irian Jaya	3
YALI	Papuan	Highlands of Irian Jaya — Baliem Valley	4

Table 14.1 Vocal Interlock — New Guinea

Of the 11 groups above that "tested positive" for interlock, all are Papuan speakers and all but one are highlanders. Since 23 groups in the entire sample are identified as highland and 22 as coastal or lowland (with an additional 13 I have not yet been able to locate accurately), there does appear to be a strong correlation between the musical evidence and the genetic/linguistic evidence, distinguishing an indigenous highland population, with roots in the early Out-of-Africa migration, from a much more recently arrived coastal/lowland population, associated with Austronesian languages and culture.

The picture for Island Melanesia, is not so simple, however, as the "lowland/highland" dichotomy is not always clear, and many native "Papuan" groups now speak Austronesian languages. Nevertheless, Island Melanesia also contains many instances of the African Signature, as evidenced by Audio Examples 18 and 22 (see Chapter Nine), and the following, truly remarkable, recording of vocal interlock, accompanied by

175

pipes, from the island of Buka, north of Bougainville, in the Solomon Islands: *Audio Example 57: Buka Singers with Pipes* (from *Emap FM – Music from Oceania*).

Australian Homogeneity

Melanesian music is by no means limited to P/B-related styles, and is in fact one of the more diversified musical areas on Earth. In contrast, Australia is among the most musically homogeneous regions in the world. Australian aboriginal singing is characterized by tense, nasal vocal style, either solo or unison, the frequent iteration of single notes, with sticks or boomerangs beaten together to produce relatively simple one-beat rhythms or simple variants of the one-beat pattern:
Audio Example 58: Western Australia (from *Emap FM – Music from Oceania*).
From the Yuendumu Community, Central Australia: *Audio Example 59: Traditional Song* (from *Traditional Aboriginal Music:Sounds from the Bush*, Arc Music, track 20).
From Northeast Australia: *Audio Example 60: CapeYork* (from *Emap FM – Music from Oceania*).
More or less the same general performance style pervades the entire continent, though occasionally one hears something more complex, with traces of polyphony. The only important musical instrument is the Didgeridoo, which was traditionally found only in the west and may be a relatively recent innovation. Drums, plentiful in Melanesia, are all but absent in Australia. The above descriptions are deceptive, however, as Australian singing and Didgeridoo playing are among the most sophisticated musical art forms in the entire world. Many of the texts that go with these songs are also remarkable examples of highly sophisticated, allusive and complex poetry.
Considering the importance of Australia as the bearer of the earliest archaeological evidence of modern humans outside of Africa, evidence which so strongly supports the Out-of-Africa model, the absence of any trace of the "African signature" in any of its indigenous music is difficult to explain. If the Out of Africa migrants were singing and playing in some version of P/B style, then what could have happened when they got to Australia that made them lose their musical traditions and develop such different ones? And since, as we've seen, we do in fact find many instances of the African signature in New Guinea and Island Melanesia, its absence in Australia is especially difficult to understand. Coupled with all the other evidence for major discrepancies, morphological, genetic, linguistic, etc., we are faced with an extremely perplexing mystery.

I would like to propose an explanation that might resolve all or most of the contradictions, which again, like so much else in this book, should be seen as exploratory, speculative and provisional. Let's begin with some provocative clues:

A Divided History

It has long been thought that the Tasmanians, tragically exterminated during the initial stages of the colonial era, might have been direct descendants of an initial wave of immigration that preceded the entry of australoid peoples. This notion was revived by anthropologist Joseph Birdsell and his associate Norman Tindale, who promoted what they called a "tri-hybrid" theory of Australian history involving three successive waves of migration (Birdsell 1967). According to Birdsell, the first immigrants, the "Barrineans," were Negritos, and it is their remains we see in the "gracile" Mungo Lake skeletons, the earliest (ca 45,000 ya) fossil remains in Australia. The next wave were what he called the "Murrayians," with "caucasoid" features resembling the Ainu. And the last wave were the "Carpentarians," the now dominant "australoids," with affinities to the australoids of India. Birdsell's research confirmed the almost mythic existence of Pygmies in Australia, which made it logical for him to conclude that they were most likely descended from the original "Barrineans."

See Figure 14.3

For Birdsell, the early Tasmanians, who may have had a similar morphology, judging from various remains, had also been Negritos, and therefore must also have been descended from the earliest immigrants. Birdsell's "tri-hybrid" theory has been disputed and is no longer a part of mainstream anthropology, possibly due to "political correctness" concerns, as it flew in the face of a popular movement promoting the idea that all aboriginals were descended from the original inhabitants of the continent.

Male vs. Female

An ongoing theme in the genetic story from this part of the world is a surprising male-female distinction, and Australia is no exception. As reported in Ingman and Gyllensten 2003,

> a striking difference between the genetic history of females and the reported history of males in the Australian Aboriginal population. . . Kayser et al. (2001) proposed that the high frequency of a unique [Y

chromosome] haplotype in Australia is the result of a population expansion that started from a few hundred individuals. In this case, the predominance of a unique Y-chromosome haplotype in Australia would be the result of a founder effect. *However, there does not appear to be a corresponding loss of genetic diversity resulting from a bottleneck seen among mitochondrial lineages* (p. 1604 — my emphasis).

In other words, the major discrepancy between Australian Y and mtDNA diversity suggests a bottleneck in the former, yet none in the latter, which seems puzzling — unless males and females have a very different history on this continent. (Remember, the Y chromosome is found only in males and can represent only male lineages.)

> Our mitochondrial [i.e., female line] data imply that some lineages from the populations of Australia and New Guinea have shared a common history since the initial colonization of Sahul. . . . [However,] [t]he lack of a common Y-chromosome haplotype found both in Australia and in the New Guinea highlands (or in any other Melanesian population) argues against the concept that the New Guinean and Australian populations are derived from the same migration event (Kayser et al. 2001). *However, the Australia-specific Y chromosome haplotype could have arisen after the colonization of Sahul and therefore is absent in other populations.* (my emphasis)

Passage from India?

For many years, anthropologists have speculated regarding what appear to be striking physical similarities between Australian aboriginals and the Vedda of southern India and Sri Lanka, many of whom have a distinctly "australoid" physiognomy. While such comparisons have often been dismissed, recent findings suggest that they could have a genetic basis after all – but, interestingly enough, only on the male line.

In an article titled "Gene Flow from the Indian Subcontinent to Australia: Evidence from the Y Chromosome" (Redd et al., 2002), the authors present "strong evidence for an influx of Y chromosomes from the Indian subcontinent to Australia . . .":

> In sum, we found that 50% of the Y chromosomes sampled from aboriginal Australians [haplogroup C*] share common ancestry with a set of Y chromosomes that represent less than 2% of the sampled Indian subcontinent paternal gene pool. . . . (p. 676)

While only 2% of the male gene pool for India might seem insignificant, it's important to remember that the C* haplogroup is found only among certain tribal peoples in south India and Sri Lanka (where we find many australoid types today). It would be very strange indeed if the figure were much higher than 2%, since Australian aborigines bear little physical or cultural resemblance to East Indians generally. However, the figure shoots up to 50% in Australia, a remarkably strong representation. While these results are indeed suggestive, the connection may be relatively recent. According to their estimates, C* dates only to the mid-Holocene, roughly 8,000 years ago, which places this particular migration well past the Out of Africa exodus.

It would be much easier to argue for an Indian-Australian cultural connection if there were any distinctive musical similarities between Tribal India and Aboriginal Australia, but that does not seem to be the case. However, I recently came across a remarkable youtube clip of dancing among the Chenchu hunter-gatherers of South India that strongly resembles certain types of Australian Aboriginal dance: *Video Example Seven — Children of the Forest*. While the very opening contains some interesting moves, the most remarkable similarities with Australia can be found at the 1:30 and 2:30 marks. [This video is no longer available via youtube.]

Compare the above with the Australian Aboriginal dancing seen in portions of *Video Example Eight: Dance During Initiation Ceremony* (skip to roughly 30 seconds in).

A Hypothetical Reconstruction

On the basis of the analysis presented above, along with a considerable amount of additional evidence not presented here, but available via my blog, *Music 000001* (http://music000001.blogspot.com/) (Grauer 2007b — see especially Posts 297-310), I've been able to put together an admittedly very speculative hypothesis, roughly consistent with Birdsell's "trihybrid" theory, which could account for all or most of the odd discrepancies, morphological, genetic, linguistic and musical, between New Guinea and Island Melanesia on the one hand, and the Australian Aboriginals on the other. Here's what I think could have happened:

1. Early entry into Sahul by island hopping from Sunda, in the immediate wake of the Out of Africa migration. The earliest immigrants would have been a small band of HMP (Hypothetical Migrant Population) descendants, who would have retained an African morphology and an African culture and value system, based largely on HMC. These early immigrants would not

have been seriously affected by the population bottleneck(s) I've associated with the Toba eruption (or some equally devastating event), as they would presumably have been living far enough to the east of India at the time to be only minimally affected, and therefore would have retained their original African characteristics to at least some significant degree.

2. It seems reasonable to think in terms of a fairly rapid expansion along the coast of the entirety of Sahul, followed by a very long period of stability, in which these relatively peaceful and cooperative hunter-gatherer descendants of HBP and HMP could have lived together in harmony for literally tens of thousands of years.

3. On the basis of the genetic evidence for both a highly contrastive history for males and females in Australia and a close Y chromosome association between Indian and Australian australoid populations, we can posit a second migration, occurring many thousands of years later, of mostly male australoid hunter-gatherers, whose ancestry would have stemmed from the South Asian centered bottleneck posited in Chapter Ten. According to Redd et al (2002),

> The divergence times reported here correspond with a series of changes in the Australian anthropological record between 5,000 years ago and 3,000 years ago, including the introduction of the dingo; the spread of the Australian Small Tool tradition; the appearance of plant-processing technologies, especially complex detoxification of cycads; and the expansion of the Pama-Nyungan language over seven-eighths of Australia. Although there is no consensus among anthropologists, the former three changes may have links to India, perhaps the most relevant of which is the introduction of the dingo, whose ocean transit was almost certainly on board a boat. In addition, Dixon noted some similarities between Dravidian languages of southern India and Pama-Nyungan languages of Australia.

4. We can now extrapolate backward to speculate on how the arrival of these strangers could have led to the conditions we now see. And the first thing to consider is the fact that, in order to produce the largely australoid population we see in Australia today, the more recent immigrants would have to have mated with the "native" women, probably forcibly at first, and at the same time largely either killed, displaced or enslaved the native men, wherever they encountered them. This would explain the "different histories" of males and females we see in the genetic evidence. The mtDNA (female line) picture would not reflect the presence of men from a completely

different population, but the Y chromosome evidence would — and that does seem to be the case.

Over time, as the more aggressive and belligerent newcomers expanded throughout the continent, the original inhabitants would have done what so many relatively non-aggressive, non-competitive, non-violent peoples have done throughout history — retired to easily defended or undesirable refuge areas. This would explain the special status of Tasmania, which could have served as a last stand for some of the natives as they retreated southeast to the point farthest away from the most likely point where the newcomers would have arrived, the northwest. And since Tasmania was originally a kind of peninsula with a fairly narrow land bridge, that might have worked for them as a last line of defense until the sea level rose and they became completely isolated.

5. Since Australia is relatively flat and easily traversed, the indigenous males would not have had much chance of survival, but could have been hunted down and slaughtered or enslaved, and their women appropriated as wives. Northeast Queensland contains a tropical forest, which was until recently, according to Birdsell's research, the home of a few small groups of Pygmies, who may have originally retreated to this area as a refuge, possibly many thousands of years ago. But the most obvious refuge area would have been to the north, in what is now New Guinea, and it is the highlands of New Guinea that we can posit as the most likely refuge area for the majority of the retreating natives. If the newcomers had arrived while New Guinea was still attached to Australia, the refugees could have made their way north by land, but if the sea had already separated the two regions, they could have retreated in boats or rafts, at least while the distance was not too great. The australoid invaders would have followed them, and at that time taken over the New Guinea coast, while the natives retreated into the highlands.

6. The next important event in the history of this region is the advent of the so-called "Austronesians," who are thought to have migrated to various points in New Guinea and Island Melanesia anywhere from 6,000 to roughly 4,000 years ago. The newly arrived Austronesians appear to have displaced most of the australoids along the coastal regions to the north and east. Their only recourse would have been a retreat into the highlands, which would therefore have come to harbor a mixed population, partly of "negrito" and partly of australoid origin. Since these groups would have formerly been bitter enemies, it's not difficult to see how the endemic warfare we now see in the New Guinea highlands could have originated at this point, although many of these populations seem ultimately to have merged, both physically and culturally.

If my scenario is correct, then the current situation in the former Sahul could be described in the following terms:

1. in Australia, the descendants of males from the second wave of migration and females from the first, with australoid morphology, speaking, for the most part, a *Pama-Nyungan* language; 2. in New Guinea, descendants of the original "negrito" settlers, with a degree of australoid intermixture, now surviving mostly in the highlands, but also along portions of the coast, living as foragers and part-time horticulturalists, speaking a wide variety of very different "Papuan" languages, and retaining at least some of their original African traditions, including, in some cases, P/B-related musical styles; 3. in New Guinea, descendants of population 1, formerly based on the New Guinea coast, now living for the most part in the highlands as forager/horticulturalists, possibly intermixed with population 2, both biologically and culturally — also speaking "Papuan" or in some cases Austronesian languages; 4. relatively recent Austronesian immigrants, speaking Austronesian languages, and inhabiting, for the most part, the northern and eastern coastal and lowland areas of New Guinea.

Chapter Fifteen: Upcoast, Downcoast — from Asia to the Americas

According to most anthropologists, humans first entered the Americas via a land bridge linking northeast Asia with Alaska. Certain dissenters have nevertheless pointed to evidence suggesting more direct trans-Pacific links. Among the most notable was Paul Rivet, founder of the *Musée de l'Homme*, who argued that "the dark skinned people of New Guinea, New Caledonia, Vanuatu, and Fiji, as well as the inhabitants of the Polynesian archipelagos — Maoris, crossed the Pacific Ocean in their canoes, and arrived in Central and South America, from where their descendants spread all across the Americas" (*Paul Rivet, New World Encyclopedia Online http://www.newworldencyclopedia.org/entry/Paul_Rivet*).

Rivet's theory was based on physical similarities, such as bone structure and blood type; similar traditions, such as head hunting; and certain linguistic parallels. Other investigators, such as Joseph Needham, have noted striking cultural similarities suggesting an ancient Chinese influence on groups such as the Northwest Coast Indians and the high cultures of Central and South America. Over the years a considerable body of evidence for trans-Pacific contacts of various kinds has accumulated, but the topic remains controversial in the extreme.[1]

Musical Cognates

An especially compelling argument for trans-Pacific migrations could be made on the basis of musical evidence alone. Various wind ensembles involving pipes, panpipes, flutes, whistles, horns and trumpets abound not only in Africa, Southeast Asia and Melanesia, as we have learned, but also Central and South America. Ensembles of this sort are not found north of the Rio Grande, suggesting that carriers of these traditions may have arrived via the south Pacific.

Cross cultural comparisons by some of the early pioneers of ethnomusicology tended to support the trans-Pacific model. In a review of Erich von Hornbostel's 1911 paper "Über ein akustisches Kriterium für Kulturzusammenhänge" ("On an acoustic criterion for cultural association"), no less an authority than Edward Sapir expresses his conviction in no uncertain terms. For Sapir, Hornbostel's comparative study of Melanesian and Brazilian panpipe tunings demonstrated that

> the pan-pipes of Melanesia and South America *are* historically connected, not merely because they are pan-pipes but because their detailed musical construction is too closely alike to be explained by

convergent evolution. Here at last we have clear evidence of a cultural contact between these two parts of the world (*Collected Works of Edward Sapir*, de Gruyter, 1994 (1913), p. 158).

Since musicologists of that era were fixated on tuning systems and scales, they paid little attention to either the manner in which the instruments are performed or how they sound when played together. If they had, the trans-Pacific associations would have been even more convincing. In almost all cases, from Africa to Melanesia to the Americas, the music played by such instruments is divided into at least two hocketing/interlocking parts. In the case of pipes, whistles, trumpets and horns, each instrument is capable of producing only one or two notes, but even in panpipe or flute ensembles all instruments perform in closely interactive hocketed interlock.

Unlike Western counterpoint, but very similar to certain practices found in Africa, what we hear is not the intertwining of independent lines, but a *resultant* melodic/ polyphonic texture produced by the juxtaposition of interlocking parts. In almost all cases, from both Melanesia and the Americas, the instruments are symbolically divided into two complementary groups, one male, the other female.

To get a visceral sense of how closely some of these very widespread practices resemble one another, let's hear some examples from both sides of the ocean:

Hocketing bark horns of the *Aitape*, northern coast of New Guinea: *Audio Example 61: Pig Hunting Song*

Hocketing bark horns of the *Piaroa* Indians of the Upper Orinoco, Venezuela: *Audio Example 62: Piaroa Horns* (from *The Columbia Library of World Music*, Venezuela, recorded by Pierre Gaisseau).

Panpipes of the the Buma people, on the island of Malaita, in the Solomons: *Audio Example 63: Panpipes of Buma* (from *Spirit of Melanesia*).

Compare the above with this closely interlocking pipe duet of the Cuna Indians, from Panama (as already presented in Chapter Nine): *Audio Example 23:Cuna Pipes* (*Primitive Music of the World*, Folkways).

Curiously Andean-sounding panpipes of the Are'are people of the Solomon Islands (as already presented in Chapter Nine): *Audio Example 22:Are'are pipers* (from *Solomon Islands:The Sound of Bamboo*, recorded by Buaoka & Sekine).

Compare with these Andean panpipes, from Bolivia: *Audio Example 64: Kacharpaya Kantu* (from *Bolivia-Panpipes – UNESCO*, track 4).

Hocketing flute duet, Sepik Region, New Guinea: *Audio Example 65: Sepik Flutes* (from *Spirit of Melanesia*).

Hocketing flute duet, Iawa Indians, upper Amazon Basin, Peru: *Audio Example 66: The Mayantu* (from Music of the Upper Amazon, Lyrichord LL157, recorded by Bertrand Flornoy).

Compare the above with this duet from the Madang region of northern New Guinea: *Audio Example 67: Nubia-Sissimungum* (from *Windim Mambu:Sacred Flute Music from New Guinea, vol. 2,* track 5, recorded by Ragnar Johnson).

Here's a somewhat different sounding flute duet, featuring repeated tones, also from Madang: *Audio Example 68: Gomkail Flutes* (from *Windim Mambu:Sacred Flute Music from New Guinea, vol. 2,* track 1).

Compare with the repeated tones in this flute duet, from the Camayura of the Amazon basin, Brazil: *Audio Example 69: Camayura Sacred Flutes* (from *Anthology of Central and South American Indian Music,* Smithsonian Folkways 4542).

In both New Guinea and South America, such flutes are played in pairs, with the larger considered "male" and the smaller "female." According to Ragnar Johnson, who recorded the Madang flutes, "each player blows in turn; one flute is blown and the other alternates. It requires all the air in a man's lungs to blow a flute, so one player inhales while the other is blowing his flute." The Madang flutes "are made, owned, played and kept secret by adult men.

Women and children are forbidden to see the flutes and are told that the cries of the flutes are the voices of actual spirits" (see *Audio Example 67,* accompanying pamphlet, p. 1). Essentially the same taboo applies in South America as well — paralleled by very similar restrictions regarding the Mbuti Pygmy *molimo* trumpet, also considered a spirit voice and also forbidden to women and children (Turnbull 1961:82).

Remarkably close similarities can be found among percussion ensembles as well, since very similar types of slit drums and stamping tubes are found abundantly in both Southeast Asia/Melanesia and South/Central America.

Canonic/Echoic Style

The musical "cognates" are not limited to instrumental music. Many groups in both regions sing together in roughly coordinated canons or rounds, a highly distinctive style I've referred to as "Canonic/Echoic" ("haplogroup" B1 in the Phylogenetic Tree presented in Appendix B). This style, based on the interlocked imitation of similar motives to produce a kind of "echo" effect sounds to me like a variant of certain types of Pygmy/Bushmen canonic interlock ("haplogroup" A4), the principal difference being that the latter is rhythmically precise and tightly coordinated while the former tends to be rhythmically imprecise and uncoordinated.

Since both styles are based on essentially the same musical principle, the temporal displacement of a single motive or melody among two or more singers, "Canonic/Echoic" style (C/E) could be a *development* from P/B, as suggested by the Phylogenetic Tree – and in that sense we could say that it too, like the instrumental styles discussed above, carries the "African Signature." On the other hand, I am not aware of any examples of C/E anywhere in Africa, suggesting a post-bottleneck origin.

Let's first listen to the sort of thing that might have served as its prototype, a three part Mbuti Pygmy "canon" in classic P/B style: *Audio Example 70: Amabele-o-iye* (from *On the Edge of the Ituri Forest*, recorded by Hugh Tracey, track 16).

The following imitative duet, from the Kaluli people of Bosavi, in the New Guinea highlands, is quite similar, but loosely coordinated rhythmically, as is characteristic of C/E: *Audio Example 71: Ulahi and Eyobo sing at a waterfall* (from *Bosavi: Rainforest Music From Papua New Guinea*, Smithsonian Folkways, recorded by Steven Feld). According to Steven Feld, the Kaluli refer to this type of singing as "lift-up-over sounding."

Compare with this similarly ragged "canon" from an Iawa Indian ceremony, in Peru: *Audio Example 72: The Kaputio* (from *Music of the Upper Amazon*, Lyrichord LL157, recorded by Bertrand Flornoy).

Here's a very similar duet, a lullaby from the 'Are'are of the Solomon Islands: *Audio Example 73: Lullabye* (from *The Solomon Islands:Sounds of Bamboo*, track 36).

Finally, one more example of C/E, from Venezuela, a trio of Warao shamans, loosely echoing one another: *Audio Example 74: Hoarotu Shamans* (recording by Dale Olson, accompanying the book, *Music of Many Cultures*, Elizabeith May, Ed.).

A Distinctive "Style-Trace"

In a little-known but extremely important Cantometric study of Amerindian song style, Alan Lomax's anthropological collaborator, Edwin Erickson, identifies a substyle corresponding quite closely with that illustrated above, which he designates "Specialized South America-Mexico." On the basis of strictly statistical, computer-based research (Erickson was an anthropologist, not a musicologist), he describes it as follows:

The bounding of the style domain, the distribution of its diagnostic traits and the patterning of resemblances all suggest that the underlying style trace has isolated a very old and generalized diffusion sphere . . .

If the appearance of these distinctive traits, especially in multiples, were the result, for example, of independent invention, or elaboration of old and broadcast American Indian styles, there would be no reason to expect the sharp bounding of the distribution area (Erickson 1969-70: 301).

After considerable discussion of various anthropological and archaeological ramifications of this style, he speculates regarding a possible association with the panpipe:

The distribution [of panpipes] in South America, thus, goes beyond the compass of the specialized South American style domain, but not very far beyond. . . Clearly, pair-playing of panpipes is a powerful sorting device for specialized South American style (ibid. 329, 331).

The Homogeneous North

The musical picture presented so far is completely different from that of North America, or to be more precise, America north of Mexico, where there are basically three instrument types, the drum, the rattle and the flute, and a remarkably homogenous vocal style, characteristic of the great majority of native North American tribal groups, regardless of language, subsistence type, environment, etc.

Exceptions, though rare, can be found among the tribal groups of the Northwest Coast, where we find a wider variety of musical instruments than is typical for North America, and also certain groups in California, notably the Hupa, who employ a form of shouted hocket resembling certain types of Ainu vocalizing. Panpipes made from metal or ceramic materials have been unearthed by archaeologists in so-called "Mound Builder" sites, dating roughly from 3,000 to 1,000 years ago. There is strong evidence that these instruments, along with many other artifacts and customs, such as head flattening, ear plugs, the use of mica, etc., even the practice of mound building itself, could have originated in Mexico, specifically the La Venta culture of Veracruz (see Silverberg 1968:222-27).

At least six principal sub-families have been identified for this region: Northwest Coast-Eskimo; California-Yuman; Great Basin; Athabascan; Plains-Pueblo; Eastern Woodlands (Nettl 1965:157-162). Songs from each such family can often be distinguished from the others by certain specific traits, such as the wide-ranging "terraced" melodies of the Plains and Pueblos, the melodic rise characteristic of the California-Yuman family, or the call and response patterns typical of the Eastern Woodlands.

Especially interesting is the manner in which characteristic "nonsense" vocables are deployed in almost all of these traditions, so that, for example, a Navajo song almost always ends with the syllables "he-ney-yan-ga," while "he-ya-ha-ya" is more characteristic of Plains songs. The music of each "family," and in many cases each tribe, can often be identified on the basis of its favored nonsense vocables alone. To my knowledge, this is a situation unparalleled in any other musical region of the world.

While each North American "family" has its own idiosyncrasies, the differences appear minor compared to the many commonalities that make this region, along with Australia, among the most musically homogeneous in the world. The most prominent shared characteristics would appear to be: unison singing; relatively straightforward percussion accompaniment on drums and/or rattles, usually based on a simple one-beat pattern; a preponderance of "nonsense" vocables; wide intervals; moderately tense voices; and an idiosyncratic manner of forming melodies, where most notes are squarely on the beat and the iteration of the same pitch over different vocables is common, especially at phrase endings.

Variants of more or less the same style can be found among many Central and South American Indian tribes as well. But such qualities tend to be rare among the groups identified above, i.e., those with the strongest trans-Pacific links – which also happen to be those bearing the "African Signature."

While no one recording could be considered typical for all North American groups, the following example of Salish (so-called "Flathead") performance, illustrates some of the most typical features discussed above: *Audio Example 75: Powow Dance* (*American Indian Dances*, Smithsonian Folkways.)

An excellent assortment of authentic North American Indian performances, including Navaho, Apache, Ponca, Sioux, Taos, Kiowa, etc. can be found on the CD *American Indian Ceremonial & War Dances*, published by *Legacy International*. Brief clips from each can easily be streamed, giving a good general sense of some of the differences between each group and also the many commonalities, as enumerated above.

A Disconcerting Discontinuity

Given the many differences between the musical styles of the American north and south, the mainstream theory by which all Native Americans arrived via a northern land bridge becomes especially difficult to maintain. Before attempting to deal with this very problematic issue, I'll complicate it a bit more:

If the Americas had been populated directly and unproblematically via a Bering Strait land bridge in the manner usually presented, we would expect there to be a clear stylistic continuity between the music of the Paleosiberians of Siberia and the Amerindians of North America. But in fact there is no such continuity. There are certainly resemblances. The two traditions are definitely related. But Paleosiberian singing is usually solo, usually unaccompanied, often noticeably glottalized, whereas Amerindians often sing in unison, with little to no glottalization, and usually accompanied by various types of drums and/or rattles, while the frame drum of the Arctic Shamans appears to be the only instrument native to Paleosiberia.

Significantly, we find only a very few instances of Paleosiberian "breathless" style[2] among Amerindians, with none at all in the north, where one would expect to find that highly distinctive trait quite frequently if these groups were simply displaced Paleosiberians, as implied by the dominant theory.

In other words, between regions once connected by a land bridge, where we would expect to find continuity, we find discontinuity; and between regions separated by the vast reaches of the Pacific Ocean, where we would expect to find discontinuity, we find continuity. Such a situation would seem to demand serious reconsideration of all those theories postulating ancient trans-Pacific voyages.

Did the Earliest Americans Arrive via the Pacific Ocean?

Sorry to disappoint you, but that won't wash either. In literally every case where archaeological research provides us with dates for possible trans-Pacific contacts, these are relatively recent. Pre-Columbian to be sure, but not really all that old, certainly not old enough to account for long-distance Paleolithic era migrations. It's not outside the realm of possibility, or even probability, that certain artefacts, traditions, crops, animals, artistic or architectural styles, etc. may have infiltrated the New World via sporadic contacts with Polynesian voyagers, or possibly even, as Needham suggests, Chinese vessels. But there is no evidence that any of these voyages could have taken place at any time prior to roughly one or two thousand years ago, and in all likelihood much later.

There is no question that Polynesian sailors were capable of making long voyages of this kind. If they could reach Easter Island, it is often argued, then why not the western shores of South America? But Easter Island was not

settled until, at the very earliest, 700 AD (*Easter Island*, Wikipedia - http://en.wikipedia.org/wiki/Easter_Island#History). Even the westernmost reaches of Polynesia are thought to have been populated no earlier than 2,000 years ago (*Polynesia*, Wikipedia
http://en.wikipedia.org/wiki/Polynesia#History_of_the_Polynesian_people).

Since even the most conservative estimates for the first arrival of humans in the Americas date to 10,000 years ago and more, we can't rely on Polynesian sailing skills to account for the earliest settlement of the New World. And there is absolutely no evidence for trans-Pacific voyages prior to the advent of the Polynesians.

(I must add, by the way, that there is also no real evidence for an "African Signature" in Polynesian music, which has its own very distinctive style. While panpipes have been found at archaeological sites, they are apparently no longer being played, so it's not possible to assess performance style. There is, in any case, little to no sign of anything resembling P/B style hocket or interlock in any of the instrumental traditions, although we do find slit drums. Polynesian vocal style can be characterized as "social unison," i.e., all singers sing in more or less the same rhythms at the same time, either in harmony or unison. The most common types of polyphony are parallel harmonies or drones. Contrapuntal interplay of the sort associated with the "African Signature" is not found. It's important to make this clear, in case anyone might want to assume that the P/B elements found in the music of certain Central and South American groups could be due to relatively recent Polynesian influence.)

The First Wave

In a recently published paper, Neves et al (2005) present compelling physical evidence for an African-Melanesian-American link and at the same time offer a convincing alternative to the Trans-Pacific theory. Noting that the cranial morphology of the earliest American settlers is "distinct from that displayed by most late and modern Native Americans," they find it closer to what "can be seen today among Africans, Australians, and Melanesians"; thus, "South America, Central America and possibly North America were populated by human groups with a more generalized cranial morphology before the arrival of the Mongoloids." Since a more "Australo-Melanesian-like" morphology "was also present in East Asia at the end of the Pleistocene," they go on to conclude that "transoceanic migrations are not necessary to explain our findings."

We postulate that after reaching southeast Asia, this stem [Out-of-Africa] population gave rise to at least two different dispersions. One took a southward direction and arrived at Australia around 50 Ka. Sometime between 50 and 20 Ka a second branch dispersed towards the north, and arrived in the Americas by the end of the Pleistocene, bringing with it the same cranial morphology that characterized the first modern humans.

A similar picture can be found in the genetic evidence. Already in 1995, Zago *et al.* (1995:4) had identified:

three predominant [Alpha]-globin gene haplotypes among Brazilian Indians [, a distribution that] has some features in common with the distributions observed in Southeast Asia, Polynesia, Melanesia and Micronesia.... The frequency of haplotype IIe among the Amazon Indians is the highest thus far observed in any human population. It occurs regularly in Oceanic and Southeast Asian populations but is absent in Europeans and sub-Saharan blacks.

[Additionally] all examples of haplotype IIa identified in our sample contained...a variant [which] when present is commonly associated with haplotypes IIa or IId in Southeast Asia, Polynesia, Micronesia and Melanesia.

After considering all this evidence, along with a considerable amount of additional genetic data gleaned from the research of others, the authors conclude: "the similarities between native [South] Americans and populations from the Pacific Islands are probably the consequence of ancient common origins that predate the peopling of the Americas and Oceania" (*ibid.*:5).

A "Beachcomber" Legacy

Stephen Oppenheimer (2004:300-13) holds a very similar view of the earliest migration into the Americas, but takes it one step farther, to accommodate the effects of the Ice Age maximum, which produced a huge glacier ca 20,000 years ago. According to him, if North America had been initially populated prior to the Ice Age, that population would have either been wiped out or forced to move as the glacier expanded — some to refuges in the South, others back where they'd come from in the northwest where at that time there lay a large land mass relatively free of ice, in the vicinity of today's Bering Strait, which he refers to as the "Beringian refuge."[3] Those already based in the southern part of North America could have continued south, possibly by sea, along the western coast, to Central and South America. This would have been the first "paleoindian" wave described by Neves.

The second wave of Asian immigrants proposed by Neves, those with a more "Mongoloid" morphology, would have been stalled in Beringia until the glacier receded, thus raising the possibility that the two populations may have mixed, both genetically and culturally. As the glacier receded, North America would have been repopulated by groups from both Beringia and the south, while Central and South America would, for the time being at least, have retained its original "Australo-Melanesian-like" first-wave population. Ultimately, the largely Mongoloid or mixed populations from the north would have migrated into Central and South America, displacing the first-wavers to marginal refuge areas in the densest jungles and highest mountains, to produce the physically and culturally diverse situation we find there today.

To summarize, the Americas may have originally been populated by at least two different groups: an offshoot of the original Out-of-Africa "beachcombers," steadily progressing from Indonesia, up the coast of Eastern Asia to the extreme north; a now very different group from Central Asia, which had already broken off from the main line thousands of years earlier. Both might have made it across the arctic land bridge prior to the Ice Age maximum, but only certain groups might have made it far enough south to be safe from the maximum when it finally arrived.

Could these have included direct descendents of the original beachcomber group, bringing with them the canonic/echoic variant of P/B singing style and their hocketing panpipes? If so, then, as they progressed further south, they would have populated certain areas in Mexico, Central America, the Andes, and the Amazon Basin, where their descendents would be living today. According to this line of thought, we do not find panpipes, hocketing horn and trumpet ensembles or canonic/echoic singing north of Mexico because any stragglers from that group would not have survived the worst of the Ice Age.

The groups taking refuge in Beringia may have consisted of two other populations traced by Oppenheimer, whose history had taken them on a different course, through Central Asia and Siberia, where they could have lost touch with the original P/B traditions, since there is now, outside of the Inuit "Throat Singing" tradition (Nattiez 1999), little trace of P/B style singing, or panpipes, north of Mexico. Possibly due to their shared experiences in Beringia during the Ice Age, these northern groups may have developed strong musical and linguistic affinities that would have persisted after they diverged, making America north of Mexico an unusually homogeneous area in both respects.

Mapping American History

Since the history outlined above may be somewhat confusing, I've made an attempt to depict it in a series of three maps:

See Figure 15.1

The uppermost map traces, in red, the progress of Oppenheimer's Out-of-Africa "beachcombers," appropriately named, since, according to his model, we can trace their slow but steady progress along the coastlines of, first, the Indian Ocean and then the Pacific, all the way up from Southeast Asia to Beringia and beyond, continuing down the coast of North America. The red line makes more sense if we assume these were not only "beachcombers" with a taste for seafood, but also seafarers of sorts, whose relatively primitive vessels would have had no problem so long as they didn't venture too far beyond sight of land. The blue arrows trace some of the later, post-bottleneck migrations discussed in Chapters Ten and Eleven. Note the two groups in Northeast Asia, poised at the doorstep of the New World. But, as the map suggests, the "beachcombers" may have already beaten them to it.

The map on the lower left highlights, in yellow, the "Beringian refuge" referred to above. Geological research suggests that it was not glaciated during this period, and would have thus been capable of sustaining human life. The large green area represents the extent of the icepack during what is known as the "Last Glacial Maximum," thought to have lasted roughly between 20,000 and 15,000 years ago. The blue arrows on the left represent the two waves of "post-bottleneck" migration into Beringia posited by Oppenheimer.

The two red arrows pointing northwest represent possible back migrations by "beachcomber" stragglers retreating to Beringia in the wake of the developing glacier. According to Oppenheimer, Beringia may have afforded a refuge to such groups, and other late arrivals, for thousands of years, prior to the glacier's melting, during which time they would have had the opportunity to interact and presumably intermingle into a single "proto-Amerindian" population. Meanwhile, as indicated by the red arrows to the south, those "beachcombers" whose momentum had carried them beyond the reach of the glacier would have continued on their journey down the west coast of both continents, possibly all the way to the tip of South America.

193

The third map represents the repopulation of the Americas from Beringia in the wake of the now receding glacier. The red globs represent various "Beachcomber" colonies in Central and South America that would have already been in place for some time. It is, of course, these groups that would still be maintaining African traditions long lost by their distant cousins to the north.

A Mystery Solved?

The complex, but nevertheless convincing, scenario offered by Oppenheimer accounts not only for the distribution of hocketing wind ensembles and canonic/echoic singing but also the proliferation of instruments generally in Central and South America. According to this theory, the Out of Africa nomads would have maintained ancestral traditions rooted in HMC as they traveled north along the coast of East Asia, passed quickly through Beringia and made their way along the eastern Pacific coast down to Central and South America.

The paucity of instruments in the north could be explained by the effects of the Ice Age maximum, which would have covered most of North America, thus wiping out most of the groups living there and forcing the survivors back into the only relative warmth of Beringia. According to Oppenheimer, life would have been brutally difficult for those survivors, in an environment that would have offered very few materials from which to build instruments. Thus, when the descendants of these groups were finally able to move down into North America proper after the Ice Age, it makes sense that they would have lost most of their instrumental traditions.

This explanation is both a bit complicated and necessarily speculative. But what we know about the musical aspect does seem to fit. Oppenheimer's theory, for better or worse, does offer a meaningful explanation of how musical traditions bearing the "African Signature" could have made it all the way to Central and South America but not survived in the North.

---

1. Much of the evidence, pro and con, is reviewed in the book *Trans-Pacific echoes and resonances: listening once again*, by Joseph Needham and Gwei-Djen Lu (World Scientific, 1985).

2. For a definition of Breathless Style, see references to haplogroup B2 in Appendix B.

3. Oppenheimer's notion of a "Beringian refuge" is supported in Tamm et al (2007:1), whose research "suggests that ancestors of Native Americans

paused when they reached Beringia, during which time New World founder lineages differentiated from their Asian sister-clades."

Sidebar 4: Update

In Chapter One, when comparing African Pygmy and Bushmen populations, I wrote as follows:

> Both peoples have long been thought to occupy a much older historical layer, with far deeper roots – though until recently no one had any idea *how* deep. More significantly, they are based in completely different parts of Africa, within totally different environments, and are thought to have remained isolated throughout most of their history from all other humans – and certainly from one another – for many thousands of years.

However, a newly published paper (Batini et al. 2011) based on a thorough study of the Y chromosome (male lineage) evidence, calls into question the notion that Pygmies and Bushmen have in fact been completely isolated throughout most of their history (as was previously thought on the basis of the mitochondrial evidence). While this paper reinforces the overall genetic picture presented in Chapter Two, affirming that Pygmy and Bushmen genomes occupy the oldest branches of the Y chromosome (male) tree, consistent with the mtDNA (female line) evidence, it also finds "evidence for further complexity in the evolutionary relationships among African hunter-gatherers."

> Our extensive phylogeographic and dating approach has provided evidence for *relatively recent contact* both among Pygmies and between them and San groups from southern Africa. Our current estimates for the coalescent time between Eastern and Western Pygmy specific Y chromosome clades (10-15 Kya) are compatible with post-LGM [last glacial maximum] contact among the two groups, with evidence for recent bottlenecks in the demographic histories of the two groups (see also Patin et al. 2009, Batini et al. 2011). Otherwise, *the very recent common ancestry detected among Western Pygmies and San* (3-4 Kya) suggests that this could be the signature of Khoe-speaking pastoralist mediated contact among the two groups, rather than resulting from retention of ancient traits. (my emphasis)

This new finding adds a very interesting wrinkle to the genetic evidence, somewhat complicating the picture I've presented in a manner that calls for further analysis and discussion.

Let's take a closer look. In the new paper, Batini et al identify

> evolutionary links between western Pygmies and San in both A and B clades [see the Y chromosome tree presented in Chapter Two], developing the initial findings presented in Wood et al. (2005). Hg A2, found among SA [Southern African] Khoisan speakers [i.e., Bushmen] at 25-45% (Wood et al. 2005; Table S9), was detected for the first time in the present work at non trivial frequency (5%) among the Baka Pygmies from Cameroon and Gabon. On the other hand, B2b4 was present at 6-7% among Khoisan speakers but reached 45-67% in both Biaka and Baka Pygmies (Wood et al. 2005; Table S9). (p. 14)

Reading up to this point, my assumption would be that the Bushmen-Pygmy connections most likely date from the time of earliest divergence, estimated at approx. 60 to possibly over 100 thousand years ago. However, "[w]e dated the TMRCA [Time to the Most Recent Common Ancestor] among the western Pygmies and San [Bushmen] specific sub-clades of these two haplogroups to between 3 and 4 Kya." One possible explanation: "the very recent common ancestry detected among Western Pygmies and San (3-4 Kya) suggests that this could be the signature of Khoe-speaking pastoralist mediated contact among the two groups, rather than resulting from retention of ancient traits." (p. 20) The pastoralists referred to are most likely a currently extinct Khoisan speaking group, the so-called "Hottentots," known as herders rather than hunter-gatherers, but nevertheless closely related genetically to Bushmen.

Close Encounters of the First Kind

Is it possible that one or more groups of Hottentot males may have encountered Pygmies in their wanderings over the last few thousand years? And is it also possible that a group of Pygmy males may have wandered out of the forest to encounter a Bushmen encampment? Since the Y chromosome evidence suggests encounters of this kind occurred and since such a possibility seems reasonable, I see no reason to doubt it. The question is: what could such encounters have meant, and what sort of cultural exchanges could have taken place that might account for some (or all?) of the similarities I've rooted in HBC?

To put things in perspective, it's important to remember that the mtDNA evidence presents a very different picture: "[p]hylogeographic analyses of mtDNA point to an ancient separation among ancestral populations, with *limited or no subsequent gene flow* after the split" (my emphasis — Batini et al, p. 20). The "ancient separation" applies not only to Pygmies and Bushmen, but also to Western and Eastern Pygmies, thought to have diverged roughly 20,000 years ago. Since mtDNA reflects female population patterns, this means there is little or no evidence of any significant exchange of females between either Western and Eastern Pygmies or Pygmies and Bushmen, since their initial divergences, deep into the African Stone Age. If so, then we would expect to see typically Pygmy haplotypes intermixed with typically Bushmen haplotypes in the mtDNA evidence, but that is not the case.

While we do find a certain amount of such evidence in the male line, it seems likely that sexual encounters among the three populations were incidental, since only a small percentage of relatively recent "alien" haplotypes (5-7%) is represented in the Y chromosome data for any of them. (We must also remember that there is a significant difference between males and females with respect to reproduction. While the offspring a single female may produce is limited, the number of children potentially sired by a male is, in principle, both unrestricted and unpredictable — thus Y chromosome evidence is much more difficult to assess than mtDNA.)

It seems unlikely, therefore, that any Bushmen (or Hottentot) group might have actually merged for any significant length of time with a Pygmy group, or vice-versa, at any time since TMRCA (the Time to the Most Recent Common Ancestor). While the Y chromosome evidence suggests that encounters between Pygmy and Bushmen, or Western Pygmy and Eastern Pygmy, males and females may have taken place from time to time, there is no evidence that such encounters were of the sort that would be likely to engender any significant degree of acculturation. *Nevertheless,* social contact of even the most limited sort might entail cultural influence, and such a possibility cannot be dismissed.

Cultural Diffusion vs. Archaic Survival

I must admit, in this regard, that the new evidence for recent contact somewhat weakens what I had originally considered an "iron-clad" case for P/B as an archaic survival, rooted in the culture of our mutual ancestors (HBC). If, as I had assumed, there were no real possibility of any contact at all between any Pygmy and Bushmen groups subsequent to their ancient divergence, then the likelihood that P/B could have developed in one group only and spread to the others via cultural diffusion was essentially nil. While my argument is no longer quite as iron-clad as before, I must nevertheless insist that cultural diffusion in this particular case remains highly unlikely.

For one thing, we are talking about a highly distinctive tradition shared by many different groups in widely dispersed, relatively isolated pockets of Africa, surrounded by other, very different groups, more powerful and influential, with very different cultures and musical styles. Assuming that one or more Pygmy or Bushmen males from one of these groups had intercourse with females from another, and assuming the females were so impressed with their music that they decided to teach it to their children, it's nevertheless very difficult to understand how such a practice could thereafter have spread to so many of the other Pygmy and Bushmen groups via similar chance encounters.

Considering that the divide between proto-Pygmies and proto-Bushmen has been estimated at over 65,000 ya and the divide between Eastern and Western Pygmies anywhere from 15,000 to 20,000 years ago, it's especially difficult to understand how events taking place only 3 or 4 thousand years ago could have led to a distribution of so complex and distinctive a tradition among so many populations that would, by that time, have almost certainly become widely dispersed.

Secondly, we must take into consideration the strong affinities between this particular musical style and the highly integrated social structure/value system so characteristic of so many groups of Pygmies and Bushmen, as discussed in Chapter Three. It's one thing to assume that a group of males might have taught some songs to a group of females, it's another to assume that such an encounter could have led an entire society to alter its social structure and value system to conform to the requirements of the musical style embodied in these songs, especially when, as in this case, a particular lifestyle and a particular musical style appear to have developed in tandem, to the point that P/B is a pervasive part of everyday life among both Pygmies and Bushmen, embracing literally everyone in the community.

Reconsidering the Baseline

The situation may not be so clear, however, with respect to other traditions included in the baseline. Beehive huts are almost always constructed by women, so it's unlikely this tradition could have been transmitted via an encounter with foreign males. Deeply rooted traditions associated with core values are also unlikely to have originated via more or less incidental contacts. More specific practices and artifacts are a different story, however, so it's difficult to be quite so confident when it comes to things like certain musical instruments, certain tools, practices such as scarification, or even certain practices associated with shamanism, which could conceivably be due to recent outside influences.

In almost all such cases, however, it's still very difficult to explain how any of them could have diffused so widely over such a large area and among so many relatively isolated groups. The "triangulation" method I used in constructing the baseline encompasses three populations living in three widely separated regions, who, according to both the mtDNA and Y chromosome evidence, diverged from a common ancestral population many thousands of years ago. It's difficult to see how any cultural commonalities among so many of these groups could be the result of relatively recent, relatively incidental, contacts.

Of all the cultural elements listed in the baseline, the bow and arrow is the most open to questions of this sort. It's conceivable that this technology, always associated with males, may have been invented at a later time, and diffused among the various Pygmy and Bushmen groups via a relatively recent encounter of the sort implied by the Batini paper. In this case, the tradition could have been spread throughout Africa generally as part of the Bantu expansion, of ca. 3 to 4 thousand years ago. As I see it, much depends on the associated use of poison tips, which, since found among so many Pygmy and Bushmen groups, does appear to have originated with HBC (though more research on the distribution of this practice is needed). It's possible, of course, that an earlier tradition of poison tipped spears may have been transmitted to arrow points at a much later date, so the issue remains very much up in the air.

Batini et al have raised some interesting questions with regard to the consequences of relatively recent contacts among hunter-gatherers, which may or may not have a bearing on certain issues raised in this book. Reluctant as I am to invoke an old saw, more research is definitely needed before the meaning of this evidence can be more fully assessed.

Chapter Sixteen: Missing Links

In Chapter Four, I described my "baseline" (HBC) as a kind of observatory from which all subsequent societies could be viewed; and in the following chapters I demonstrated how it could be put to use for that purpose. In this chapter, I'll swing the "telescope" around by 180 degrees for a peek in the opposite direction. Instead of looking forward toward what, for our ancestors, would have been the future, I'll be looking backward toward their past.

It's important to remember that our *Most Recent* Common Ancestors (MRCA) were not all that special in themselves, but simply, and due largely to chance, the group from which the ancestors of today's Pygmies and Bushmen diverged, roughly 60,000 to possibly well over 100,000 years ago. From this very broad perspective, it should be clear that the ancestral culture I've been treating as originary is itself the product of historical and evolutionary forces that preceded it, leading all the way back to the first "modern" humans, the earliest archaic humans, and beyond, to the ancestors we have in common with our closest primate relatives.

Is there any evidence that might link the already advanced culture of HBC with that of these much earlier, and decidedly more primitive, societies? Would it surprise you if I answered "yes"? At this point, I suppose not. And would it surprise you if I were to once again claim that the most promising evidence lies within the realm of music? I could be wrong, but as I see it the musical evidence contains some tantalizing clues that I can't resist exploring.

Out on a Limb

What sort of music might have existed *before* the already highly developed musical language I've posited for our most recent common ancestors? In other words, what could have happened in the many thousands, indeed millions, of years leading up to the development of P/B? Since this style is already so complex and sophisticated, it's difficult to imagine how it could have been created out of whole cloth. Something much simpler must have preceded it. And here I'll be literally going out on a limb, to consider the vocal behavior of our cousins, the apes.

In the fascinating book, *The Origins of Music* (Wallin, Merker and Brown 2000), neuroscientist Björn Merker specifically relates the vocalizations of certain primates to the early development of human music:

Synchronous calling . . ., that is, true cooperative synchronous calling rather than synchrony as a default condition of competitive signaling, requires a motivational mechanism for mutual entrainment. We assume that such a mechanism was selected for in the course of hominid divergence from our common ancestor with the chimpanzee, and was retained to the present day in the form of our propensity to join in and entrain to a repetitive beat. . . Indeed, if the present argument should turn out to have any merit, this adaptation for entrainment supplies an irreducible biological root of human music.

While, according to Merker, true synchrony is absent among chimpanzees, it can apparently be found in bonobos. Referring to a study of bonobo vocalizations by the noted primatologist, Franz de Waal, Merker points to "a loud and explosive sound called staccato hooting." According to de Waal, "during choruses, staccato hooting of different individuals is almost perfectly synchronized so that one individual acts as the 'echo' of another, or emits calls at the same moments as another. The calls are given in a steady rhythm of about two per second." (pp. 318-319).[1]

Research by Gottfried Hohmann and Barbara Fruth, who studied Bonobos in the wild, in the Lomako Forest of Central Zaire, is consistent with de Waal's observations:

> From analyses of simultaneous high- hootings of mature pairs, it became apparent that calls of both apes were given often in more or less perfect alternation, indicating a remarkable degree of behavioral coordination between them. Jordan (1977) and de Waal (1988) mention a high degree of synchronization between vocalizations of different individuals, and the latter author emphasized the gibbon-like nature of long-distance hooting. (Hohmann and Fruth 1994)

In a fascinating paper by Ellen Dissanayake (2008), the author makes much of certain musical features of human mother-infant interactions. Significantly, she points to "interactive behaviors" between mother and child that

> take place . . . sequentially, in bouts of 1.5 to 3 seconds, on a time base, so that each partner in the dyad reacts and responds contingently to the other's signals *within one-half second or less*, anticipating and participating in an ongoing, changing, cocreated engagement. I propose that the dyadic coordination developed in

mother infant interaction is likely a precursor of human music in which individuals mutually coordinate their voices and body movement in temporally and dynamically structured sequences (my emphasis, p. 177).

Since, according to de Waal, a very similar type of interaction, at essentially the same pace (2 per second), is characteristic of bonobos, Dissanayake's observations seem consistent with the notion of a possible link between human and bonobo vocalizations, reflected in the structure of the mother-infant bond.

Synchronous Calling – Some Examples

On Franz de Waal's website, based on his book, *Our Inner Ape* (http://www.emory.edu/LIVING_LINKS/OurInnerApe/faq.html), we find an audio clip where the "chorusings" of multiple bonobos and chimpanzees are compared: *Audio Example 76:Bonobos and Chimps.* In both cases we hear highly interactive calls; and the bonobo interactions do, as predicted, seem somewhat more precisely timed than those of the chimps.

As indicated by de Waal, as referenced above, the "long-distance hooting" of bonobos resembles that of certain gibbons, and fortunately there are some excellent videos of gibbons interacting vocally. Here is a very interesting youtube video featuring a common type of not- so-distant "duetting" between a pair of Siamang *Gibbons. Video Example Nine:Siamang Gibbon Calls*

Here's another example, also *Siamangs: Video Example 10:Siamang Singing.*

Shouted Hocket

While not as precisely synchronized as a well rehearsed musical performance, these highly interactive duets are good examples of the "synchronous calling" invoked by Merker and de Waal. In addition to Merker's insightful speculations, what interests me especially about this sort of behavior is its strong resemblance to a highly distinctive form of human vocal interaction I've called "Shouted Hocket." (Definitions of the term "hocket" can be found in Chapter One and *Appendix A.* Shouted Hocket is an extreme simplification of essentially the same principle, based on the rapid interlocking and/or interchange of shouted, hooted or yodeled tones.) To better understand the connection, let's examine a copy of the phylogenetic map presented in *Appendix B:*

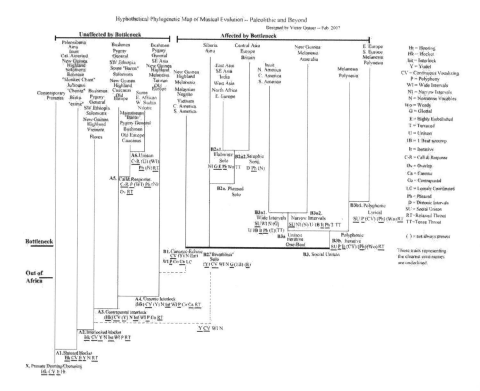

Figure 16.1 Phylogenetic Map of Musical Evolution. (For details on how it was constructed and how to interpret it, see *Appendix B*.)

The tree is rooted at the lower left with a musical "haplotype" labeled "X - Primate Duetting/Chorusing." X is characterized by four markers: Hk for "hocket," CV for "continuous vocalizing," It for "iterative" vocalizing, and Ht for "hooting," a type of vocalization closely related to yodel. Just above and to the right, we find "A1- Shouted Hocket," a form of "synchronized calling," very similar to that of bonobos and gibbons, only performed by humans. A1, also characterized by hocket, continuous vocalizing and iteration, is remarkably close to X.

Let's listen to some audio clips of Shouted Hocket from various parts of the world, keeping in mind the bonobo, chimp and siamang examples we've just heard. Before continuing, however, I want to make clear that it is not my intention to equate the music of any of these people with the calls of apes or gibbons. Most of their music is in fact far more complex and sophisticated than the brief excerpts I'm quoting here.

We've already heard some examples of simple two part interactions in Chapter Fourteen:

From the Huli people, Southern Highlands of New Guinea: *Audio Example 54: Huli Yodeling* (from *Emap FM – Music from Oceania*).

From the Dani, also a highland New Guinea group: *Audio Example 55: Dani* (from *Emap FM – Music from Oceania*).

An "esime" (shouted interlude between more elaborate songs), from the Aka Pygmies of Africa: *Audio Example 56: Aka esime* (from *Musical Anthology of the Aka Pygmies, recorded by Simha Arom*).

Here's a more complex example of Shouted Hocket from Brazil. *Audio Example 77:Mehinacu*. Listen especially to the closely interactive hocketing at the very end of the clip, reminiscent of the bonobo and chimpanzee chorusing heard in Audio Example 76 (From Saydisc, *Disappearing World*.)

Here's an example of beautifully yodeled "duetting" from the Island of Madagascar, where the Mikea hunter/gatherers have traditionally been considered the indigenous inhabitants. *Audio Example 78:Mikea* (From the Ocora CD, *Madagascar, Pays Mikea*.)

An especially interesting and intricate hocketed vocal interchange, sometimes called "throat singing" can be found among many Siberian groups, where it is associated with shamanic traditions, and also among the Inuit (Eskimos), where it is currently regarded as a game.

From Kamchatka, in Siberia: *Audio Example 79:Kamchatka.*
From the Inuit: *Video Example 11:Eskimo Inuit Throat Singing.*

Compare with this shamanic ritual from the Ainu indigenes of Japan: *Audio Example 80:Ainu*. Something similar, but thousands of miles away, from the Hupa, a native American tribe of Northern California: *Audio Example 81:Hupa* (from Lee Productions).

Halfway between A1, Shouted Hocket, and A2, Interlocked Hocket, we find more complexly interactive vocalizations, close in some ways to the chorusing of both bonobos and chimps, as heard above, but more precisely synchronized. Listen, for example, to this excerpt from an extended initiation ritual among the Ju'hoansi Bushmen: *Audio Example 82:Tcoqma* (from *Namibia:Chants des Bushmen Ju'hoansi*, recorded by Emmanuelle Olivier). To my ears there are some truly remarkable similarities between this African ritual and the now familiar "Monkey Chant" of Bali: *Audio Example 83:Ketjak* (from *Golden Rain*, recorded by David Lewiston).

A Musical Link

Can we understand Shouted Hocket (which includes not only unpitched shouting, but also pitched hooted and yodeled "shouts" as well) as a kind of "missing link" between pre-homosapien vocalizing, represented by the duetting and chorusing of bonobos, chimps and gibbons, and our musical "haplogroups," A2, A3, and A4, characterized by more complexly interwoven parts, in counterpoint and/or canon? In other words, was there, at some time deep into the African "Stone Age," some sort of evolution from something resembling the coordinated vocalizing of today's primates to the far more sophisticated and intricate, but still highly interactive, musical "language" of P/B?

As described by Kisliuk (1998), the Pygmy *Esime* is a shouted or hooted interlude of the sort often found between more complexly organized interlocked songs. Could it be a survival of an original, unpitched, pre-musical type of vocal interchange? The example we've heard from the Dani people of New Guinea combines a very rhythmic shouted interchange with some softer yodeling heard in the background. The Huli example is very similar but this time clearly yodeled and also pitched, alternating tones a major third apart.

The Mehinacu example is shouted, but the Mikea example that follows is both yodeled and pitched. The example of "throat singing" from Kamchatka is clearly pitched, on three different tones, but the Inuit example is all on one note, more closely resembling primate duetting. Note also the audible breathing in these examples, suggesting hyperventilation (see below).

Both the Ainu and Hupa songs involve both singing and shouted hocket, both with heavy breathing and suggestions of hyperventilation as well. Hyperventilation is clearly present in the Bushmen *Tcoqma* initiation ceremony, where it is associated with shamanism and trance. The Balinese Ketchak, or "Monkey Chant" is most astonishing of all. Though today it is performed largely for tourists, it is thought to have originated in shamanic trance practices that predate Hinduism.

Shamanic Links

The question now is: what can we make of all these examples? Are there other aspects of any or all of these performances that could give us some clue to their meaning, cultural, historical or both? An especially promising clue is provided by the pioneering research of semiologist Jean-Jacques Nattiez, as described in a remarkable essay, "Inuit Throat-Games and Siberian Throat Singing: A Comparative, Historical, and Semiological Approach" (Nattiez

1999). Having studied examples of throat singing from certain Siberian tribes, the Ainu of the Sakhalin Peninsula and Hokkiado, and various Inuit groups of Alaska and Northern Canada, Nattiez notes that there is a significant difference in meaning between the various Inuit traditions, understood simply as games, and the traditions of the Siberians and Ainu, where throat singing has strong associations with shamanism.

Understood strictly "in context," one might dismiss the very strong stylistic resemblances among all these different practices as of no importance since one functions merely as a game while the others have a very different function, as part of shamanic rituals. Digging deeper, Nattiez brackets the issue of function to consider more generally applicable explanations for all the many similarities, along three categories: "universalist," "diffusionist," and "phylogenetic." Rejecting the first as unlikely and the second as improbable (because the vast geographic distances all but rule out direct influence), he embraces a phylogenetic interpretation:

> Among the Inuit and the people of Asia, analogies of distribution between linguistic features . . ., archaeological artefacts . . . and genetic data . . . have been established. This strongly suggests that these connections are the result of a migration which occurred 4,000 to 5,000 years ago . . . (pp. 411-412)

He concludes that what is true for the linguistic, archaeological and genetic connections is probably true for the musical practices, especially in the light of the long series of stylistic similarities he then enumerates. They must all stem from "common protoforms, as is the case for genes and languages..." (p. 413)

Nattiez goes on to consider

> why these symbolic forms do not necessarily have these religious connotations today, particularly among the Canadian Inuit. The semiological distinction between the signifier and the signified in an historical perspective will help us to understand how a similar form (a similar signifier) gets a new meaning (a new signified) in a different culture... From this situation, we may draw broader conclusions of interest for general musicology and semiology. In sonorous symbolic forms, the form, the *signifier*, best resists transformations through time. However, the *signified*, the religious significations of the animal and nature imitations associated with these forms, are evanescent. (p. 414)

This conclusion is extraordinary, literally turning on its head the long cherished assumption that the only meanings to be seriously considered are those *signified* in the context of a particular society, meanings which, for Nattiez, must be considered "evanescent." As his research clearly demonstrates, it is the musical signifier that has the power to persist through the ages, from one social context to the next, thus offering the more reliable index of human history and, potentially, the more convincing and satisfying insight into the meaning of music in the broadest and deepest sense.

While Nattiez explodes the hegemony of the functionalist and contextualist assumptions so dear to so many anthropologists and ethnomusicologists, he clearly could not have arrived at the conclusions he did without a very deep prior investigation into the functions and immediate contexts of throat-singing as manifested in all the different cultures studied. In fact, it was the testimony of an Inuit woman, who recalled some things her grandmother had said about the association of Inuit throat "games" with hunting magic, that provided him with an important clue to the origin of such games in shamanistic practice (p. 405).

Significantly, the Balinese "Monkey Chant" is also thought to have originally been part of a shamanic ritual. The Ju'hoansi *Tcoqma* is unquestionably shamanic, associated with an all night initiation ceremony for young boys, in which many men go into trance and perform healing rituals. Among the *Ju'hoansi*, the great majority of males are considered shamans, with potentially very powerful healing powers.

A Circumpolar "Proto-form"

As Nattiez demonstrates, the circumpolar "throat-singing" tradition he's identified can be understood as a unified style family despite its being interpreted differently in different social contexts, as either a shamanic practice or a game. It's important to understand that Nattiez achieves his results phylogenetically, by working his way backward, with the aid of archaeological, linguistic and genetic evidence, to a "protoform" for all manifestations of this style, a common root dating to thousands of years in the past. Is it possible for us to connect all or at least some of the other types of "shouted hocket" we've been considering, from Melanesia, Indonesia, South America, Africa, etc., via the same protoform? And if so, would the association with shamanism still be relevant?

As should be clear by now, a significant amount of additional research into both the musical practices and cultural background of all the groups we're considering would be necessary before any solid conclusions could be drawn. Nevertheless, there is a great deal we *are* in a position to consider at this point, if only provisionally. If all these instances could indeed, in one way or another, turn out to be associated with shamanism, that would certainly strengthen the connection. But as Nattiez has shown, it's not necessary for the social function, the *signified*, to remain the same, since the same signifier may, over time, come to take on different significations.

What's most important is the ability to trace the various manifestations of the *signifier* we are examining back to a single source phylogenetically. The presence of shamanism in certain contexts might indeed provide an important clue, but, as Nattiez has taught us, the absence of any particular signified should not necessarily impinge on an investigation of the underlying signifier.

The protoform under consideration here must be understood not simply as a theoretical construct but a real musical style, practiced by real people at a certain time and place, i.e., both historically and geographically. Taking historical linguistics as his guide, Nattiez associates the throat-singing protoform with the time when three language families, *Eskimo-Aleut*, *Chuckchi-Kamchatkan* and *Altaic* were, according to certain linguistic theories, one and the same — a connection reinforced by evidence from the then nascent field of population genetics. (I'm delighted to note, by the way, that Nattiez has preceded me, not only by taking the genetic evidence into account, but also by suggesting that the musical evidence might actually have a bearing on the way the supposedly "more scientific" linguistic and genetic theories are evaluated.)

Whereas Nattiez was guided by the linguistic and genetic evidence current at that time, pointing to a circumpolar root culture 4,000 or 5,000 years old, we are in a position to take an even broader view, on the basis of the more recently developed, far more extensive, "Out of Africa" theory, with characteristic time spans ranging into the tens of thousands of years. Such research provides us with a "standard candle" based on estimates of anywhere from roughly 60,000 to over 100,000 years for the branching of proto-Pygmies and proto-Bushmen from MRCA. As I've already argued, the extraordinary similarities between the musical traditions of the Pygmies and Bushmen, combined with the genetic results, warrant a complete rethinking of our sense of how long a particular tradition may persist unchanged.

There is no reason to assume, therefore, that Nattiez's protoform is only 4 or 5 thousand years old, simply because the divergence of certain language families might date to that time. If the throat-singing complex is, as I suspect, a variant of the far more widely distributed A1 "haplogroup" I've labeled "Shouted Hocket," the protoform might well be truly archaic, traceable not only to HBC but far beyond, to some of the deepest mysteries of our distant past.

Hyperventilation

According to Nattiez, a pervasive characteristic of throat-singing is the production of a continual stream of sound through rapid alternations of audible exhaling and inhaling, "which create what can be called a 'panting style' . . . the main feature common to the three cultures under consideration" (p. 401). In a remarkable essay, "Can Hyperventilation be a trance mechanism in Nganasan ritual dance accompaniment," Triinu Ojamaa and Jaak Aru (2005) demonstrate the relation between "panting style," hyperventilation and trance in the Nganasan Bear Dance, yet another example of the shamanic circumpolar tradition explored by Nattiez. According to the authors, "Inspiration and expiration alternate in a certain rhythm. We can characterize the accompaniment as rhythmically organized panting." Their essay presents convincing evidence, both musical and biological, of the relationship between hyperventilation and trance, a pervasive feature of shamanism.

Clear signs of hyperventilation can be found in our examples from Kamchatka, the Inuit, Ainu, Hupa, and Ju'hoansi, while there are strong indications of something similar going on in the uncannily rapid, trance inducing, vocal interlock of the Balinese "Monkey Chant." There are in fact many other instances in many parts of the world where vocalizing combines shouted hocket with gutteral "panting," hyperventilation and trance, though not always associated with shamanism per se.

A remarkable variant can be found, for example, among Masai warriors, who chant, according to Malcom Floyd, in "a semi-vocalised, semi-pitched, rhythmic hyperventilation accompaniment technique" called *nkuluut*, characterized by low pitched, gutteral sounds" (*British Forum for Ethnomusicology Newsletter*, 2001, vol. 1). See *Video Example 12:Masai Warriors in Masai Mara.*

According to Floyd, this type of performance serves both as a source of arousal and containment of that arousal, in delicate balance. "It will also be noted, however, it is not uncommon for the arousal to reach depths which make containment impossible, for *nkuluut* to overpower melody, resulting in extreme cases in seizures leading to catatonic states." While such chanting can be organized according to the call and response litany format so commonly found in Africa, it can also take the form of a type of shouted interlock very close indeed to both Bushmen and Paleosiberian practice.

A bio-cultural link?

As we've learned, many non-human primates vocalize in a remarkably similar manner, as exemplified by the so-called "pant-hoots" commonly heard among bonobos, chimps and gibbons, a basis for the duetting and chorusing sequences illustrated above. There is, however, a significant difference. Their continuous, rapid-fire vocalizing is facilitated by large air sacs:

See Figure 16.2

According to a study by Gwen Hewitt, Ann MacLarnon, and Kate E. Jones,

> apes and larger gibbons may be able to produce fast extended call sequences without the risk of hyperventilating because they can re-breathe exhaled air from their air sacs. Humans may have lost air sacs during their evolutionary history because they are able to modify their speech breathing patterns and so reduce any tendency to hyperventilate ("The Functions of Laryngeal Air Sacs in Primates: A New Hypothesis," the *International Journal of Primatology*, Vol. 73, No. 2-3, 2002)[2]

Could we postulate, on this basis, a situation in the distant past where a newly speciated band of humans, no longer equipped with air sacs, were nevertheless attempting to vocalize in the "traditional" pant-hooting, duetting and chorusing manner, an effort which would have placed them dangerously near the threshold of hyperventilation, unconsciousness and trance? An essential difference between the vocalizing of their predecessors (X) and their own, newly minted, version (A1) would have been the need to work out some sort of strategy for avoiding or at least delaying hyperventilation and its effects by modifying their breathing patterns, as the article suggests.

Might the very real possibility of falling into trance while vocalizing in this manner provide a clue to the origins of shamanism? And since so much of the culture of indigenous peoples is based on experiences encountered during trance, might we also dare to attribute the origins of culture itself to an instinctive need to vocalize continually despite the loss of air sacs?

1. Merker's interest is primarily in unison synchronization rather than alternation, as in his view it is the former that must have played the greater role in the early development of music. After a brief email exchange in which I explained my views, he was unwilling to accept my position regarding the greater significance of alternation in such chorusing, as a possible precursor of hocket, which for him lacks the significance it has for me.

2. The whole issue of the role of primate air sacs in continuous vocalizing raises all sorts of interesting questions with respect to possibly related issues in musical evolution, such as the role of certain instruments requiring recycling of the breath, such as the didjeridoo, or instruments like the bagpipe, with air sacs built in.

Chapter Seventeen: In Olden Times

The Law of Pipes

> In olden times Huang-ti ordered Ling Lun to establish the *lü*. Ling Lun travelled from the western to the shady northern side of Mount Yuan Yü. He selected bamboo grown in the Chieh Ch'i valley. He chose only a piece which was hollow and of even thickness. He cut off its knots and used the hollow section between the two joints, the length of which was 3.9 ts'un. And he blew the pipe and produced the sound kung of huang-chung. He then brought twelve other pipes of different lengths down from the mountain and he listened to the sounds of the male and female Phoenix birds. He grouped their sounds into the twelve lü. There were six sounds of the male bird, and another six of the female. He related them to the kung of the huang-chung and found that the huang-chung was the foundation of the lü-lü. (As quoted in Kárpáti 1980.)

In order to understand the above passage, it is necessary, first of all, to realize that the syllable *lü* has different meanings, marked by different written characters, depending on the pitch with which it is spoken. Two of these meanings are: "law" and "pipe." Thus, the well-known Chinese myth of the Yellow Bell (huang-chung) is based on either an amusing pun or a hilarious misunderstanding. The Yellow Emporer, Huang-ti ordered Ling Lun to establish the *law* but what he actually comes up with is a *pipe*. Which suggests that the person credited with determining the tunings which were to become the basis of the Chinese tonal system was tone-deaf.

This disconcerting notion is made more probable when we consult another version of the story, as told by the 1st Century BC historian Ssii-ma Ch'ien:

> Starting from the first pipe, the author says, you construct a series of pipes either by "taking away or adding a third" from the pipes that follow. So if the length of the first pipe is 1, the next one is a third shorter, i.e. two-thirds its length, and the following one is a third longer than the previous one, that is 4/3, which will be 8/9 of the first pipe's length. (Ibid. pp. 6-7)

In other words, the tunings determining the *lü-lü* (literally "pipe-law") can be constructed purely on the basis of measurement, with no need for any pitch awareness whatsoever. The first five pipes constructed from this method will produce the first five pitches of the "circle of fifths" (e.g., C – G – D – A – E), from which the familiar *pentatonic* scale can be derived: C-D-E-G-A, or, to use the Chinese terminology: *kung, shang, chiao, chih, yü* (equivalent to our do, re, me, sol, la).

But there is more. Thanks, possibly, to the aforementioned confusion over the meanings of *lü,* the Yellow Bell

> was conceived simultaneously as a sacred eternal principle, the basis of the state and a note of definite pitch in music. . . It was considered important to find the correct pitch for each dynasty, or political disorder would be likely to ensue. (Peter Crossley-Holland, as quoted in Phillip Tagg, *A Short Prehistory of Western Music (rough version 1),* p. 15 – http://www.tagg.org/xpdfs/origins3.pdf.)

Moreover, possibly because a "law" can also be understood as a "rule," which can be extended to mean "standard of measurement" (as for example a "ruler"),

> [t]he choice of the primary pitch in China had extramusical as well as practical applications, for the length of the yellow bell pipe became the standard measure (like a metre); and the number of grains of rice that would fill it were used for a weight measure. Thus, the pipe itself was often the property not of the Imperial music department but of the office of weights and measurements. (*Encyclopedia Britannica* website, *East Asian Arts* –
> http://www.uv.es/EBRIT/macro/macro_5001_91_97.html.)

And since a "ruler" is not only an implement that measures according to a "rule," but the one who makes the "rules" (in the sense of "laws"), the Yellow Bell took on central importance in Chinese civilization, putting music "in tune with the universe."

> "Music is the harmony of heaven and earth while rites are the measurement of heaven and earth. Through harmony all things are made known, through measure all things are properly classified. Music comes from heaven, rites are shaped by earthly designs." (Ibid.)
>
> [T]he five fundamental tones are sometimes connected with the five directions or the five elements, while the 12 tones are connected by some writers with the months of the year, hours of the day, or phases of the moon. The 12 tones also can be found placed in two

214

sets of 6 on Imperial panpipes (*pai-hsiao*) in keeping with the female-male (yin-yang) principle of Chinese metaphysics. (Ibid.)

Origins

There are several things that interest me in this remarkable myth. First, it presents us with a fascinating theory about the origin of the panpipe, an instrument to which I've attached considerable importance (see, especially, Chapter Nine), and, by extension, the origins of music itself, one of the principle themes of this book. And not only the origins of music in general, but the origin of the musical notes, and the system by which they are tuned.

Significantly, it associates pipes and/or panpipes with birds (see Chapter Twelve). This is something one finds very often in the literature on panpipes, from many different regions all over the world. And indeed some of the oldest pipes described in the archaeological literature were made from bird bones.

Especially significant are the references to pipes as either male or female. Indeed the story of the Yellow Bell appears to be the source of the fundamental Chinese concept of Yin and Yang. In a great many pipe, flute and panpipe traditions, almost everywhere these instruments are found, from Africa to China, southeast Asia, Melanesia and even the Americas, the division into male and female is important.

And since the story of the Yellow Bell centers on ratios, then perhaps we can think of it also as the story of the origin of mathematics. In fact there are some remarkable similarities between the theory behind the Chinese tuning system and the Pythagorean system of the ancient Greeks. But aren't all panpipes based on mathematical ratios? In the words of sociologist Marcell Mauss, "a theory of music exists everywhere there are panpipes" (as quoted in Hugo Zemp, "Aspects of 'Are'are Musical Theory" (*Ethnomusicology* vol. 23, no. 1, 1979)).

Another thing I've noticed in the Chinese accounts is that they are not only about origins but also traditions, and the way traditions are maintained. The Yellow Bell becomes the standard for a great many things that were vital to traditional Chinese society. It began, however, as a wooden pipe and, as such, would tend to expand or contract over time. It was necessary, therefore, for the original process of its creation to be repeated at various times – traditionally at the accession of a new emperor.

One could see this custom as an insight into the nature of tradition, too often misunderstood as the rather boring insistence on continually doing things the same old way. However, as the myth of the Yellow Bell suggests, in order for traditions to continue functioning as such, they must not only be maintained, but renewed (see Sidebar One).

And speaking of origins, my favorite part of this story has to do with the possibility that the whole thing could have begun with a complete misunderstanding. I could be way off base here, and if I'm wrong I hope someone with a knowledge of ancient Chinese will step in to correct me. But if our hero Ling Lun actually was tone deaf, and as a result, actually did misunderstand an order to produce a system of "laws" as an order to produce an arrangement of "pipes," then this too could give us an insight into the meaning of many other venerable and venerated, but also rather strange and inexplicable traditions, which might well have originated in misunderstandings, deceptions, accidents, or other events of a more or less trivial nature.

A Myth is a Lie . . .

I will now proceed to weave a myth of my own, compounded from the Yellow Bell myth interwoven with some of the various yarns I've been spinning throughout the course of this book. Before I continue, however, I want to quote one of my all time favorite sayings, attributed to one of my all time favorite artists, Pablo Picasso: "Art is a lie that makes you see the truth." That for me is a truly profound observation, with enormous resonance in all possible directions. I think the same can be said for myth — so I'll say it: *A myth is a lie that makes you see the truth.*

In that spirit, I'll ask some questions that I, for one, find especially intriguing about this particular myth: who was the Yellow Emperor? where did he live? when did he live? what was the Yellow Bell? where was it first created? when was it first created? The assumption behind literally all interpretations of this story is that it takes place at some indefinitely defined "olden time," possibly 2 or 3 hundred, or two or three thousand, years BC, somewhere in China.

To better evaluate that assumption, let's examine a more recent myth about the origin of panpipes, from the United States:

> A story handed down by ex-slaves claims that one evening a slave was feeling low in spirit and heard a plaintive cry of a night bird. The sound inspired the slave to get a piece of cane from a canebrake and cut some holes in it. He then commenced to play a "blues" on his whistle. As time went by, the instrument evolved into a set of "quills." ("The Birds and the Blues," by Max Haymes – http://www.earlyblues.com/featured_article.htm.)

216

According to this myth, the panpipe, or as it was sometimes called by African-American bluesmen, the "quills," originated in the United States. We know that can't be true, however, because of overwhelming evidence that this instrument antedates the founding of the United States and, indeed, the discovery of the Americas. So the person inspired by the bird could not have been an African-American slave, as the story implies, but someone who lived at a time far more remote than either slavery or America itself.

I believe the same critical thought process must be applied to the myth of the Yellow Emperor and the Yellow Bell. If we are to seek the truth pointed to by the myth, we must both take it seriously and treat it skeptically, tease out the "lie" behind it so we can see the truth toward which it is pointing.

All the evidence tells us the Yellow Emperor could not have been Chinese and the Yellow Bell could not have originated in China.

True Lies

According to musicologist Fritz Kuttner, the original set of wooden pipes could not have consisted of more than five. The complete set of 12 tones mentioned in the version I cited above seem to have been a much later development. Based on his systematic analysis of the terminology associated with each of the 12 tones, Kuttner concludes that the original set of five pipes could only have been produced prior to the era when tuned bells were being cast. And "Since tuned bells dating from the early Shang II period have been found in quantity, the first partial Lü system [i.e., the original five tone scale] might easily go back to Shang I times."

So far this sounds like pretty ordinary, academic stuff, but Kuttner finds his conclusion "almost shocking, because it pushes the beginnings of the traditional Chinese tone system back into pre-historic times in the direction of the legendary dynastic dates which every serious student of China's history would dismiss as naive. It seems that here we have a musicological tiger by the tail because our conclusion must be unacceptable to orthodox sinology." ("A Musicological Interpretation of the Twelve Lüs in China's Traditional Tone System," in *Ethnomusicology*, Vol. 9, No. 1. (Jan., 1965), pp. 22-38.)

Since I'll be weaving a myth of my own, it won't be necessary to examine Kuttner's reasoning too carefully. Even if it contains a flaw, it nevertheless expresses, as I see it, the simple truth hidden behind an elaborate facade. Because pipes and panpipes are found in many different parts of the world, often among indigenous peoples living in remote areas far from any possible Chinese influence.

In fact, as we learned in Chapter Seven, the distribution of these instruments can best be explained on the basis of a common cultural ancestry, dating from a period well before the origin of any of the Chinese dynasties; dating, in all likelihood to the "Out of Africa" migration itself, anywhere from 60,000 to 90,000 years ago. Assuming this musical tradition did in fact have a beginning, which would be pretty difficult to deny, it was certainly not in China.

According to *my* myth, the "Yellow Emporer" would have been African, possibly an early ancestor of the Bushmen, who are often described as having yellowish complexions (to go with the epicanthic folds in their eyelids). In certain documents he's described as the ancestor of all the Chinese people, but since in my version he's African, maybe he was everyone's ancestor, the first culturally "modern" human. His assistant, the creator of the Yellow Bell, must also have been African — though he might not have even been a single person, but possibly a group, all working and thinking together. He might not even have been a he, but a she.

Sinologists will no doubt protest, as Kuttner anticipated they would. But on what grounds? If the Yellow Emperor and the Yellow Bell both date back to some mythical, undocumented, past, then who's to say where — or when — they originated? And if anyone wants to claim the originator of the myth clearly intended it to be about China and nowhere else, then we're back where we started, with more speculation about origins — this time the origin of the myth itself. And who's to say where *that* got started — and by whom? As I see it, therefore, my version is at least as good as anyone else's. Better in fact, because, as should be clear from everything you've read up to now, it is backed up by evidence.

Sets of pipes are, indeed, an important part of the history of Chinese music, Chinese music theory and even Chinese philosophy. They go back a long way into Chinese pre-history, to at least 1100 BC, the estimated date of a set of bird bone instruments found in a tomb in Henan Province. But as the genetic evidence so strongly suggests, the Chinese *themselves* did not originate in China, but, ultimately, along with everyone else: Africa.

And, as we work our way backward in time from the earliest migration to East Asia by "modern" humans, I see no reason to assume such pipes could have been "independently invented" in that region, especially since they are now so common, not only in Africa, but so many other places along the original migration path, complete with bird associations, male-female pairing, hocketed ensemble performance, and in so many (though not all) cases, pentatonic tunings. Thus, according to *my* myth, the Yellow Bell was an African instrument, and the first tuned pipes an African invention.

But why, you ask, is this matter so important? Because, as I see it, the myth of the Yellow Bell is not only about the creation of a set of tuned pipes, but the first tonal system, thus the origin of music itself – and not only music, but also language; and not only language, but . . .

The Centrality of Pitch

In almost all speculations regarding early music and its origins, the most essential element, the use of discrete pitches, and their organization into a coherent tonal system, is either ignored or taken for granted – i.e., assumed a priori with no need to explain how it evolved. Yet if there is any one element of music that clearly distinguishes it from any other type of activity, by any other creature, it is pitch.

In the previous chapter, I discussed the manner in which certain apes and gibbons perform coordinated "duets" and/or "choruses," which, as I speculated, could represent a "missing link" between the hooted vocalizations of primates, which do not employ discrete pitches, and the yodeled vocalizations so commonly found among Pygmies and Bushmen, which do. While duetting and chorusing are, indeed, very close to "Shouted Hocket," as widely performed among many indigenous peoples worldwide, neither hooting nor shouting, no matter how highly coordinated, can, strictly speaking, be regarded as music. To clarify, let's compare an example of shouted hocket with a similarly interactive performance characterized by yodeling.

Shouted hocket: an *esime*, or interlude between songs, as performed by a group of Aka Pygmies: *Audio Example 56: Aka esime*

Yodeled hocket: performed by a group of Huli tribesmen, from highland New Guinea: *Audio Example 54: Huli Yodeling*

In the first example, I hear only unpitched shouting, while in the second I hear two distinct pitches: A# and F#. And the question is: how did we bridge the gap between the first type of vocalization and the second? And why should the difference matter? Before we can meaningfully speculate on such matters, we need to ask ourselves a more basic question: what is a musical tone?

Phonemes and Tonemes

What might seem on the surface to be a simple step, from ordinary vocalizing (as in hoots or shouts) to the singing (or playing) of discrete pitches, is in fact an enormous leap, with profound consequences for human culture and history. What we have been conditioned to hear when we sing, or play an instrument, is very different from the purely acoustical phenomena produced, as displayed on an oscilloscope or sonogram.

For one thing, the "tones" of music are not individual tones at all, but complexes of sound, with many elements, beginning with a set of overtones, combined with certain resonances, instabilities, possibly some degree of nasality, harshness, breathiness, raspiness, etc. What we think we perceive, is, in other words, very much a social construct rather than a given. This is a situation closely analogous with what happens when we hear a spoken syllable, which, for linguists, can be understood either *phonetically* or *phonemically*.

The *phonetic* is what we actually hear acoustically, much of which usually escapes our conscious awareness. The *phonemic* refers to what we hear psychologically, based on certain fundamental sets of culturally determined oppositions, or "articulations," put into play by each individual language. More generally, anthropologists often use the term *emic* (derived from "phonemic") with reference to the culturally determined aspect of any behavior or belief, and *etic* (derived from "phonetic") with reference to descriptions of a more objective nature.

There is no generally accepted equivalent terminology for music but there ought to be, because there is a strong analogy at work between what happens when we perceive musical notes as "tonemes" (to use the relatively obscure, but apt, expression coined by musicologist Charles Seeger) and when we perceive spoken vocables as "phonemes." This is not a coincidence, but an important clue to the nature of both music and language — and the relation of one to the other.

Ferdinand de Saussure, the father of "structural linguistics" and semiology, argued convincingly that language must be understood as "a system of interdependent terms in which the value of each term results solely from the simultaneous presence of the others" (de Saussure 1922:159). The deep relevance of this statement to the realm of music as well has often been overlooked. The key term is "value"—as in the tonal and rhythmic "values" of Western notation. The values of which de Saussure writes can thus be applied not only to the structure of phonemes (understood as classes of vocables) but to musical notes as well, understood "tonemically" as pitch classes, both of which are produced from field-like systems of class "identity" built on culturally sanctioned ("*emic*") distinctions.

"In Olden Times"

How does this relate to the Yellow Bell? Let's recall the myth: "In olden times," Ling Lun "selected bamboo grown in the Chieh Ch'i valley. He chose only a piece which was hollow and of even thickness." But that was only the first step. He *then* proceeded to construct a *set* of pipes by adding or subtracting a third of the original's length, thus producing a system through which the pitches of all tones are related to one another according to simple ratios defined by the smallest whole numbers, specifically the powers of 2 and 3.

In other words, he starts with a pipe that produces a discretely defined pitch, but that is not enough. In order for the pitch to be heard meaningfully, it must be part of "a system of interdependent terms in which the value of each term results solely from the simultaneous presence of the others" (see above). In other words, in order to be heard *culturally*, as a musical "phoneme," rather than simply acoustically, as either "pure sound" or "noise," it is necessary for an individual pitch to be part of a rational tonal *system*. Thus, a culturally determined system of tuned pipes is already the basis for what can only be called a "language," musical or otherwise, precisely in the sense defined by Saussure.

There's more: once you have a situation where different "tonemes" are produced by different pipes in a rationally related set, then, as with the phonemes of spoken language, each pipe has the potential to become a signifier – if for nothing else then, at the very least, the tone it will produce when played. Thus, to "notate" a melody you could line the pipes up in order of size and then point to one pipe at a time, in the same sequence as the notes of the melody you have in mind.[1] It is then only one small step to the understanding of each tone as a signifier for anything one might want to point to while playing or singing. Which puts us well on the road to a language or, if you prefer, proto-language, consisting exclusively of tonal relationships — consistent, perhaps, with what Steven Brown has called "musilanguage" (Brown 2000), in which

> the many structural features shared between music and language are the result of their emergence from a joint evolutionary precursor rather than from fortuitous parallelism or from one function begetting the other. (p. 271)

Bridging the Gaps

We are now better prepared to return to the question posed above: how did we bridge the gap between simple primate vocalizations and the singing (or playing) of systematically organized musical pitches? To which we will now want to add a second question: given a system of meaningfully organized pitches, or what we might want to call, in Brown's terms, a "musilanguage," how did we arrive at both music and language as we now know them?

There is probably no way to answer such questions definitively, as there is far too much information we don't have, and will in all likelihood, never have. But I do think we are now, after so many preliminaries, in a good position to speculate intelligently on such matters, and in that spirit I will offer the following sequence as a hypothesis worth considering:

1. Interactive "hooted" vocalizations of early primates and pre-humans, along the lines of the "duetting" and "chorusing" of certain contemporary ape and gibbon populations. The adaptational advantage of such behavior was most likely the facilitation of both long distance communication and close cooperation.

2. The morphing of pre-human "hooting" into more or less discretely pitched yodeling could have been an adaptation associated with the transition from a largely vegetarian to a largely carnivorous diet. Since many birds sing using roughly discrete pitches, there would have been an advantage for human hunters in learning how to imitate bird songs as a lure, and yodeling, closely related to hooting, may have been the simplest means of doing that.

3. At some point someone would have discovered that one could do an excellent bird call imitation by blowing into a hollow pipe. Since some of the oldest pipes found in archaeological digs are made from bird bones, this might also have involved a form of imitative magic.

4. There is no way of knowing which of the two previous steps would have come first. Perhaps yodeling and piping developed in tandem, as suggested by the following examples of vocal-instrumental hocket (as first presented in Chapter Nine): *Audio Example 19: Voice with Hindewhu,* BaBenzele Pygmies; *Audio Example 20: Hocket with Voice and Pipe,* Huli people, highland New Guinea.

5. More or less isolated pitches produced by either yodels or pipes may have made useful lures, but would still have been a far cry from what we now consider music. They would, no doubt, have been heard simply in terms of how far or close they came to the call of a particular bird. Thus, in order for music to come into existence, there must, at a certain very specific

point in human history, have come an extraordinary moment of discovery, every bit as important, in my view, as the invention of the wheel. This is the moment described in the myth of the Yellow Bell, the moment when someone selects a length of cane to make a pipe in the usual way, but then gets the idea of creating a *set* of pipes, organized according to a *system*.

It's important to understand that only through the creation of a set of systematically organized, tangible artifacts could truly musical "tonemes," as opposed to animal imitations or simple utterances, have come into existence. Regardless of its purely acoustic status, a single tone can never be a toneme. Nor would a set of vocalized pitches have had, at such an early stage, the stability to establish a system of interrelated *values*, as understood by de Saussure, over time. And since, as we know, almost every human society in the world sings and plays using tonal systems based on ratios very close to the integer ratios associated with the Yellow Bell story, the founding set of pipes would have to have been organized according to more or less the same simple ratios.

6. On the basis of the above sequence, it's not difficult to see how the development of a system of rationally related pitch "classes" or "tonemes" could have led to the development of a language of sorts, based exclusively on tonal relations. Once such a system of tuned pipes is established, we already have, as I argued above, both a "phonemic" and a "semantic" system as well. Each individual tone will now be heard "tonemically," in terms of the tonal structure embodied in the entire set, and will at the same time be in a position to function as a signifier of, at the very least, the note it produces. Could this have been how speech emerged, as a language of pure tones?

7. If the earliest "language" consisted essentially of discrete pitches, then we can see how, for early humans, the development of musical awareness, as part and parcel of linguistic awareness, would have had a powerful adaptational advantage (now lost, of course, since music no longer has the same function).

8. At a certain point this proto-language or "musilanguage" would have diverged into two independent branches — one leading directly to purely musical interactions something like these: *Audio Example 13:Mbuti Pipers* (African Pygmies); *Audio Example 21: Ede Panpipes* (Vietnamese "Montagnards") (see Chapter Nine for references); *Audio Example 84: Chek I Vendelar* (the *Ouldeme* of Cameroon, in *Flutes of the Mandara Mountains*); *Audio Example 85: Kiloloky* (the Mikea of Madagascar, from *Pays Mikea*, Ocora Records); *Audio Example 63: Panpipes of Buma* (the Buma people, of the Solomon Islands, from *Spirit of Melanesia*) — the other leading directly to the development of tone language, as the use of tonal phonemes would have persisted even after non-tonal elements were added. As Steven Brown

reminds us, the close association between the two realms can still be heard in the drum and whistle languages of today.[2]

In sum, the events alluded to in the Yellow Bell myth go well beyond the spatial and temporal borders of ancient China to a foundational moment in "deep history," a crucial first step in a refining process destined to take us from the raw acoustics of the *etic* to the first stages of an *emic* awareness that would ultimately give rise not only to music and language, but so many other aspects of culture, from religion, social organization, kinship, mathematics, astronomy, philosophy etc. to the science and technology of our modern world.

1. One could object that true music notation is permanent, whereas the process I just described is ephemeral and requires memorization. That would be true for the notation of a melody, yes. But each set of pipes can also be regarded as the notation of both a scale *and* a tuning system. And as such it *would* have some permanence, at least as much as an inscription on parchment or paper. Moreover, if the original pipes are then used as templates for the production of *new* pipes, we have a very durable system indeed. As with the digital encoding systems of today, what is "handed down" is not only an original "artifact," but the process through which the artifact can be continually reconstructed — and the tradition embodied by it renewed.

2. There is, of course, a great deal more to be said about such possibilities. While I'm not at all sure Dr. Brown would agree with everything (or anything) I've written here, I would recommend his *essay* (Brown 2000) as a thorough treatment of some of the more subtle and complex aspects of the "musilanguage" hypothesis.

Chapter Eighteen: The Legacy

Back out of all this now too much for us,
Back in a time made simple by the loss
Of detail, burned, dissolved, and broken off
Like graveyard marble sculpture in the weather
      Robert Frost, "Directive"

We shall not cease from exploration
And the end of all our exploring
Will be to arrive where we started
And know the place for the first time.
      T. S. Eliot, "Little Gidding"

BEIJING, April 5, 2004 (*Xinhuanet*) — A *historical tribute* by some 4,000 Chinese from home and abroad paid homage in Xi'an, Shaanxi Province, to Xuanyuan Huangdi (the Yellow Emperor) on behalf of more than 1.3 billion Chinese across the globe. The gathering took place outside the legendary emperor's mausoleum, and was a sign of respect to the ancestor of the Chinese nation. . .

The Yellow Emperor, a great tribal chief towards the end of primitive China, was honoured as the ancestor who helped greatly bring Chinese civilization into being. The invention of, among others, the cart, boat, bow and arrow, and Chinese medicine are attributed to him. One of his imperial historians is believed to have created Chinese pictography.

(http://www.asiafinest.com/forum/index.php?showtopic=5904)

See Figure 18.1

As is evident from the above newsclip, the story of the Yellow Emperor and the Yellow Bell is not simply about how an important tradition got started, but is also a story about how a brilliant ancestor went about establishing order, not only in the realm of music, but also economics, law, statehood, the relations between the sexes, and, last but not least, heaven and earth. While he was at it, he also invented important tools, such as the cart, the boat, the bow and arrow, medicines and even pictographic writing. Significantly, the Yellow Emperor is regarded as an ancestor due more to the traditions he established than to any biological functions he may have performed.

One reason I decided to focus on the Yellow Bell myth is because it tells us so much about the nature of both ancestry and tradition, and how closely bound to one another they are. While traditions are what are passed down from generation to generation, it is their association with the ancestors that gives them their meaning and their unique power. What is important, therefore, is not simply to keep a particular tradition going, but to honor the intentions of the ancestor who established it.

Thus the Yellow Bell, which is, after all, simply a length of wooden pipe, must not only be preserved but also, from time to time, replaced, through a process analogous to the process by which it was first established. Similarly, we find in many rituals, both "primitive" and "civilized," an effort to re-establish the original conditions under which a particular tradition first came into being, as a way of connecting with the ancestor(s) who initiated it. Even in a supposedly modern society like the United States we refer to the Constitution as the ultimate arbiter of all things legal, but need a Supreme Court to continually evaluate and re-evaluate its meaning, so the intentions of the "Founding Fathers" are preserved.

While the Chinese myth places the Yellow Emperor and the Yellow Bell well back into a vaguely defined "olden times," when China itself was being established as a state, according to *my* version of the myth tuned pipes originated at a much earlier time, before modern humans voyaged out of Africa — and well before that, to the time before humans learned to speak to one another. And despite all the many tens of thousands of years from that primeval time to this, we still find ensembles of pipes and panpipes, still cut from lengths of cane, still tuned, in a great many cases (though not all), more or less according to the system described in the story of the Yellow Bell, based on the simple whole number ratios, 2/3 and 4/3.

Remarkably, we still find, all over the world, musical traditions, both instrumental and vocal, based, more or less, on those exact same ratios.[1] And just as the Yellow Bell became the foundation of so much that was central to Chinese civilization, so did the ratios long ago established in the "law of pipes" become the foundation of so much of importance in other civilizations, as, for example, in the pioneering mathematics and physics of the ancient Greeks, where the exact same ratios were "discovered" by Pythagoras.

Such a tradition did not simply come from nowhere. And even though it must have originated well before the existence of China or the Chinese people, as they now define themselves, it most likely did in fact, as the Chinese myth implies, have a very definite beginning, at the hands of a very real, flesh and blood, but also very mysterious "ancestor," whose identity is shrouded in the mists of deep history.

Which returns us to the questions posed in the Introduction, for which I am now in a position to offer some meaningful, though admittedly speculative, answers: "who were our ancestors, what were they like, what part of their legacy has survived, and what lessons can we derive therefrom?" My responses will give us an opportunity to review some of the most important ideas already covered in preceding chapters.

MRCA

As far as the "who" is concerned, there are in fact a great many ancestors. Our parents are our most recent ancestors, and our grandparents our next most recent. When we speak casually of "our ancestors" we are usually invoking a vaguely defined abstraction, either a long list of ancestors, accumulated over many thousands of years, or else a single founding ancestor or ancestral group that we assume must have existed at some distant point in a now mythical past. Since so many peoples so strongly identify with a particular territory, kingdom or nation, the ancestors that most concern them are invariably associated with specific places, if not specific times.

According to ancient Chinese documents, the Yellow Emperor lived in "olden times," in Shaanxi Province, well within the boundaries of what is now China. In the Old Testament, we learn that Abraham was the first Jew, thus the ancestor of all Jews. He is said to have lived in *Ur of the Chaldees* at some time roughly around *2,000 BC*. However, the ancestors of Abraham and all other humans living at his time would, from the Old Testament perspective, have to have been Noah and his wife, since all humans other than they and their progeny would have been destroyed in the flood. Moreover, Noah and his family also had ancestors, going all the way back to the Garden of Eden. And before Adam and Eve was "God the Father", who could be considered the ultimate ancestor, as far as the Judeo/Christian tradition is concerned.

So much for the Chinese and Hebrew traditions — but just about every society in the world has its ancestors, who in most cases are completely different from one another. One might conclude from this that, as far as mythology is concerned, we are living in a world where every group has its own unique history and its own unique ancestry, tied to the land where it presumably originated.

As far as science is concerned, however, there is a different story to tell. As we've learned, there is now good reason to believe we all ultimately share exactly the same ancestry, known technically as "MRCA," i.e., the Most Recent Common Ancestors of everyone now living on planet Earth. This is the group I identified in Chapter Four as HBP, or Hypothetical Baseline Population. The notion that such a group might actually have existed in flesh and blood is relatively new, based on genetic research associated with the so-called "Out-of-Africa" model.

The Multiregional View

Anthropological thinking for a great many years was dominated by various versions of a very different theory, known as the "multi-regional" model, which was based largely on "racial" differences, with each of the major "races" originating in a different part of the world, implying either no MRCA at all, or an MRCA so remote in time that it represented little more than an abstraction. According to this model, "Caucasoids" would have descended from European Neanderthals, "Mongoloids" from Asiatic Homo Erectus and "Negroids" from a long line of archaic human and pre-human species in Africa.

Multiregionalism in its purest form holds that almost all human commonalities are due to "convergence," based on certain evolutionary and/or biological universals, making the development of things like language, music, dance, kinship systems, religion, and even our characteristically "modern" anatomy, the inevitable products of a common destiny shared by archaic humans in widely disparate regions of the world, while "racial" differences can be traced to multiregional origins.

Since such an idealized and in fact racialized view of human history is so strongly at odds with both the genetic evidence and the postmodern *zeitgeist* generally, it can no longer be seriously maintained. Most multiregionalists have fallen back on a sort of compromise in which the various "racial" groups originated in their respective regions, but exchanged both genes and cultural elements through millions of years of continual cross-continental migration.[2]

Partly because there is no archaeological evidence for such migrations, partly because the alternative, Out-of-Africa, model is so strongly reinforced by so much of the genetic research, the multiregionalist position has, for the most part, faded into the background. While multiregionalism is nevertheless still vigorously defended by a small but highly active and vocal group, the view of human history presented here is consistent with the mainstream "Out-of-Africa," or "recent African origin," model developed over the last 25 years or so by population geneticists, as described in Chapter Two.

A Phylogenetic Model

In contrast to multiregionalism, Out-of-Africa is essentially a *phylogenetic* model, based on the Darwinian notion of "descent from a common ancestor," meaning that when we refer to MRCA we are referring to a very specific group that lived at a very specific time and place, and not simply to a theoretical abstraction. As noted in Chapter Two, various estimates date the divergence[3]of the oldest mitochondrial haplogroups found in modern humans, labeled L0 and L1, to roughly between 90,000 and 150,000 years ago.

And since all haplotypes directly derived from L0 and L1 are found almost exclusively among peoples now living in Africa, it seems reasonable to conclude, as have the great majority of population geneticists, that MRCA most likely lived somewhere on that continent, at some time during the Middle Paleolithic (or Middle "Old Stone Age"). Pretty vague, I admit. But nevertheless something. In fact, much more than we had any reason to expect even 20 or 25 years ago, when population genetics was still in its infancy.

While the dates may be vague, the existence of MRCA is marked by a very specific event, the moment when a group of proto-Bushmen or proto-Pygmies broke away (the technical term is "diverged") from the population of which they had formerly been a part. This need not have been a momentous occasion, but more likely a relatively minor split, now considered significant only in retrospect. MRCA were thus the population from which this breakaway group diverged. What makes them especially interesting is the fact that they can be characterized, both biologically and culturally, by their status at the moment of divergence.

It must be stressed, however, that MRCA is by no means the end of the line, because they too had ancestors — and if you want to compare humans with great apes, you can posit an MRCA for these two groups as well – and on down the line: prior to humans, apes and monkeys we find more primitive mammals and prior to them lizards, insects, bacteria, etc., all the way back to the earliest life form, which can be considered the ultimate ancestor.

In a sense, therefore, the question of "who" our ancestors were becomes a kind of tautology: our ancestors are the ones from whom we are descended, all the way back to the beginning of life. But such a definition would never satisfy those many peoples throughout the world for whom the notion of "ancestor" holds such great meaning. As I noted above, we can't really separate such ancestors from the traditions with which they are associated, which tells us that the traditional notion of "ancestor" is at least as much cultural as biological: the ancestors are simultaneously those from whom we are descended and those from whom our traditions stem.

And if we wish to get beyond the ancestry of any particular group to the common ancestry, both biological and cultural, of all such groups, then we have no choice but to consider the group I've been referring to as MRCA. For all practical purposes, the MRCA identified by the geneticists can be regarded as our common ancestors and their culture can be regarded as the source of some of most venerable traditions now being perpetuated among so many societies, both "primitive" and "modern," of today.

There are, additionally, two other ancestral groups of special importance to the story I've been telling: the Out-of-Africa migrants discussed in Chapter Seven, who appear to have been the ancestors of all non-Africans; and what I've referred to as the "post-bottleneck" population(s), the earliest survivors of the cataclysmic event hypothesized in Chapters Nine and Ten, which may have triggered much of the large-scale diversity, both "racial" and cultural, we see in the world of today.

So much for the "who."

What Were They Like?

While the genetic research has identified "mitochondrial Eve" as our most recent common female ancestor, and "Y chromosome Adam" as our most recent common male ancestor, it has nothing to say about what either of them, or the group (or groups) to which they belonged, were like – in other words, what sort of society were they a part of, and what sort of culture did they possess?

While archaeologists have attempted to reconstruct at least certain aspects of the culture of "early man," little or no attempt has been made to reconcile the various bits and pieces with one another, not to mention the genetic findings — and in fact, many of the "bones and stones" they study are from populations whose lineages may well have gone extinct thousands of years ago and can hardly be regarded as "ancestral" as far as any of today's peoples are concerned.

Which is, as I see it, why the approach I've taken in this book is potentially so useful. In the spirit of the revolutionary methods of the population geneticists, I've managed to construct a tool for the "excavation" of the ancestral culture by extrapolating backward from the present to some of the deepest recesses of our common history. And while the geneticists have been unable to reconcile "mitochondrial Eve" and "Y chromosome Adam," who seem to have lived during two very different eras, the

Hypothetical Baseline Culture I've managed to cobble together (see Chapter Four) points to a single, specific ancestral society, which in all likelihood existed prior to the L0-L1 divergence, and appears, on the basis of my "triangulation" method, to have maintained (if not necessarily originated) certain highly distinctive and uniquely interesting cultural traits and traditions.

A Lost History

While the whole idea of extrapolating backward from present to past has been anathema to most anthropologists for some time, I am not completely alone. In a similar spirit, and informed by essentially the same set of genetic findings, Nicholas Wade's *Before the Dawn:Recovering the Lost History of Our Ancestors* (Wade 2006) is equally ambitious in its attempt to reconstruct ancestral culture. Wade's logic is simple and convincing:

> [S]ince people in societies around the world behave in much the same way, the principal elements of human nature must already have been present in the ancestral human population before its dispersal into Africa and the world beyond.
>
> Despite the fact that "not a trace of these first people has yet been found by archaeologists," nevertheless, "a surprising amount can now be *inferred* . . ." (p. 52 – my emphasis).
>
> By analyzing the behaviors common to societies around the world, particularly the hunter-gatherers who seem closest to the ancestral people, anthropologists can describe how the ancestral population probably lived and what its people were like. (ibid.)

In elaborating his theory, Wade points to two very interesting "ways of developing a portrait of the ancestral human population; one is through the Universal People, the other through the Real People." He first considers "universal human behaviors" ranging from "cooking, dance and divination to fear of snakes" facial expressions, and, more importantly, language, all "found in societies throughout the world . . ." (p. 65) He goes on to list a range of behaviors and traditions apparently shared by all peoples and thus likely to have been a part of ancestral culture.

In addition to the Universal People, it is possible to consider a very specific group of Real People, such as the "San," i.e., Bushmen, who "as members of the L1 [actually it's L0] branch of the mitochondrial tree may be the closest living approximation to the ancestral human population" (p.66). As you can see, Wade's thinking is in some ways remarkably similar to my own. Indeed, as he paints a fairly detailed portrait of the !Kung San (aka Ju/'hoansi) Bushmen, he lists many of the same characteristics highlighted in these pages, especially chapters Three and Four.

Of course, he is not so naïve as to assume that everything we find in Bushmen culture can be attributed to the ancestral population, and in the following section, entitled "Ancestral Portrait," he judiciously weighs the possible differences. As he does so, however, some limitations of his approach become evident.

In contrast to the many specific, well documented details of !Kung life he's already enumerated, his "Ancestral Portrait" is highly speculative and vague, based on untested and in certain cases inaccurate assumptions. Clearly the !Kung in and of themselves cannot be a reliable model, because we have no way of knowing the degree to which any aspect of their culture is due to the specific conditions under which they now live. For example: does their communal reciprocity stem from an ancestral tradition, or is it simply a strategy for holding the community together in the face of a harsh, resource-scarce, desert environment?

As far as the Universal People are concerned, while it's true that many elements of culture do in fact seem universal, it would take a very ambitious research project to confirm that. Do we really know that cooking, dance, divination, fear of snakes, standardized facial expressions, etc. are found in literally every society, or even a significant majority? How could we go about testing such a hypothesis? Moreover, it is by no means self-evident that the absence of a certain trait in certain societies means it must have been absent in the ancestral society. Wade rules bows and arrows out because we don't find them among the Australian aborigines without considering the possibility that this technology could have been lost at some point in their history, for any number of reasons.

The most serious problem I have with Wade's approach is his continual reliance on the behavior of "hunter-gatherers" as an index of ancestral culture. As we learned in Chapter Five, there are a great many different types of hunter-gatherers, with a wide variety of often very different value systems and survival strategies. And, again, as with the Universal People, any attempt to identify cultural elements held in common by all or even most hunter-gatherer societies would require a research project of major proportions.

The dangers of such an approach become especially evident when he concludes that the ancestral people must have "engaged in constant warfare, defending their own territory or raiding that of neighbors" (p. 74), because he sees strong evidence of violence and endemic warfare among such "hunter-gatherer" groups as the Australian Aborigines, the tribal peoples of

New Guinea, the natives of the Andaman Islands, the Yanomamo of Brazil, etc., supplemented by widespread evidence of head-hunting and cannibalism throughout the hunter-gatherer world.

As far as the allegedly "harmless" Bushmen are concerned, he cites reliable evidence that "the San fought regularly with their pastoralist Bantu neighbors" and were found to have an internal homicide rate "some three times that of even the United States."

According to Wade, the tendency of the ancestral people, and, by implication, humans generally, to engage in territorial aggression, warfare and raiding, was hard wired into their genes as a legacy from our primate ancestors. Such a conclusion might seem odd in light of the fact that the great majority of today's primates do *not* engage in such behavior, but Wade has chosen to focus his attention on chimpanzees, the only other creatures in the animal kingdom[4] with "a strong propensity to kill their own kind" (p. 148). Since Wade is already convinced that the earliest humans were inherently violent and warlike, he has little problem deriving such behavior from a "joint human-chimp ancestor" (p. 141).

Methodological Issues

Wade's book is an intelligent, well written and perceptive overview of a large body of meaningful evidence, including some of the most recent genetic research, pertaining to a great many important aspects of human culture and evolution, and on that level I highly recommend it. I take exception, however, to the methodology he has employed in his attempt to recreate the ancestral culture, which is, as I see it, far too vague, and far too dependent on untestable or inadequately tested assumptions – notably the assumption that certain commonalities in the behavior of today's "hunter-gatherers" can be extrapolated into the behavior of a common ancestor. Especially problematic is the repeated harping on a supposedly inherent human tendency toward violence, which I find both misleading and potentially harmful.

Why am I so convinced Wade must be wrong? All the issues raised above have been extensively discussed in these pages, especially Chapters Four, Five and Six. In Chapter Four, I explicitly question the tendency of many anthropologists

> to lump all hunter-gatherers together, as though there were some universal ahistorical force that unites them, simply because they maintain hunting and gathering traditions. As we will learn from the

following chapter, this is far from the case. All 'immediate-return' societies do *not*, in fact, look alike.

In Chapter Five, as promised, I describe a wide variety of different hunter-gatherer societies (including some of the simple "horticulturalists" included on Wade's list, who share many forager characteristics), with a range of very different behaviors and social structures, from some, like the Pygmies, Bushmen and Hadza, who are acephalous, egalitarian, communal and relatively non-violent, to others, such as the New Guinea tribes cited by Wade, dominated by aggressive "Big Men," characterized by fierce competition for status and endemic warfare. As I concluded, it is a mistake to "accept the commonly held view of 'hunter-gatherers' as representative . . . of some sort of universalized essence of 'Stone-Age Man'."

In Chapter Four, under the heading "Core Values," I distinguish between violent *behavior*, as found among certain individuals in literally all societies, and *institutionalized* violence, in which violence is woven into the fabric of the society as a whole, where it is both tolerated and in many cases encouraged. The three populations I've drawn on to produce the baseline ancestral culture outlined in Chapter Four lack any of the trappings one would expect to find in such a society (see below).

In Chapter Six, I explicitly address the unfortunate comparison between early humans and chimpanzees, which can be sourced to a highly influential, but seriously misleading book, *Demonic Males*, by Richard Wrangham and Dale Peterson (1997). As does Wade, the authors assume that all hunter-gatherers have always engaged in endemic warfare, which makes the comparison with the aggressive and violent behavior of male chimpanzees seem particularly apt. While noting that bonobos, close cousins of chimps, have a very different, essentially non-violent, culture, the authors' preconceived notions of what our "Stone-Age" ancestors must have been like make the comparison with chimps seem far more likely.

The theories of Wrangham and Peterson have been widely accepted and are exerting a significant influence on many of our leading thinkers. An especially disturbing example can be found in a recently published book by the well known political scientist Francis Fukuyama, *The Origins of Political Order* (Fukuyama 2011), a work which is sure to have a powerful influence on decision makers throughout the world. A key section of Fukuyama's book is in fact titled "Chimpanzee Politics and its Relevance to Human Political Development."

According to Fukuyama, who confidently cites Wrangham as a basic source, "[we] know that both human beings and modern chimpanzees are descended from a common chimplike ancestor . . ." He continues, noting, reasonably enough, that our earliest human ancestors were, like Chimpanzees, highly social (as indeed are many of their primate cousins), making the perfectly valid point that sociability has most likely been a part of human nature from the beginning.

Even more significant, in his view, is the observation, again based on Wrangham, that chimpanzee behavior is inherently violent, with "groups of male chimpanzees in the wild ranging beyond their territories to attack and kill chimps from neighboring communities" (p. 31). On this basis, and this basis alone, he ultimately concludes, with equal confidence, that "violence is rooted in human nature," as "one of the most important points of continuity between ancestral apes and human beings," thus endorsing Hobbes' famous dictum "that the state of nature was a state of war of 'every man against every man.'" This dubious conclusion becomes the fundamental basis for a theory of socio-political evolution colored throughout by a highly cynical, deeply pessimistic view of human nature.

I cannot agree, and find such conclusions alarming, to say the least. As I wrote in Chapter Six,

> the Pygmy and Bushmen groups on whose traditions I've drawn for the construction of an ancestral baseline, are nothing like chimps. Indeed, when we examine those cultural elements shared by so many Pygmy and Bushmen groups . . . [it] looks, in fact, as though our ancestors were closer to bonobos than chimps.

Since writing this passage, I've come across a remarkable video that makes my point quite dramatically: *Video Example 13:Bonobos Like to Share*. The "subject" is not only willing to share, but goes to the trouble of unlocking another Bonobo's cage to make sure his pal can also get to the food.

Compare with the following description of Aka Pygmy sharing, by Michelle Kisliuk:

> On another occasion I brought a tomato to the Bagandou camp . . . I gave a wedge to Bandit sitting beside me, expecting him to pop it in his mouth. Instead, he proceeded to call for a knife and cut the wedge into about sixteen tiny pieces, sharing it with everybody in sight (Kisliuk 1998:132).

There are many other notable similarities between bonobo culture and the baseline culture I constructed in Chapter Four, including synchronized vocal interlock, female assertiveness, non-hierarchical political structure and yes, most certainly, a tendency to avoid violent behavior, none of which are characteristic of chimpanzees. Thus, one way of answering the question of what our ancestors were like might be, very simply: bonobos!

The HBC Model

In attempting to paint a relatively comprehensive picture of our common ancestry, we must first, as we have seen, reject theories based on universals and/or "hunter-gatherer" behaviors and customs, including the notion that MRCA must, like chimpanzees, have been inherently violent and warlike.

The long neglected musical evidence presented in Chapters One and Three has led us to a very different conclusion, based on a radically different approach, as elucidated in Chapter Four. Thanks to an important clue provided by the remarkable affinities between the highly distinctive musical traditions of those populations in the world with the deepest lineages, the African Pygmies and Bushmen, coupled with the equally remarkable manner in which the organization and performance style of their music reflects certain key elements of the social organization and cultural values of both groups, it has been possible to move out from the realm of music to the realm of culture generally, to speculate meaningfully on what the common ancestors of the Pygmies and Bushmen might have been like.

And since the genetic evidence so strongly suggests that the common ancestors of these two groups are the common ancestors of everyone else as well, we have opened the door to a meaningful (though necessarily provisional) consideration of what MRCA might have been like.

For a full accounting see Chapter Four, where you'll find a listing headed "The HBC Model Thus Far." Briefly, what my triangulation method reveals is an ancestral culture that is, in some ways, almost embarrassingly "Utopian," with an economy very close to what Marx called "primitive communism"; a non-hierarchical, acephalous, highly egalitarian political structure based on close interpersonal cooperation rather than coercion by leaders; a high degree of both group integration and personal freedom; a spiritual life refreshingly free of dogma or institutionalized thinking; a "complementary" relation between the sexes, in which women are relatively, though certainly not completely, equal to men; finally, despite a high degree of interpersonal contentiousness coupled with occasional episodes of violent behavior, we see no sign of *institutionalized* violence.

While certain Pygmy or Bushmen individuals have acted violently, and certain Pygmy or Bushmen groups have, from time to time, engaged in warfare (invariably stemming from relatively recent external pressures), "[w]hat we do *not* see, and would not therefore expect to find in HBC, are evidences of: cannibalism, head-hunting, endemic warfare, exploitation of women or children, female mutilation, prostitution, slavery, blood-feuds, raiding."

Migrants, Bottlenecks and the Origins of Institutionalized Violence

As for the two other ancestral groups considered in this volume, I've made an effort to characterize the Out-of-Africa migrants in Chapter Seven, where my ideas regarding their culture are summarized in an extensive table (see Table One), while the socio-cultural effects of the bottleneck event hypothesized in Chapter Ten are considered under the heading "The Toba Effect."

While there are many fascinating things to consider regarding the nature of both the migrants and the post-bottleneck survivors, one single issue looms largest for me: the origins of violence and warfare — or to be more specific, institutionalized violence and endemic warfare. Since I cannot agree with the now widely held view that violence is programmed into our genes, and see no evidence that MRCA either encouraged or tolerated it, then, as far as I am concerned, the origins of violence and warfare as socially sanctioned behaviors are yet to be determined. Initially I planned to devote a chapter to this problem, but ultimately decided against it simply because I lacked the time and resources to do the necessary research, and didn't want to wander off too far into the realm of vague speculation. Nevertheless, the topic is of sufficient interest and importance as to warrant a certain amount of discussion here, however incomplete and tentative.

Assuming I am correct about the essentially pacifist nature of HBP, then the next question for us to consider is whether the Out-of-Africa migrants (HMP) shared similar values or, at some time prior to their African exodus, had adopted the very different values of a warlike society. As I noted in Chapter Seven, geneticist Eduardo Moreno has argued in favor of the latter alternative, referring to them as "The Migrant Warriors that Colonized the World" (Moreno 2010). Moreno's work is of special interest to me since he has approached such issues from a perspective so close to my own.

To review some of the points already made in Chapter Seven:

Moreno sees *no* correlation between those populations characterized by the ancestral mitochondrial haplogroups L0, L1 or L2 (mostly African Bushmen or Pygmies) and a warlike ethos, supporting my view that our common ancestors were essentially non-violent. On the other hand, he *does* find such a correlation with hunter-gatherer groups carrying haplogroup L3, and its M and N descendents, who tend to exhibit either patently warlike behavior or the presence of competitive rituals, games, etc. that appear consistent with an essentially warlike value system. On this basis, he arrives at the conclusion that the high degree of violent behavior so characteristic of so many non-African hunter-gatherers is most likely due to cultural values inherited from their L3 ancestors, the Out-of-Africa migrants.

At this stage, I'm not completely convinced, though I find Moreno's approach impressively original, sympathetic and promising. There are too many hunter-gatherers in too many different parts of the world who are distinctly *non*-warlike, regardless of whether they might or might not engage in competitive rituals or games. Moreno's focus on such competitions is nevertheless suggestive and certainly deserves further consideration, but as I see it, there is not yet enough evidence available on which to base a strong hypothesis one way or the other.

If in fact HMP had retained the values of their HBP ancestors and were *not* warlike, that could possibly account for the many non-African hunter-gatherer groups that have traditionally tended to avoid violence, and would, moreover, explain why so many have apparently retreated into marginal "refuge areas," such as forests, islands and mountains, where they have, until recently, been able to pursue their traditions in relative peace. If that is the case, however, then we are still left with the question of where, and how, very different traditions supporting institutionalized violence originated.

Tradition!

As I see it, in order to understand the origins of socially sanctioned violence, regardless of where or when it originated, we need to arrive at a clearer understanding of traditions in general, how they originate, the manner in which they are propagated, and the conditions under which they can be altered. And since the lasting power of age-old traditions over the human mind and psyche has been a persistent theme throughout this book, it makes sense, at this point, to do some reviewing.

As the musical evidence considered in Chapter One so strongly suggests, certain traditions can persist essentially intact for tens of thousands of years. While such a conclusion is certain to trigger skepticism among social scientists, the evidence (see especially Appendix A) cannot be ignored. And if we are willing to consider such a conclusion, however provisionally, then we are faced with the question of why certain traditions fail to "evolve" or "develop" while others apparently do.

I deal with this question in its most general form in the first "Sidebar," under the heading "Cultural Continuity." While this analysis is presented as "preliminary," it is, in fact, based on conclusions drawn as a result of all the research that went into this book, which convinced me that the traditional approach to continuity and change is based on a serious oversimplification of both culture and history.

As I see it, there is no such thing as "cultural evolution" in the sense of some sort of inbred, natural tendency for traditions to change over time. "Cultural drift," when it does occur, almost always pertains to relatively superficial elements, such as, for example, all the many variants we can find of a particular folk song as it makes its way through both time and space. When we consider deeper issues of musical style and structure, which was, of course, Alan Lomax's great innovation, we see no significant change at all.

Thus we find the salient characteristics of, say, ballad style, remaining virtually unchanged from country to country and even continent to continent, implying relative stasis over many thousands of years. The same is true of more practical traditions such as, say, archery, where we find many different types of bow and arrow developing over the centuries while the basic principle remains precisely the same.

According to this model, real change, when it does occur, is due either to external forces, such as natural disasters, wars, or the influence of neighboring groups; or, in the case of more highly developed societies, the desires (or whims) of powerful leaders, or competition among specialists, which can drive innovation. In the case of non-specialized hunter-gatherer societies, the origin of traditions supporting violence cannot be due to powerful leaders, as such societies are typically acephalous, nor competition among specialists, since there are no specialists; nor can it be due to war, or the influence of neighboring societies with a warlike culture, since we are considering the *origin* of such a culture, which would not yet have existed elsewhere. It seems logical, therefore, to look for the origin of institutionalized violence in the effects of a natural disaster. Which is one reason I've attached such great importance to the "bottleneck event" highlighted in Chapter Ten.

Whether produced by the Toba eruption or some other comparably significant occurrence, the effects of a major ecological disaster, as we well know from recent experiences with floods, earthquakes and tsunamis, could have been profound and lasting. Under such conditions, as I wrote in Chapter Ten,

> Instead of an egalitarian ethic steeped in non-violence, a new system of values, based on the survival of the strongest, most assertive and most competitive individuals, and their subservient followers, could emerge. Once such a tradition is established, it would be almost

impossible to go back to the old way of doing things and even of thinking. Even if things might improve over time, to the point that the society is no longer stressed, and no longer dependent on strong, aggressive leaders, it might not matter, because traditions tend to perpetuate themselves long after they have lost their original purpose and even their meaning.

Thus, if under dire circumstances, a situation is created whereby only the most aggressive and violent individuals are likely to survive, then, as I see it, we have good reason to expect that traditions supporting competitive, violent and warlike behavior could suddenly emerge from an originally nonviolent base. And once such traditions are established, then, as I argued above, they will tend to persist indefinitely until they, in turn, are confronted with a more powerful external event or influence.

Whether such a theory is adequate as an explanation of the origin of violence remains to be seen. As I stated above, much more evidence would be necessary before any firm conclusion could be reached. Nevertheless, from evidence presented in Chapters Ten through Fifteen, there is good reason to see the bottleneck event as a major turning point, both biological and cultural, for large segments of the human race, for whom the bottleneck survivors would have constituted an especially significant ancestry.

The Legacy

Now that we have a clearer (or more confused?) notion of who our ancestors were and what they were like, we can move on to the next question: what part of their legacy has survived? And here I must admit to having begged the question, because it's not at all self-evident to what extent any such survivals could be regarded as a "legacy," rather than a simple curiosity, of interest only to antiquarians.

Here's how I put my feelings a few years ago, in an essay entitled *Echoes of Our Forgotten Ancestors*:

> The highly integrated, interlocked, freely polyphonic, improvised and playfully hocketed yodeling of the various Pygmy and Bushman groups of Africa would seem to constitute a perfect reflection of their social order: intensely group oriented, but also individualized — acephelous, egalitarian, more or less gender equal. . . If humankind is, indeed, "innately" aggressive, violent, and competitive, that information seems never to have reached the gentle aborigines of Africa.

Can the Pygmy/Bushman model be applied to the earliest musical and social state of *homo sapiens sapiens,* prior to its "Out-of-Africa" adventure? If true, such a finding would be of immense importance, not only to ethnomusicology and anthropology, but all of us, simply as human beings — which is to say: as the inheritors of a certain *legacy* — of cooperation as opposed to competition; gentleness and mutual support as opposed to aggression and violence — a legacy of interactive play, pleasure — and joy. (Grauer 2006, p. 44)

Is there evidence that any aspects of such a legacy could have indeed survived to the current era? My answer is, very simply: yes. For one thing, this book itself is based on the premise that such survivals exist. If I saw no indication of that, then I'd have had nothing to work with in extrapolating backward from the present to the past. What we see as we look around us on a global scale is abundant evidence of survivals from a long distant past, most obviously in the cultures of so-called "indigenous" societies, which, until very recently, were still very much alive and if not thriving, then at least managing, and in many cases struggling, to preserve at least some of their most valued traditions.

What I see in each of these societies is a kind of palimpsest, i.e., an overlay, of sometimes very different and even contradictory cultural elements. And in this palimpsest it is often possible to identify traditions stemming from the three ancestral sources I've highlighted in these pages: HBC, the Hypothetical Baseline Culture of our most recent common ancestors (MRCA); HMC, the Hypothetical Migrant Culture of the Out-of-Africa migrants; and, finally, a culture, or group of cultures, originating, as I suspect, in some of the profound changes stemming from the "Bottleneck" event discussed in Chapters Nine and Ten. The most recent layer, is, of course, the layer formed by the profound and often negative influence of the more "advanced" cultural forces now impinging on them. As I see it, none of these layers has been entirely lost when "supplanted" by the next, which is one of the reasons such societies can seem so complex and contradictory to outsiders.

Let me now pose a particularly challenging question, especially meaningful, I'd imagine, to those reading here: Can we tease out the various layers of such a palimpsest from the so-called "developed" world, the society of automobiles, airplanes, computers, cell phones and Internet blogs? In other words, does the story I've been telling in these pages have any immediate relevance for *us*? Is the ancestral legacy *our* legacy too, or largely a matter for professional anthropologists and the indigenous peoples they study?

As far as music is concerned, I've pointed, in Chapter Twelve, to signs of the "African Signature" in Europe, not only in certain folk traditions featuring vocal interlock, hocket and canon, but in the liturgy of the medieval church, clearly influenced by some of these traditions, for which such vocal interplay became common, forming one basis for the development of the polyphony we now take for granted in the "classical" tradition to which it gave rise. I confess that, now that I'm attuned to it, I hear a great many "echoes" of Pygmy/Bushmen style in the classical music I love, from Medieval motets, to Renaissance madrigals, Bach fugues, Beethoven string quartets, all the way to "modernist" works, such as Stravinsky's *Rite of Spring* and the intricately hocketed counterpoints of Webern, Boulez, Berio, Stockhausen, etc. I hear it in much popular music as well, including Hip Hop. Especially Hip Hop. But this is another story for another day.

I sometimes wonder whether the ideals that now form the basis of modern democracy could be a part of that same legacy. Notions such as "life, liberty and the pursuit of happiness," or "all men are created equal," supposedly stemming from the Eighteenth Century European "Enlightenment," are perfectly in tune with the "Utopian" values of the ancestral culture I've postulated. If such values are indeed at the basis of a common cultural ancestry, and if, as I've argued, our most valued traditions tend to persist, even in the face of the most powerful and persistent obstacles, then the egalitarian values of our ancestors, like their egalitarian music, may have persisted unnoticed and unrecognized in the psyches of countless individuals who, under even the most oppressive conditions, have persisted in their belief that a luminous "golden age" of equality and freedom might someday return.

Such thinking has been sternly rejected of late, as part of a reaction against supposedly naïve and romantic characterizations of indigenous peoples. To choose one example among many, here is Roy Grinker commenting on views expressed in Colin Turnbull's popular, *The Forest People*:

> *The Forest People* . . . is in many ways a thinly veiled attempt to use the idea of the "Pygmies" as a way to make universally valid statements about human nature. Turnbull played upon a deep-seated need throughout much of the West to invent a "primitive" and original form of human society, and toward this goal he draws

an idealized picture of the Mbuti living a romantic and harmonious life in the bountiful rain forest of the Congo (Grinker 1994:6).

A similar view is expressed by Francis Fukuyama, in the book referenced above:

> The idea that violence is rooted in human nature is difficult for many people to accept. Many anthropologists, in particular, are committed, like Rousseau, to the view that violence is an invention of later civilizations, just as many people would like to believe that early societies understood how to live in balance with their local environments. Unfortunately, there is little evidence to support either view. (Fukuyama 2011:73)

Aside from the fact that, as I have demonstrated, there *is* indeed considerable evidence to support such views, both Grinker and Fukuyama fail to address a key question that goes to the heart of the issues they've raised. If in fact there is "a deep-seated need . . . to invent a 'primitive' and original form of human society," and if "the idea that violence is rooted in human nature is difficult for many people to accept," one is tempted to ask: why? Why is it that so many people in our society have such a "deep-seated need" to think in such idealized terms, and why is it so "difficult for many people to accept" that humans are, at base, cold-blooded killers? If human nature is as essentially ruthless as Fukuyama claims, then one would assume the great majority of humans everywhere would have no problem at all with such characterizations, and in fact point to them with Klingon-like pride.

If most people have a "deep-seated need" to idealize certain indigenous societies as "primitive and original" "noble savages," one can only wonder where that need comes from. What is there in us that responds so strongly to stories, books and movies about the adventure filled, freewheeling lifestyles of Tropical Forest Pygmies, Bushmen of the Kalahari, Hadza, etc.? Are such values the product, simply, of overactive imaginations? Or might they themselves be survivals from our distant past? Could what Carl Jung once referred to as the "collective unconscious," an innate, universal feature of the human psyche, be better understood as an "historical unconscious," located not so much in the human mind, as in the vast field of culturally transmitted norms and values that condition it?

In this regard, I suspect that some of the most fundamental values may have always been conveyed most powerfully and effectively through music. While certainly not a "universal language" in the sense once generally accepted in the West, music does have certain unique properties that make it an especially effective communicative tool, even across the most profound cultural and social divides. Despite the media dominance of pop, rock, country, hip-hop etc., many different kinds of music are enthusiastically appreciated and even cultivated in our society, to the point that recordings of some of the most esoteric musical practices from the most remote corners of the world have been widely available for many years.

Because of its unique properties and extraordinarily important social role, music has been widely documented in a manner that is special, totally unlike just about any other type of human behaviour one could name. Listening with an open mind for ancestral echoes still present in the authentic music of the traditional peoples of today may be the first step toward the understanding and appreciation of a long neglected, infinitely valuable, legacy.

Cultural Equity

Assuming a portion of our ancestral legacy has survived, we must now deal with the final question: what lessons can we derive therefrom? No one worked harder to convince the world of the importance of such a question than the controversial father of Cantometrics, Alan Lomax. The phrase "Cultural Equity" was coined by Lomax in a seminal essay (Lomax 1972), in which he identified a cultural "grey-out," destined to "fill our human skies with the smog of the phoney and cut the families of men off from a vision of their own cultural constellations." He descried an "over-centralized electronic communication system" that was "imposing a few standardized, mass-produced and cheapened cultures everywhere," promoting "the swift destruction of culture patterns all over the planet."

As one might expect, musical traditions played a special role for Lomax, who had devoted so much of his time and energy to their preservation:

> Scientific study of cultures, notably of their languages and their musics, shows that all are equally expressive and equally communicative. They are also equally valuable; first, because they enrich the lives of the culture or people who employ them and whose psychic balance is threatened when they are destroyed or impoverished; second, because each communicative system . . . holds important discoveries about the natural and human environment; and third, because each is a treasure of unknown potential, a collective creation in which some branch of the human species invested its genius across the centuries. . . [Thus, we are in

danger of destroying] a system of interaction, of fantasy and symbolizing which, in the future, the human race may sorely need.

While Lomax saw cultural equity in terms of justice and equality, I wonder whether he also considered that other meaning of the term "equity," the one that's used when we invest in a stock. As he had strong socialist sympathies, this notion, with its capitalist overtones, may not have appealed to him. But aren't the traditions Lomax championed a kind of equity in that sense as well, as a sort of "common stock" in which our ancestors have been investing since the dawn of humanity, and in which we *all* share an interest?

In that case, what's at stake is not only a matter of fairness, equal *justice* for all modes of cultural expression, as important as that surely is, but the preservation of a common *heritage*, an infinitely precious cultural legacy of incalculable value to every living human being. As Lomax implies several times in his essay, there is a strong analogy at work linking our efforts to preserve the natural environment, all but universally applauded, with the need for similar efforts on the cultural front, equally important for the well being of our *human* environment, but unfortunately far less well understood.

Are Indigenous Cultures "Frozen in Time"?

If by "cultural equity" we simply mean "fairness" to various and sundry remote and exotic cultures, each seen as both unique and also set apart, "frozen in time" in a world of its own, then one might feel a responsibility to preserve each of these separate worlds in its own pristine "authenticity." If, however, we see "cultural equity" as something in which we too hold a stake (i.e., *equity*), as a spiritual investment made by generations of ancestors, going all the way back to the beginnings of our species — which, as I've been arguing, does appear to have a common source, and, therefore, a common cultural heritage — then we cannot separate indigenous peoples off from ourselves in exotic and remote worlds of their own, but must see them as part of a dynamic ongoing process that concerns everyone now alive — and our descendants after us. This is especially significant in view of the fact that it is the same so-called "indigenes" who have been most concerned, if not obsessed, with both the preservation and cultivation of tradition. These are the ones whose lessons we must be prepared to learn if we are to profit from the "equity" that's been accumulating for so many generations.

All well and good, one might say, but when we get down to specifics we seem to be confronted with an enormous number of totally different traditions, each appearing to us as something rigid, indeed "'frozen in time," sometimes irrational, often fragile and even brittle, difficult to understand

and even more difficult, therefore, to connect with. While I've been emphasizing that which is admirable in our ancestral traditions, it's impossible to deny that in many cases there is a dark side as well.

Indeed, tradition can be a force for repression, control, exploitation and a host of other practices that many find disturbing, if not evil. The problem is indeed immense, and there are many different ways of addressing it. The path I've been following here represents my own effort to dig down deeply enough through all the historical and cultural clutter to find something we can all agree is worth not only studying and learning from, but also preserving, encouraging and developing. Once we arrive at this point, we may be surprised to see traces of this ancient heritage cropping up in many unexpected places.

A good example might be the young girl in the film "Whale Rider," who identifies so strongly with her Maori heritage, in spite of the opposition of tribal "traditionalists," even her own grandfather, who object to her activities because females have traditionally been excluded from playing the roles to which she so longingly aspires. I think that story has great meaning for those who are trying to sort out what is valuable about tradition, what is destructive about it, and why the differences are so important.

What is especially interesting to contemplate is whether the girl represents tradition or is resisting it. On the one hand, she is attempting to overthrow age-old traditions by doing the sort of things usually reserved for males. On the other hand she appears to be the only young person in the village with a real interest in perpetuating the very traditions threatened by her involvement in them.

As I see it, this story can be understood not so much as an opposition between generations, or a new or old way of seeing things, but as the opposition between certain relatively new traditions (new, that is, from the perspective of deep history), concerned primarily with social control, which have, indeed, become frozen in time; and older, more fundamental traditions stemming from a much deeper cultural layer, which promote social integration, fairness, equality — *and* adaptation to new and different conditions where appropriate. The elders are trapped in the former, while the girl is tuned in to the latter and behaves accordingly — in a manner that eventually wins the day, transforming the consciousness of all involved, including the film's viewers — one of which, I'm pleased to say, was me.

Oh and One More Thing

There is one more lesson to be learned, a lesson of special relevance at this particular moment in history, when our economic system appears on the verge of collapse, and our way of life with it. One of the basic principles of classical economics is that all humans are ultimately, whether we like to admit it or not, motivated by self-interest, which in turn drives competition, the basis for our "free market economy." This is a view once widely, and uncritically, accepted in the post-Soviet, "free market" driven world of today. Here's one particularly clear statement, by Mark Perry, of what was, until recently, regarded as unquestionable wisdom (Perry 1995):

> In a capitalist economy, incentives are of the utmost importance. Market prices, the profit-and-loss system of accounting, and private property rights provide an efficient, interrelated system of incentives to guide and direct economic behavior. Capitalism is based on the theory that incentives matter!

Why do incentives matter? Human nature, for one thing: "By failing to emphasize incentives, socialism is a theory inconsistent with human nature and is therefore doomed to fail." For another, the need for maximum efficiency due to the scarcity of resources: "In a world of scarcity it is essential for an economic system to be based on a clear incentive structure to promote economic efficiency." Which leads, inevitably, to competition: "Without competition, centrally planned economies do not have an effective incentive structure to coordinate economic activity." Thus, "Without incentives the results are a spiraling cycle of poverty and misery."

Yet, as has been clear to those who have studied the Pygmies and Bushmen of Africa, their remarkable societies appear, through most of their history, to have lived collectively, sharing goods on an equal basis, shunning competition, and yet managing to survive peacefully and harmoniously among themselves, for the most part, with little if any trace of regimentation or coercion, for what now appears to have been literally tens of thousands of years!

Elizabeth Marshall Thomas, in her book *The Old Way* (Thomas 2007), writes with glowing admiration of the !Kung Bushmen's "almost obsessive sense of equality and sharing. . . In daily matters, sharing was the way of life. Everybody shared" (p. 108).

If sharing can be a way of life for societies that have flourished for tens of thousands of years, then a need for personal incentives based on competition cannot be grounded in "human nature." And if life in the Kalahari desert, where Bushmen groups have survived for centuries at least, is marked by extreme scarcity of both food and water, then Perry's assertion that "In a world of scarcity it is essential for an economic system to be based on a clear incentive structure to promote economic efficiency" cannot be true.

Why is this important? Because, as we now know, it is not only Soviet style socialism that has collapsed, but also the brand of "free market capitalism" so enthusiastically promoted by Perry — and so many others.

Perry was able to conclude, with some confidence, back in 1995:

> Capitalism will play a major role in the global revival of liberty and prosperity because it nurtures the human spirit, inspires human creativity, and promotes the spirit of enterprise. By providing a powerful system of incentives that promote thrift, hard work, and efficiency, capitalism creates wealth.
>
> The main difference between capitalism and socialism is this: Capitalism works.

Which reminds me of those famous words of Gordon Gekko: "Greed is good. Greed is right. Greed works." As we now know, to our sorrow and grief, Perry was not only wrong about societies "where all things are held in common," to quote More's *Utopia*. He was also wrong about the capitalist Utopia he was promoting. "Free market" capitalism does not work. Greed does not work, and therefore cannot be good for anything at all. Despite the continual litany of complaints and rollings of the eyes we've been getting for so long from fashionably revisionist academics, there *is* something we can learn from those "primitive" Pygmies and Bushmen after all. The only question is: will the message reach us in time?

---

1. It has often been argued that these ratios are derived from the harmonic overtone series, which would explain their universality as a manifestation of "nature," rather than the perpetuation of a human tradition. If this were the case, however, then we would expect to find these same ratios employed throughout the natural world, in the vocalizations of all sorts of animals, and especially the songs of birds. But that is not the case. In fact, humans are the only animals who use them.

2. For a vigorously argued presentation of this version of multiregionalism, see Templeton 2002.

3. Estimations of genetic divergence dates are based on a technique known as "coalescence." For a definition and discussion of this topic, see the online Wikipedia article on *Coalescent Theory* (http://en.wikipedia.org/wiki/Coalescent_theory).

4. According to evolutionary biologists Richard Wrangham and Dale Peterson, as already quoted in Chapter Six, "Out of four thousand mammals and ten million or more other animal species, this suite of [violent and

warlike] behaviors is known only among chimpanzees and humans. . ."
(Wrangham and Peterson 1997:24).

Appendix A: The Musical Evidence

NB: This appendix presents a more detailed examination of the comparison between Pygmy and Bushmen music presented in Chapter One. Some of the material is technical and some requires a familiarity with music notation. No prior knowledge of Cantometrics is required.

Musicological Evidence

Based on earlier studies of Pygmy and/or Bushmen music,[1] supplemented by additional research of my own, I have compiled a list of musical commonalities shared by most Pygmy groups, both eastern and western, and at least some Bushmen groups. I will, where appropriate, associate each of these distinctive features with references to the following musical transcriptions:

See Figures A1 – A3 on blog, plus Figures A4 and A5 below

Mbuti--Amabeli-o-i-e

Figure A4: Mbuti Pygmy song, recorded by Hugh Tracey, transcribed by Victor Grauer.

Figure A5: Ju/'hoansi Bushmen female duet, — recording by Emmanuelle Olivier, transcribed by Victor Grauer.

1. An underlying rhythmic cycle that regularly repeats (see Figs. A1 – A5).

2. A basic "theme," sometimes heard, more often implied, that serves, along with the rhythmic cycle, as an underlying organizational element. (The "theme" is labeled as such in the first three figures.)

3. Interlocking or interweaving "contrapuntal" parts (evident in all examples).

4. The frequent presence of "hocketing" effects, in which melodic fragments in different voices closely interact with one another. (See for example, the interaction between parts A and C, and parts D and E, in Figure A1, the interplay of voices 1 – 4, in Figure A2, and the close interplay between the two voices of Figure A5.)

5. The crossing of parts, sometimes referred to as *Stimmtauch* (as most clearly exemplified in the relation between voices A and B in the first "measure" of Figure A1, the continual crossing of parts a and c in Figure A3, and throughout Figures A4 and A5).

6. Resultant effects, due to the close interchange of continually crossing parts.

7. Additive structure (see explanation below).

8. Pitch displacement. (Note, for example, the octave displacement of the two A's in voice C of Figure A1. Also, in Figure A3, where voice b displaces certain notes of voice a at intervals of a fourth or fifth.)

9. Temporal displacement. (I've added brackets to highlight displacements in Figures A1 and A2 — diagonal lines serve the same purpose in Figs. A3 and A4.)

10. Ostinato effects, based on the repetition of brief motives. (See parts D and E, in Figure A1; voices 1, 2, 7 and 8 of Figure A2; and the bracketed motives of Figure A4).

11. Improvisation (most clearly exemplified in the variations on the opening motive in Figure A4).

12. Disjunct melodic lines (see voices C and D of A1, and throughout A2, A3 and A5).

13. The dovetailing of parts, linking the ends of one phrase to the beginning of the next, to produce a continuous flow of sound.

14. Vocal polyrhythm (evident in Figs. A1, A2 and A3);

15. Polyrhythmic handclapping.

16. Predominance of "Nonsense" vocables, mostly vowel sounds (as in Figures A1 and A4).

17. Little to no embellishment.

18. Precisely defined rhythms, with no trace of rubato.

19. Yodeling.

20. Polyphonic vocalizing.

21. Heterophonic vocalizing.

22. The conflation of polyphony and heterophony (see below).

23. Little to no distinction between melodic and harmonic intervals. (As is evident from all five examples, any scale tones can be either horizontally or vertically juxtaposed.)

24. Secundal dissonance. (See for example, the fourth beat of the first "measure" of Figure A1, where pitch classes c, g, d and e are sounded together, or the many instances in Figure A2 where g and f sound together).

25. The encoding of multiple parts in monodies, and, conversely, monodies derived from multipart models. (In certain repertoires, as reported in Kisliuk 1998 for the *Aka* Pygmies, and England 1995 and Olivier 1998 for the *Ju'hoansi* Bushmen, multiple parts are frequently derived from melodies, often transmitted via dreams or trance states. In addition, solo performances can be derived from multipart models. In both traditions, therefore, the same songs can be realized in either solo or multipart form.)

Only nine items (1, 2, 10, 11, 14, 15, 17, 18, 20) can be considered characteristic of African music generally. The remaining sixteen are atypical for any but Pygmy and Bushmen groups.[2]

Several transcriptions of Pygmy and Bushmen polyphonic vocalizing were systematically analyzed and compared in my paper, "Concept, Style and Structure in the Music of the African Pygmies and Bushmen" (Grauer 2009). At the heart of this effort was a demonstration that the many similarities that seem so striking to the ear are based on deeply rooted conceptual and structural affinities that are not always immediately apparent. To better understand what this means, let us take a closer look at some of the features listed above.

According to Michelle Kisliuk (1998),

[t]he first line of melody [as presented in her transcriptions of Aka Pygmy songs] is what I call the "theme" . . . a melodic phrase on which the song and most of its associated variations are loosely based. This theme, which repeats cyclically, provides an underlying time line and a harmonic frame for the song, whether or not the theme itself is actually voiced. (p. 112)

The existence of a remarkably similar structural concept underlying the singing of the Ju/'hoansi Bushmen is apparent from the writings of Nicholas England (1967, 1995), and a collaborative study by Susanne Fürniss and Emmanuelle Olivier (1997, 1999). As in Pygmy music, such themes are associated with a continually repeating cyclic structure, resembling what would, in Western classical music, be called "variations on a ground."

Another, especially significant, similarity is the "additive" manner in which the music is organized, also fundamental to both traditions yet only rarely found elsewhere, where anyone at any time can join in to add his or her own independent voice to the overall texture, with the result that there are usually as many unique parts as there are performers. Additive form reflects an important aspect of social structure: independent and creative participation in many aspects of life, not only music, is expected of everyone present.

One of the most characteristic and significant aspects of Pygmy/Bushmen style is the use of a technique often referred to as "hocket." This term, coined during the Middle Ages in Europe, literally means "hiccup," a derisive reference to a practice popular in the church music of the time. Strictly speaking, *hocket* can be defined as the tossing of a single melodic line back and forth between two or more performers. In extreme cases, as in a bell choir, or certain African wind ensembles, each performer plays only one or two notes. The term is usually extended to include more complex practices, such as the tightly coordinated polyphonic/heterophonic interlocking of brief, complementary motives, as found in both Medieval hocket and the contrapuntal vocalizations of both Pygmies and Bushmen. While hocketed

253

interplay is not uncommon in African instrumental music, it is relatively rare in the vocalizations of any but Pygmy or Bushmen groups.

Possibly the most interesting and unusual common feature of both traditions hinges on a practice known as *heterophony*. A *polyphonic* performance can be characterized as made up of tonally (and sometimes also rhythmically) independent parts, singing in harmony; on the contrary, when everyone sings in *unison*, all voices perform exactly the same melody with no harmonization at all. The term *heterophony* is used to describe a situation somewhere between the two, where each voice or instrument presents essentially the same melody, but each in its own way, with a certain degree of rhythmic independence. In some cases one part performs the basic tune while another performs a more highly embellished version; in other cases, all parts can be regarded as variants of an underlying melody that may never be heard in its simplest form. Harmonies can sometimes occur incidentally, but they can usually be explained on the basis of variation or, in some cases, temporal displacement, rather than tonal independence.

What we find in a great many Pygmy and Bushmen performances is an extremely unusual and indeed remarkable tendency to *conflate* both polyphony and heterophony in a manner difficult to describe, not always easy to hear, but clearly demonstrable through musical analysis (see Grauer 2009). Pygmy/Bushmen heterophony can easily be mistaken for polyphony, since two or more versions of the same melody or melodic segment can be precisely coordinated, yet independent in terms of both rhythm and melodic contour.

Fig. A5 (see above) illustrates the manner in which polyphony and heterophony can be conflated in a single performance:

Ju/'hoansi Lion Song
Recorded by Emmanuelle Olivier
Transcribed by Victor Grauer

(Gradually moves up one half-step)

The first four measures are polyphonic, i.e., the two interlocking lines are completely independent, both rhythmically and tonally. The following two measures, however, represent the sort of thing Emmanuelle Olivier has characterized as "the illusion of polyphony."[3] While the two voices may seem independent and are precisely coordinated rhythmically, they sing, for the most part, the same notes, either in unison or octaves, as indicated by the vertical lines I've added. Very similar types of contrapuntal interaction, both polyphonic and heterophonic, are commonly found in Pygmy music as well — as indicated, for example, by the vertical lines and brackets in Figure A1. Ultimately, what we discover through careful analysis of various examples from both Pygmy and Bushmen repertoires is that the traditional opposition between polyphony and heterophony, i.e., music conceived either "vertically" or "horizontally," is far from absolute.

With regard to this dichotomy, a very different interpretation has been offered by Susanne Fürniss and Emmanuelle Olivier, for whom "the conception that the Ju/'hoansi have of their music is radically opposite to the Aka's" (1999:201), since for them the contrapuntal vocalizations of the Aka Pygmies are truly polyphonic, "based upon four constituent parts," while, for the Ju'hoansi Bushmen, "counterpoint is generated . . . from a [single] constituent part, i.e., a monody."[4] This constituent part is usually performed simultaneously (with variations) in three tessituras." Among the Aka "the superimposition of the four constituent parts ipso facto gives rise to a contrapuntal model," while among the Ju'hoansi, "counterpoint is constructed on the basis of a single melodic line through the procedures of rhythmic delay, imitation and transposition by the interval of a fourth and fifth above and below" (Ibid.:129–31). Since she perceives Bushmen multipart music as fundamentally monophonic, with all parts either heterophonic variants or rhythmic displacements of a basic theme, Olivier has characterized their group vocalizations as producing "the illusion of polyphony" (Olivier 1998).

Puzzled by what struck me as a very strange conclusion, yet intrigued by some of the genuine insights expressed in their writings, I decided to conduct a thorough review (Grauer 2009), which led to the following conclusion:

> The opposition posed by Fürniss and Olivier with respect to music conceived either polyphonically or linearly represents, as I see it, a meaningful, if misapplied, insight. An axis of opposition exists, but as we have seen, it cannot be placed *between* the musical practices of the Pygmies and Bushmen, since both conceptions influence the practice of both groups. The opposition must therefore be placed

among them, as two aspects of a musical universe common to both (p. 418).

As can be easily demonstrated through study of the transcriptions reproduced in Figures A1-A5, heterophony *and* polyphony are typically conflated in the music of *both* groups, in a complex, highly idiosyncratic manner common to both, implying an even closer bond than had previously been suspected.

For example, the uppermost vocal part of the Aka Pygmy song "Makala," as transcribed by Michelle Kisliuk (Fig. A1), is labeled "Theme" and is in fact the basis for most of the other parts. While voice "C" may look like an independent polyphonic part, it is actually a heterophonic variant of the theme, all pitches being either in unison or octaves with the upper voice, as indicated by the short vertical lines I've added. Voice B also appears, at first glance, to be a completely independent part, yet, as indicated by the brackets I've added, it is based, note for note, on rhythmic displacements of segments from the principal theme. Voice A combines independent polyphony and heterophony, while voice E simply repeats the first four pitches of the second segment of the theme. If it weren't for voice D, the only completely independent part, this would be an excellent example of what Olivier would call "the illusion of polyphony" — only "Makala" is a Pygmy song.

Examining the Ju/'hoansi Bushmen "Eland Song – Great," as transcribed by Nicholas England (Figure A3), we do indeed, as predicted by Olivier, find both rhythmic displacement (as indicated by the diagonals) and note for note heterophony (as indicated by the short verticals). Compare, however, with Figure A4, an Mbuti Pygmy "canon" in which very similar displacements (and, indeed, very similar melodic lines) are found. Moreover, the lowest line of the Eland song does not conform to Olivier's model, as it is a completely independent polyphonic part. And if there are any doubts regarding the ability of the Ju/'hoansi to both conceptualize and perform true polyphony, they will be dispelled by Figure A2, a transcription of a Ju/'hoansi performance consisting of eight polyphonically independent parts. For an especially clear example of the manner in which polyphony and heterophony can be conflated in a Bushmen performance, see Figure A5.

While Fürniss and Olivier deserve considerable credit for revealing many important aspects of the traditions they have studied, the conclusion they have drawn regarding a "radical opposition" between Pgymy and Bushmen music is not supported by comparative analysis. No such analysis is even attempted in either of their comparative studies, nor is there more than a passing reference in either to the extensive research of Nicholas England, whose book-length study of Ju/'hoansi music (1995) demonstrates the full complexity of Bushmen vocalizing, which, for him, is "polyphonic at its very basis" (England 1967:65).

According to England, "some singers—any of them—may contribute a countermelody that is truly independent of the basic theme(s) of a piece. There is always one such melody; often there are two, and sometimes more." Additionally, in certain other types of song, "many different melodies are meshed together to form the contrapuntal fabric . . . A desideratum is that each singer invent her own line within the framework of the period . . . Commonly a singer will sing a melody that is not being sung by the women to her right and left in the circle" (1995:225). Clearly, polyphony and monophony are conflated in *both* traditions, constituting yet another especially compelling *affinity* between the two groups.

Evidence from Cantometrics

The Cantometric coding system, conceived by Alan Lomax and developed by Lomax and myself in the summer of 1961, represented a profound break with the methods then prevalent among students of both Western and non-Western music (Lomax 1962, Lomax et al. 1968). Unlike those methods, focused on subjective evaluation of the various tonal and rhythmic components of a musical "composition," Cantometrics represents a deliberate simplification, emphasizing certain very broad, clearly audible parameters of musical *performance*. While Cantometrics is hardly a complete and definitive measure of all aspects of music, the Cantometric approach provides a systematic, relatively objective, and reasonably consistent quantitative method for the comparative statistical analysis of traditional vocal music worldwide, based on attentive listening rather than note by note analysis.

The better to understand both the Cantometric method and the manner in which Cantometrics can help to clarify the relation between Pygmy and Bushmen music, let us compare recorded excerpts and Cantometric profiles of two typical performances, an Aka Pygmy divining song, *Diye* (Audio Example One), as recorded by Simha Arom, and a Ju'/hoansi Bushman *Giraffe Dance* (Audio Example Four — see Chapter One for references.)

I will focus only on some of the most significant parameters of the Cantometric representation of the Aka song:

Diye -- Aka divining song

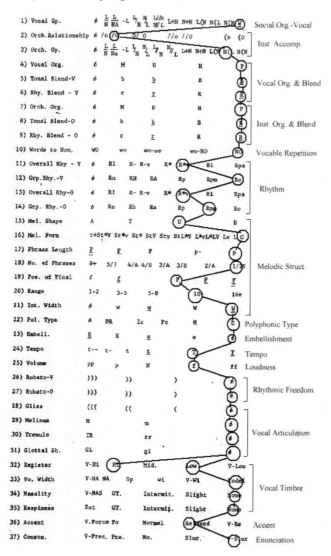

Figure A6: Cantometric Profile of Aka "Divining Song, Diye."

What the first line tells us is that the "social organization" of this performance, i.e., the manner in which the singers relate to one another, is primarily characterized by *interlocking* parts (W), coded at the rightmost extreme. Pygmy and Bushmen music is typically performed in this interlocking or interwoven manner, which has sometimes been described as a form of "counterpoint," i.e., the simultaneous interrelation of rhythmically

258

independent parts. Most African singing is characterized by various forms of antiphony, popularly known as "call and response."

Line four is coded "P" for polyphony. For many years musicologists assumed that polyphony (i.e., singing or playing in harmonically distinct parts) was a late development in the evolution of music, originating in Western Europe during the Middle Ages. It was assumed that any other instances to be found among folk, ethnic or tribal peoples must be due to the influence of Western "classical" or religious music. But this long cherished assumption was completely shattered as ethnomusicologists discovered more and more examples among indigenous peoples essentially free from outside contact. There is no longer any question but that Pygmy and Bushmen polyphony is indigenous and not in any way due to outside influence.

Lines five and six encode the degree of vocal blend along a five-point scale, from completely uncoordinated singing, on the left, to maximally blended, on the right. For both tonal blend, on line five and rhythmic blend, on line six, our Pygmy song has been coded as maximal. One of the most remarkable aspects of Pygmy and Bushmen vocalizing is the degree to which all participants match their voices with one another and synchronize rhythmically with extraordinary precision.

Line ten is not concerned with music per se, but encodes the degree to which the music is sung to meaningful words. Again, we have a five-point scale, with the most "wordy" texts on the left and the least wordy, or completely "nonsensical," on the right. "Wordiness" is measured by the relative number of unique vocables or vocable phrases in the text, so that highly repetitive texts, and/or texts characterized mostly by "nonsense" syllables will be coded on the right. If you listen carefully, you can hear that our Pygmy example consists exclusively of nonsense vocables, mostly open vowels such as "oh" and "ah." Again the heavy use of such vocables, with relatively little or no meaningful text, is typical of both Pygmy and Bushmen singing.

Lines 16 through 18 tell us, in a nutshell, that our Pygmy song appears to be organized as a kind of "canon," "round," or "hocket" ("C" on line 16), characterized by the continual interweaving of one or two short "phrases" or motives (lines 17 & 18). It's important to interject a word of caution at this point, because Cantometrics is deliberately designed to provide a simplified impression of the way in which a performance is organized, as opposed to what could be determined from a systematic analysis. If it were necessary for the coder to analyze every song in detail, each coding would take far too long, and the many problems attendant on precisely categorizing each performance within hundreds of possible structures would make comparative study all but impossible. What Cantometrics tells us is what the general impressions of the coder were, given the (necessary) limitations posed by the coding system itself. Suffice it to say that the Cantometric representation of the musical structure of a great many Pygmy and Bushmen songs is a crude simplification of what is in fact a highly intricate structure, in which short motives can not only be repeated but freely varied, within the context of a larger melodic-rhythmic cycle that uniquely defines each song. Ultimately, as should be clear, Cantometrics must be regarded as an essentially informal, heuristic methodology, which should, whenever possible, be supplemented by more detailed analysis (see above).

Line 20 concerns the overall vocal range of each performance along a five point scale. "Diye" has been coded as 10+, indicating a range roughly between one and two octaves. As indicated by line 21, which measures "interval width," the distance from one tone to the next within any given part is typically very wide, ranging from leaps of a third, to fourths, fifths, sixths and octaves.

Lines 24 and 25 encode tempo and loudness, according to six point and five point scales, respectively. In this case "Diye" has been coded as both moderately fast (T) and somewhat loud ("f" stands for *forte*). Note that Cantometrics makes no attempt to define either parameter objectively, in terms of either the metronome or the decibel meter. Metronome markings are meaningful only in the context of notated music, and the decibel meter will give very different results depending on the conditions under which each performance was recorded. Since both measures must necessarily be subjective, there will always be some room for disagreement and, thus, a certain amount of inconsistency.

Lines 26 through 31 are all coded at the rightmost end of the scale, which in these cases is the null value. In other words, "Diye" lacks any degree of rhythmic freedom (i.e., "rubato"), glissando, melisma, tremulo or glottal shake. This, coupled with the null coding on line 23, "Embellishment," tells us that this performance, like so many other examples of Pygmy/Bushmen style and, indeed, so many other types of African music generally, is unusually straightforward, clear and "clean," both rhythmically and vocally. The impression is reinforced by lines 34 and 35, where both nasality and rasp are also coded as absent.

Line 33 represents "Vocal Width," or the degree to which the throat is either constricted or relaxed while singing. In this case what might look at first glance like a simple six-point scale is apparently complicated by the inclusion of the term "Yodel." Since true yodeling (as opposed to falsetto) is possible only if the throat is extremely open and relaxed, we decided to include it on this line as an extreme case. Wide open voices that do not yodel are coded as point five on this scale (*V-Wi*), while yodeling voices are coded as point six (*Yodel*). That "Diye" must be coded at this extreme is evident from the recording, where yodeling is clearly recognizable from the outset. Along with *interlock*, coded as point 13 (*W*) on line one, *Yodel* can be regarded as an especially distinctive characteristic of both Pygmy and Bushmen vocalizing.

We may now compare the Pygmy and Bushmen profiles side by side:

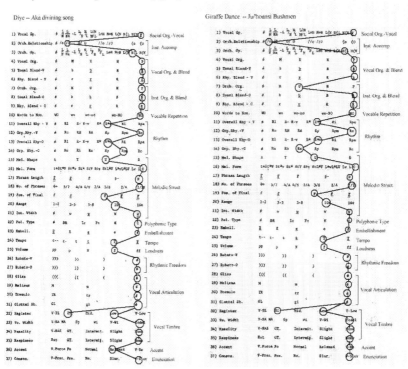

Figure A7: Pygmy and Bushmen Profiles Displayed Side by Side

The auditory impression of stylistic similarity is supported by the strong visual resemblance of the two profiles. Indeed, the songs are coded identically on 33 out of 37 lines. The presence of interlocking and yodel in "Giraffe Dance," as coded on lines 1 and 33, should be evident from the outset of the recording – as in "Diye," the yodeled parts interweave fluidly and seamlessly. Closer listening will reveal that, like the Pygmy example, the Bushmen performance is characterized by a high degree of tonal blend, which makes it almost impossible to distinguish the voices from one another, in addition to remarkably precise rhythmic coordination. As is clearly evident from the recording, the text of the Bushmen example also consists exclusively of "nonsense" vocables, as coded on line ten, employing most of

261

the same vowels as in "Diye." Melodically, the "Giraffe Dance," like "Diye," is coded as "C" on line 16, with a high degree of repetition evident in both recordings. The Bushmen voices, in terms of both articulation and timbre, are coded identically to those of the Pygmies in literally all instances, as evidenced by the array of "null" cases we see in lines 23, 26-31 and 34-35. The strong similarities in terms of timbre, vocal fluidity, yodel, clarity of articulation, etc. should be strikingly apparent to the attentive listener.

Tables A1 and A2 summarize the Pygmy and Bushmen samples as a whole (45 and 20 songs, respectively)[5]:

Table A1: Cantometric Percentage Table, African Pygmies
(Baka, Biaka, Bedzan, Binga, Mbuti)

(N. B.: The percentage figures on each row will, in some cases, total more than 100%, since it is sometimes necessary to select more than one point for a single parameter.)

		1	2	3	4	5	6	7	8	9	10	11	12	13
1	Scl Org V-Gp		4.44%		4.44%		2.22%	2.22%	4.44%	2.22%	2.22%	11.11%	2.22%	82.22%
2	Scl Vcl-Orch	26.67%	22.22%	31.11%						6.67%			8.89%	6.67%
3	Scl Org Orch	26.67%	2.22%			6.67%	22.22%					11.11%	31.11%	
4	Msc Org Vocl				4.44%									95.56%
5	Tonal Blend	4.44%								15.56%				80.00%
6	Ryth. Blend	4.44%			2.22%						2.22%			91.11%
7	Msc OrgOrch	26.67%			2.22%			15.56%						55.56%
8	Orch. Tone	28.89%							4.44%		11.11%			55.56%
9	RhyCrdnOrch	28.89%							2.22%		4.44%			64.44%
10	Reptn of Txt				2.22%			6.67%			20.00%			73.33%
11	Vocal Rythm						66.67%			26.67%		6.67%		2.22%
12	Ryth Rln Vcl	4.44%		11.11%						6.67%		4.44%		75.56%
13	Orch. Rythm	26.67%		22.22%			35.56%			17.78%		8.89%		
14	RythRln Orch	28.89%		13.33%				20.00%		6.67%		33.33%		2.22%
15	Mel. Shape									82.22%				26.67%
16	Mel. Form							2.22%	2.22%		2.22%	11.11%	6.67%	80.00%
17	Phrase Lngth							13.33%			28.89%			66.67%
18	No. Phrases											11.11%		88.89%

#	Feature	1	2	3	4	5	6	7	8	9	10	11	12	13
19	Pos. Fnl Ton	42.22%			6.67%					37.78%		11.11%		22.22%
20	Melodic Rnge				4.44%			20.00%			51.11%			24.44%
21	Intrvl Width							22.22%			31.11%			51.11%
22	Polyphnc Typ	6.67%		2.22%			2.22%		6.67%		4.44%			84.44%
23	Embellishmnt													97.78%
24	Tempo					20.00%				62.22%		17.78%		
25	Volume				20.00%			31.11%			53.33%			
26	Vocal Rubato	2.22%								2.22%				95.56%
27	Orch. Rubato													100.00%
28	Glissando	15.56%				8.89%				17.78%				57.78%
29	Melisma	57.78%						15.56%						28.89%
30	Tremolo													100.00%
31	Glottal	13.33%						6.67%						80.00%
32	Register	11.11%			62.22%			46.67%			44.44%			11.11%
33	Vocal Width						2.22%		8.89%		37.78%			60.00%
34	Nasality				2.22%			17.78%			15.56%			64.44%
35	Rasp				13.33%			11.11%			31.11%			55.56%
36	Accent				11.11%			13.33%			55.56%			28.89%
37	Enunciation							2.22%			22.22%			77.78%

Table A2: Cantometric Percentage Table, Bushmen (Ju/'hoansi)

#	Feature	1	2	3	4	5	6	7	8	9	10	11	12	13
1	Scl Org V-Gp		15.00%				5.00%	5.00%				5.00%		75.00%
2	Scl Vcl-Orch	20.00%	25.00%	25.00%					10.00%	10.00%			10.00%	5.00%
3	Scl Org Orch	20.00%	20.00%				40.00%						15.00%	10.00%
4	Msc Org Vocl				15.00%						5.00%			85.00%
5	Tonal Blend	15.00%			5.00%						5.00%			75.00%
6	Rythmc Blend	15.00%			5.00%									80.00%
7	Msc Org Orch	20.00%			5.00%		55.00%							20.00%
8	Orch. Tone	40.00%									5.00%			55.00%
9	Rhy Crdn-Orch	40.00%					5.00%							55.00%

10	Reptn of Txt				5.00%							15.00%		80.00%
11	Vocal Rythm						25.00%			40.00%		20.00%		20.00%
12	Ryth Rln Vcl	15.00%		10.00%		5.00%						30.00%		65.00%
13	Orch. Rythm	20.00%		20.00%		5.00%	25.00%			35.00%				5.00%
14	Ryth Rln Orch	40.00%		45.00%				10.00%				10.00%		5.00%
15	Melodic Shape									85.00%				20.00%
16	Melodic Form	25.00%										15.00%	5.00%	75.00%
17	Phrase Lngth				20.00%			15.00%				35.00%		55.00%
18	No. Phrases	25.00%										5.00%		85.00%
19	Pos. Fnl Ton	30.00%			15.00%					45.00%		5.00%		15.00%
20	Melodic Rnge				10.00%			10.00%				50.00%		30.00%
21	Intrvl Width											15.00%		85.00%
22	Polyphnc Typ	15.00%							10.00%					75.00%
23	Embellishmnt													100.00%
24	Tempo	5.00%				30.00%				40.00%		25.00%		
25	Volume				55.00%			35.00%				5.00%		5.00%
26	Vocal Rubato	20.00%												85.00%
27	Orch. Rubato	5.00%												100.00%
28	Glissando	30.00%								20.00%				50.00%
29	Melisma	30.00%						10.00%						60.00%
30	Tremolo													100.00%
31	Glottal	25.00%						10.00%						65.00%
32	Register	15.00%			75.00%			35.00%				65.00%		10.00%
33	Vocal Width			5.00%			5.00%		10.00%			20.00%		75.00%
34	Nasality				5.00%			15.00%				5.00%		75.00%
35	Rasp	5.00%						5.00%				30.00%		60.00%
36	Accent				15.00%							40.00%		45.00%
37	Enunciation											5.00%		95.00%

Table A3 summarizes the Cantometric codings for all non-foragers (farmers and/or herders) in the sample for Sub-Saharan Africa (875 songs):

Table A3: Cantometric Percentage Table, African Farmer-Herder Populations

		1	2	3	4	5	6	7	8	9	10	11	12	13
1	Scl Org V-Gp	0.23%	18.86%	0.34%	13.37%	2.63%	6.51%	2.40%	21.49%	3.20%	29.94%	10.06%	8.11%	10.06%
2	Scl Vcl-Orch	25.37%	24.80%	17.26%		3.77%	0.69%		6.40%	1.71%			10.51%	12.34%
3	Scl Org Orch	25.37%	18.40%		0.34%	14.97%	20.91%	1.37%	0.80%	0.11%	0.11%	4.46%	10.86%	3.66%
4	Msc Org Vocl	0.57%			20.11%			28.00%			5.49%			50.17%
5	Tonal Blend	20.00%			2.51%			16.80%			28.00%			34.29%
6	Rythmc Blend	20.34%			3.09%			9.14%			23.54%			45.71%
7	Msc Org Orch	25.26%			9.60%			24.00%			0.34%			41.03%
8	Orch. Tone	43.43%			0.91%			8.23%			12.91%			33.60%
9	Rhy Crdn-Orch	44.00%			0.57%			2.63%			11.31%			41.94%
10	Reptn of Txt	5.60%			18.86%			38.29%			30.74%			9.14%
11	Vocal Rythm			1.03%		0.11%	56.80%			7.54%		28.23%		10.63%
12	Ryth Rln Vcl	20.34%		60.23%	0.11%	3.43%		6.63%		2.29%		1.71%		12.00%
13	Orch. Rythm	25.37%		13.37%		0.11%	48.46%			7.77%		5.94%		2.17%
14	RythRln Orch	44.34%		14.17%		0.69%		14.29%		11.54%		15.54%		1.83%
15	Mel.Shape	8.11%				0.23%				68.23%				35.31%
16	Mel. Form	9.26%	10.06%	4.34%	1.71%	4.69%	6.74%	13.14%	6.74%	3.66%	22.51%	12.34%	9.71%	6.63%
17	Phrase Lngth	2.29%			7.54%			33.26%			53.03%			29.49%
18	No. Phrases	22.74%		3.54%		3.66%	1.94%		2.97%	1.71%		21.37%		50.74%
19	Pos. Fnl Ton	50.86%			31.89%					18.86%		5.71%		2.40%
20	Melodic Rnge	1.26%			17.49%			44.80%			31.20%			4.80%
21	Intrvl Width	1.37%			9.03%			47.66%			42.40%			7.43%
22	Poly. Type	49.14%		3.66%			7.77%		17.26%		9.49%			16.00%
23	Embellishmnt	1.49%			3.77%			11.20%			18.97%			66.17%
24	Tempo	0.23%		3.77%		13.26%				48.23%		35.77%		3.31%
25	Volume	1.71%			17.26%			46.74%			38.17%			5.71%
26	Vocal Rubato	9.60%				4.80%				12.57%				75.89%

#												
27	Orch. Rubato	3.43%			0.46%					4.80%		92.57%
28	Glissando	4.34%			21.14%			0.11%		46.74%		28.00%
29	Melisma	10.51%					32.91%					57.71%
30	Tremolo	2.51%					8.11%					89.83%
31	Glottal	4.34%					20.00%					76.34%
32	Register	6.29%		34.86%			67.66%				37.03%	4.23%
33	Vocal Width	1.26%	15.20%			20.11%			51.54%		29.37%	5.03%
34	Nasality	9.26%		35.89%			33.14%				16.57%	13.49%
35	Rasp	6.51%		35.31%			38.74%				15.20%	11.66%
36	Accent	4.23%		31.09%			46.86%				22.86%	3.77%
37	Enunciation	0.34%		7.43%			27.20%				60.11%	11.89%

Note that the percentage tables for both Pygmies and Bushmen (A1 and A2) are characterized by strong modes — 60% or more for the great majority of parameters — consistent with a high degree of stylistic homogeneity within each group. The percentage table representing non-foragers (A3) is, on the other hand, far more evenly distributed, with relatively few modes of 60% or higher, consistent with a range of different styles.

A comparison of modal profiles drawn from the above percentage tables is shown in Figure A8:

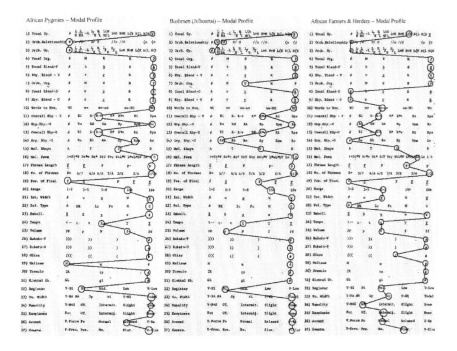

Figure A8 – Modal Profiles for African Pygmies, Bushmen and Farmer-Herders Compared (based on Tables A1-A3)

The modal profiles representing Pygmies and Bushmen are in strong accord, with identical modes for 26 of 37 lines, and significant differences on only five: 7, 14, 19, 25 and 29. Note as well the strong similarities between the profiles for the individual songs, as presented in Figure A7, and the respective modal profiles. On the other hand, the modal profile representing farmers and herders is contrastive with both the Pygmy and Bushmen profiles, with only 15 points of identity with the Pygmy profile and 12 with the Bushmen; and significant differences on 12 and 14 points, respectively. When we add the relative lack of strong modes in the farmer-herder sample, the contrast with the Pygmy and Bushmen samples becomes even greater.

Some of the most important differences: line 1 – P/B voices coded mostly as interlocked (82% and 75%); Farmer-Herders (F/H) coded mostly as leader-chorus antiphony, with only 10% interlocked; line 10 – the great majority of P/B vocalizations contain little to no meaningful text (73% and 80% coded as NO), while the mode for F/H is at the midpoint for this parameter (wo-no); line 16 – P/B coded mostly as C (interwoven, short motives – 80% and 75%), while F/H sing in a variety of different forms, with the mode at simple litany (LV – 23%); line 20 – vocal range for P/B (a 9th or more) is significantly greater than that for F/H (fifth to an octave); line 21 – P/B characterized by

267

large interval widths, of a fourth, fifth or octave (*W*), while the mode for F/H is diatonic (*w*); line 22 – the great majority of P/B songs are coded as contrapuntal (C – 84% and 75%), compared with only 16% of F/H songs – many other F/H performances (49%) are solo or unison; line 33 – the great majority of P/B songs are characterized by yodeling (60% and 75%), compared with only 5% for F/H.

As is apparent from Table A4, the two most distinctive Cantometrically encoded features of Pygmy and Bushmen singing, interlock and yodel, are combined far more commonly among African foragers than any other region in the worldwide sample:

Table A4: Interlock and yodel combined in the same performance, by world region.

	Sample Size	% Interlock & Yodel Combined
AFRICAN FORAGERS	95	39%
MELANESIA	524	3%
BLACK AFRICA	1335	2%
SOUTH AMERICA	284	1%
EUROPE	842	1%
MALAYSIA	552	1%
AMERICAN HUNTERS	355	1%
POLYNESIA	197	1%
WESTERN ASIA	699	0%
EASTERN ASIA	427	0%
AUSTRALIAN FORAGERS	43	0%
SIBERIA	121	0%
AMERICAN VILLAGERS	124	0%
NUCLEAR AMERICA	146	0%

(NB: among African foragers, only the five Pygmy groups included in this survey, the Ju'hoansi Bushmen, and the Mikea foragers of Madagascar have been coded as vocalizing with interlocking and/or yodel. Neither interlock nor yodel has been found in any of the other foraging groups: "Twa" Pygmies; "Khwe" Bushmen; Hadza; Sandawe; El Molo – though our sample for each of these groups is small and the picture could change in future. For more on the world distribution of interlock and yodel, see Grauer 2007.)

1. The following works were consulted in the compiling of this list: Rouget & Grimaud 1956 (accompanying pamphlet); Lomax 1959, 1962, 1968; England 1967, 1995; Frisbie 1971; Arom 1976, 1991; Olivier & Fürniss 1997, 1999; Locke 1996; Kisliuk 1998; Fürniss 2006.

2. While all of the most distinctive traits can commonly be found in most Pygmy and at least some Bushmen groups, some can also be found among other African groups as well, but to a limited degree and only under certain circumstances. For an analysis of the distribution of elements of Pygmy/Bushmen style among African farmers and herders, see Grauer 2009:421-422.

3. My observations regarding the conflation of polyphony and heterophony owe much to an insight of Emmanuelle Olivier, who has stressed the significance of precisely coordinated "contrapuntal" heterophony in Bushmen singing, and the manner in which it can produce the "illusion" of polyphonic interplay (Olivier 1998). (While Olivier has argued that Pygmy music is organized in a completely different manner, there are in fact many examples of Pygmy singing in which very similar effects can be found – for a discussion of our differences on this matter see below, in the text.)

4. Literally, "counterpoint is generated single from a constituent part, i.e., a monody," which appears to be a misprint. I have rearranged this sentence in the interest of clarity.

5. The Pygmy table represents the Baka, Biaka, Bedzan, Binga and Mbuti Pygmies of Central Africa (45 songs in all) and the Bushmen table represents the Ju/'hoansi Bushmen of the Kalahari Desert (20 songs). Although "Twa" Pygmies and "Khwe" Bushmen are also represented in the Cantometric sample, both groups are known to have been assimilated with Bantu groups for many years, as reflected in both the historical and genetic evidence, and were therefore excluded from this survey. As far as I've been able to determine, the music of both groups shows strong Bantu influence and little if any relation to Pygmy/Bushmen style.

Appendix B: A Musical Tree

Some years ago, in order to get a clearer sense of how the various bits and pieces of musical evidence relate both to one another and to the overall historical picture as it was emerging from the genetic evidence, I managed to put together a hypothetical phylogenetic tree of musical style. The tree represented my own best thinking thus far, based to some extent on the Cantometric data, but also on other aspects of musical style of which I was aware. There are many years of research behind this, so I do think it's meaningful — but it is also somewhat subjective, in the sense that it is *not* automatically produced by the raw data itself. I'm not sure how accurate it is, and it will almost certainly require alteration over time, but for now it will, hopefully, convey some sense of my thinking regarding the musical "big picture":

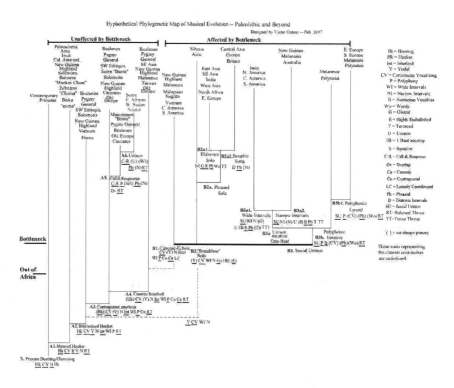

Figure B1 – Phylogenetic Map of Musical Evolution – Grauer

Note the column on the right, a listing of various musical characteristics, mostly drawn from Cantometrics but not all. In the map I treat these as analogous to genetic markers, roughly the equivalent of mutations. All

270

"haplogroups" beginning with the letter A represent styles or style variants originating in Africa and surviving more or less intact in other parts of the world to this day. All those beginning with "B" represent styles that appear to have originated as the result of the bottleneck event considered in Chapters Nine and Ten.

Root and Branches

At the lower left, you'll find the "root" of the tree and some of the earlier branches. Since it is customary when designing genetic trees to root the tree in the lineage of the closest primate (usually the Chimpanzee), I've considered that possibility for music and discovered that in fact there *might* be some basis for rooting my tree in the "musical" culture of certain primates. This aspect is of course an extremely speculative, but also, I think, quite interesting, feature of the tree.

Moving upward and to the right, we find the *human* root of the tree, labeled "A1," or "shouted hocket." A more complete description of each style family (or musical "haplogroup") is provided in the abbreviations located just below each label. The key to these abbreviations can be found in the rightmost column. Under "Shouted Hocket," we find the following markers: Hk CV It Y N RT. Hk stands for "hocket," which I've already defined as a musical procedure in which an idea, usually a brief motive, is broken up between two or more parts, often but not always dovetailed with one another. CV stands for "continuous vocalizing," i.e., the production of a continuous stream of sound, with no pauses and no coordination between breathing and any aspect of musical structure, e.g, phrasing. CV tends to sound like the musical equivalent of a run-on sentence. Where more than one performer is involved, the breathing is usually staggered and we hear no pauses. If there is only one performer, the musical flow is often interrupted by audible gasps for breath at arbitrary points in the melody.

"It" stands for the continual iteration of a single note. Y stands for yodel. N stands for the frequent use of "nonsense" vocables. Since in many cases we can't be sure if any given vocable has a meaning or not, Cantometrics defines "nonsense" largely in terms of repetition. (If the same vocable or set of vocables is regulary repeated it is coded as "nonsense" regardless of whether or not it might carry some meaning.) RT stands for "relaxed throat," as opposed to TT, the tense throated vocalizing so characteristic of Middle Eastern and East Asiatic singing. These six traits are by no means the only ones characterizing shouted hocket, but they do seem among the most prominent and easily identified. However, I still need to explain why I called this "shouted hocket" in the first place and why it's located at the root of our musical tree. Since there's no substitute for actually listening, here's an example, from the CD set "Musical Anthology of the Aka Pygmies," recorded by Simha Arom : *Aka esime* (Audio Example 56).

This is a brief example from the end of a much longer track, of a type of Aka vocalizing called (according to Michelle Kisliuk) "esime," which, as she describes it in her excellent book *Seize the Dance*, functions as a kind of interlude between songs. As such, it is often overlooked and has, in fact, only rarely been recorded. What particularly interests me are the places where the shouting is tossed rapidly, and rhythmically, back and forth between the "leader" and the group. Compare with an example of a similar practice from the Dani people of the Eastern Highlands of New Guinea: *Dani Hocket* (Audio Example 55). This is, in fact, a type of vocalizing found quite commonly among certain indigenous groups, in Africa, New Guinea, Island Melanesia and elsewhere. I think it could be important, first because of its worldwide distribution among so many peoples whose ancestry might well go back to the original "Out of Africa" migration; second, because it's easy to see how it could be the prototype for the more intricate varieties of contrapuntal hocket we find so often among the same groups; and third, because of its striking similarity to certain types of primate vocalization.

If you follow the vertical line upward to the list of tribal groups at the top, you'll find the groups for whom I have examples, either in the Cantometric database, or from additional listening experience (usually both), which vocalize in some version of the "shouted hocket" style. That style may not be the most important or most commonly found in those groups, but it is known to be at least present among all of them.

Let's now move up to the next branch of the tree, "A2. Interlocked Hocket." You'll notice that one of the "Shouted Hocket" traits is missing: It, or iteration, which is characteristic only of the simplest type of hocket, which lacks any melodic structure. Instead, we have, in addition to all the other traits, some new ones: Int, for "interlock," WI, for "wide intervals," and P, for "polyphonic."

The Bottleneck Effect

Looking more generally at the tree as a whole, it's important to recognize that it is broken down into two different segments, the first labeled "Unaffected by Bottleneck," the second "Affected by Bottleneck." This fundamental break makes my tree very different from any other I'm aware of. We have a strong tendency to think of evolution in terms of gradual change, but there are very good reasons to see the evolution of early music in a different light.

Note, by the way, that all the African groups are located in the leftmost section, "Unaffected by Bottleneck." There are no African groups in the rightmost section. In my view, this is an extremely important aspect of this tree. Note also that there are many non-African indigenous (or "folk") groups along with the African ones listed at the top of the leftmost section. As I see it, the close connection of these groups with variants of Pygmy/Bushmen style (haplogroups A1 through A4) is possibly of great significance, as they most likely, as I see it, represent survivals from the musical practice of the original "Out of Africa" migrants.

Music from A to B

If we concentrate only on what could be called "superhaplogroup A," i.e., all the categories labeled A1 through A6, on the left side of the display, we see a clear continuity from one branch to the other on the phylogenetic tree. In most cases each branch differs from the one immediately adjoining it by only one or two traits. Note that the symbol Y, for yodel, is in parenthesis for A3 and A4, meaning the trait is not always found there. This reflects the fact that yodeling can be commonly found among almost all Pygmy groups as well as many (though not all) Bushmen groups, but is only rarely associated with P/B style among other African groups, even among those peoples whose vocalizing is interlocked in a manner strikingly similar to Pygmy or Bushmen polyphony.

Note also that A5, Call and Response, associated with the Bantu "mainstream," is located relatively high on the tree, reflecting estimates that the so-called Bantu groups genetically diverged from their P/B ancestors at some point roughly around 18,000 years ago. Another very important feature of the Bantu "mainstream" is the extraordinary development of instrumental music, but as the tree is limited to vocal styles, that isn't shown. What's implied by the tree is that P/B style can be regarded as prototypical for Bantu mainstream style, with polyphonic call and response seen as an outgrowth from hocketed interlock.

In and Out of Africa

Looking now to the far left column of the diagram, we see the phrase "Out of Africa," with a horizontal line marking the approximate point in history where, hypothetically, the first band of "modern" humans left Africa for Asia. Everything below this point can be understood as representing the state of music prior to that event. It should also be noted that style families A1 through A4 were apparently spread to other parts of the world via the

"Out of Africa" migration. Again, instruments are not represented here, so it's important to recall that, in all likelihood, the first "Out of Africa" migrants were probably carrying sets of endblown pipes (unbound, but also possibly bound into panpipes), whistles, horns, trumpets, slit drums, stamping tubes, all performed in "P/B style," i.e. with interlocked hocket; also endblown flutes, musical bows, harps and zithers, simple xylophones and simple membranophones (skin drums).

Note the break between "haplogroup" A4 and the families just above it, to the right, i.e., B1, B2 and B3, all rooted at the same place, the thick horizontal line representing the "Bottleneck." Note also that there is no solid line connecting any of the A families with any of the B families. What is represented here is a break in continuity. What could this mean? If "modern" humans originated in Africa, with one small group migrating from that continent to populate Asia, Europe, Oceania and the Americas with their descendents, then it's only logical to assume their music would have migrated with them. According to this straightforward "Out of Africa" model, we would expect that either the original African style families would persist, or gradually evolve, or both. However, the expected continuities simply aren't there.

For example, let's consider style family B2, "Breathless Solo." What is this style and why is it important? By "breathless" I refer to an unusual and highly characteristic feature of this type of vocalizing, in which a solo singer produces a continuous stream of notes as a sort of musical "run-on" sentence. Breathing often appears arbitrary in this style, i.e., not coordinated with the melodic structure. In many cases, the singer appears to be attempting to continue for as long as possible and then audibly gasps for breath with no apparent regard for where he or she is in the melody. We called this style "breathless" because it doesn't seem to take the singer's need to breathe into account. This is radically different from what we would ordinarily expect, since the coordination of the breath with important syntactic junctures is a very much taken for granted aspect of both the musical and linguistic phrase in the great majority of cultures. Other distinctive features of this style are the use of nonsense vocables, wide intervals and a voice quality characterized by heavy glottalization.

"Breathless Solo" appears to be the dominant style for a very widespread family of so-called "Paleosiberian" reindeer-oriented hunting societies stretching across the length of northern Eurasia, from Scandinavia (the Saami Laplanders) through vast stretches of northern Russia and Siberia (Samoyed, Evenk, Yukaghir, Kamchatka, etc.) to the northernmost island of Japan, Hokkaido (the Ainu). As with the Pygmies and Bushmen of Africa, the very widespread distribution of such a distinctive musical style (not to mention

274

lifestyle) over such a vast and difficult terrain, strongly suggests a common cultural root dating back, in all likelihood, to the upper paleolithic.

So how do we go from the mellifluous, flowing, highly integrated, interlocking, polyphonic style of A2 through A4 to the rather singsong, runon, monophonic vocalizing of the Paleosiberians represented by B2? If the Out of Africa model is correct, the Paleosiberians must share a common genetic root with the African migrants. Could something have happened during the long migration through the southern coast of Asia that might have suddenly caused such a drastic musical change among their ancestors? Yes, or at least that's the theory.

That "something" would have been what I've been calling the "bottleneck," i.e., a drastic reduction in population size that would have wiped out much if not all the genetic variation in a given population, with the possibility of an equally drastic alteration of its culture. There are several references in the genetic literature to a major population bottleneck thought to have occurred at some point between 30,000 and 130,000 years ago. As we've seen, Steven Oppenheimer is more specific, attributing such a bottleneck to the historically verified super-explosion of Mt. Toba, in Sumatra, roughly 72,000 years ago.

Mapping Music History

The following maps represent an attempt to apply the musical "haplogroups" of my phylogenetic tree to a hypothetical recreation of the evolution of musical style consistent with the "Out of Africa" migration, as pictured by so much of the genetic research:

See Figure B2

In the first little map, titled "Out of Africa," all the arrows are red, representing the four variants of "Pygmy/Bushmen" style (A1 - 4 on the Phylogenetic Tree) that, as I see it, must have spread along with the original "out of Africa" migrants, following the southern route, all the way to southeast Asia, Sundaland and the Sahul (New Guinea and Australia), with some groups continuing north along the east Asiatic coast. Note the offshoot into northern Pakistan, as indicated by the arrow pointing directly upward, representing the possibility of a bifurcation of the migration path, with one group veering north along the Indus valley. I'll have more to say on this presently.

While the arrows of the first map represent a continuous migration of groups vocalizing in P/B style (A1-4) along the entirety of the Indian Ocean coast, the second map, titled "Bottleneck Event," is intended to depict the disruptive effects of a highly localized disaster that could have, among other things, eliminated all trace of the A haplogroups from most of Pakistan and all of India — but, as indicated by the presence of A1-4 in southeast Asia, could have left much of the region to the east of the Indian border relatively unaffected.

Since Toba is the most likely "culprit," I decided to represent it here – however, a Tsunami centered somewhere southeast of the tip of India might have had a very similar effect, as would a serious drought, or a catastrophic flood along the Indian coast. As I've argued, any of these events could have triggered one or several population bottlenecks in South Asia, but at least partly spared those who had already made it beyond the Indian border, to Myanmar, the Malay Peninsula, Southeast Asia and the Islands to the East of Sundaland. We can regard both a possible Tsunami and the Toba eruption as equivalent as far as their bottleneck producing effects are concerned.

Note the isolated presence of A3&4 in northern Pakistan, representing the possibility of an offshoot along the Indus River during the earliest phase of the migration. An isolated branch of the Out of Africa migrants based on the northern banks of the Indus might have been able to survive the effects of Toba with their African traditions more or less intact. Such a survival is almost necessary if we want to explain how certain elements of the "African signature" could have made it to Europe, where some very important P/B related traditions can still be found in refuge areas throughout that continent.

This hypothesis is supported by the fact that a great many tone languages are spoken in this region (Punjab and Kashmir Provinces), the only area in the entirety of the South Asiatic subcontinent where tone languages are commonly found. If the language spoken by HMP were tonal, then that would explain the presence of tone language in this area today, as an African survival. A3&4 are placed in parentheses because the presence of these musical "haplogroups" in this area at that time is purely hypothetical – hardly any trace of P/B remains anywhere in South Asia today.

Canonic-Echoic Style

Moving to the third map, labeled "Aftermath," the rise of style families B1, B2 and B3 is depicted, all presumably rooted in significant changes, biological, environmental, social and cultural, that could have left their mark on whatever individuals would have survived the disaster depicted in the second map. B1, or "canonic-echoic" style, is of special interest because, unlike B2 and B3, it appears to be derived from A4, "canonic interlock," as indicated by the scored lines connecting the two "haplogroups" in the phylogenetic tree, and can be understood as a variant of P/B. Comparing the list of markers for A4 and B1, we see only one important difference, the presence of LC, "loose coordination."

Unlike what we find so commonly in Africa, the voices in a typical B1 performance are not precisely synchronized rhythmically and can often drift rather freely in relation to one another. I've placed the "root" of B1 in the vicinity of Myanmar and Thailand since, as with P/B generally, it has not been found anywhere in India, Pakistan or the Middle East. Since I have never found any trace of B1 in Sub-Saharan Africa, it seems logical to see it as a "post-Toba" development — but since it is so close in so many ways to P/B it must also be regarded as carrying the African signature. It seems likely, therefore, to have arisen among a population affected by the disaster, but just out of reach of its most devastating effects, thus most likely rooted in Myanmar or Thailand.

In the third map, we see B1 splitting off in three directions, one towards the Malay Peninsula, where it is currently found among certain "Negrito" groups; one towards New Guinea and Melanesia, where it is found among the Kaluli people of Bosavi, who, according to a memorable study by ethnomusicologist Steven Feld, call it "lift up over sounding," as well as certain groups in island Melanesia, notably the 'Are-Are people, whose panpipe music has been so carefully studied by Hugo Zemp. A third arrow points northward along the Pacific coast, from where, as indicated in the following map, we see it continuing all the way to Bering Strait and then, still following the Pacific coast, moving southward all the way to the jungles of South America.

"Breathless" Style and Shouted Hocket

I have already discussed B2, "Breathless Solo," at some length above. What the map implies is that this style could have had its origin on the Indian subcontinent, rather than its current home, among the Paleosiberians and Saami of northern Eurasia. It's placed in parenthesis because we currently find little evidence of it in India, or indeed anywhere in Asia south of Siberia (although a very interesting cylinder recording of Vedda singing, with a comparably "breathless" run-on quality, suggests that the style could have survived close to its original locale among these "Australoid" indigenes of Sri Lanka).

Could B2 be the result of some later event, possibly some other disaster, or the effects of the ice age? Possibly, but it would have had to be rooted very early on in human history to have made its way into the many widely

277

separated and remote places where it's found today. While B2 seems in many ways almost the opposite of any of the African A styles, there are some very interesting points in common, as indicated by the scored lines linking B2 with A2. The two styles are both characterized by yodel or yodel-like vocalizing (especially in the "joik" songs of Lapland, but also reflected in the heavy glottalization found throughout this style area), continuous vocalizing (interrupted by gasps for breath), wide intervals, and an emphasis on "nonsense" vocables. It is thus possible to see how B2 might have emerged directly from P/B, but in a post-disaster setting where communal life might have broken down and individuals could have been forced into isolation for long periods.

Note the presence of A1, "shouted hocket," close to B2 in both southeast India (where both are enclosed in parentheses since neither is found in this region today) and the circum-polar region far to the north. In this case, A1 must be regarded not as a new, post-bottleneck development, but as a rare P/B survival which could have migrated northward with the same "proto-paleosiberian" population that eventually carried B2 into Siberia. This is my way of accounting for the presence of a fascinating variant of shouted hocket among certain Paleosiberian, Ainu and Inuit groups today, known as "throat singing." While most recordings of circum-polar vocalizing available today are B2-style solos, the highly interactive throat singing tradition represents an important, though relatively rare, survival of the African signature in the far north, preserved almost exclusively by women.

The single arrow emanating westward from our parenthetical representation of A3&4 is intended to depict the migration of P/B-related vocalizing traditions from the upper Indus valley, somewhere in the vicinity of the Punjab region, into the Caucasus at a very early period (prior to 40,000 -50,000 years ago, according to archaeological estimates), during the first stages of the original settlement of Europe by descendants of HMP. While there is currently no trace of P/B in the Punjab today, the strong presence of the African signature in the Caucasus (especially western Georgia) and in so many remote enclaves scattered throughout Europe (see the expansion of A3&4 on the "Early Migrations" map) can be understood only if we infer that it must have originally been present in northern Pakistan and northwest India along with the people destined to become the first Europeans.

Let's now turn to the fourth little map, representing some of the relatively early post-bottleneck migrations. We see B2 branching in opposite directions from some point in northern Asia, as far as Kamchatka and even Hokkaido in the East and northern Scandinavia (Lapland) in the West, representing the current range – for the most part — of this style. The whole history of B2, along with that of the Paleosiberian reindeer people generally, is extremely uncertain, so what we see on the map must be taken with a huge grain of salt. Since reindeer were an important resource for humans in many parts of both Asia and Europe during the Paleolithic, even as far south as Spain, and the migrations of the "reindeer herder's" ancestors before, during and after the most recent Ice Age is largely unknown, what we see on the map must be regarded as a gross oversimplification.

Somewhat less speculative, but nevertheless extremely hypothetical, is the possibility, as reflected in the phylogenetic tree, that B2, which may well have made its way into many regions of both Europe and Asia at various times, could have been prototypical for two important types of Eurasiatic solo vocalizing, B2a1, and B2a2. The phylogenetic tree shows a derivative of B2, "haplogroup" B2a, or "Phrased Solo," an apparent development from the "breathless," unphrased singsong of Paleosiberian singing to a type of melody organized according to what we now call "phrases," i.e., syntactic elements articulated by breaths.

At least two branches of B2a survive today. B2a1, "Elaborate Solo," is a type of highly embellished solo vocalizing characteristic of many Asiatic groups. The Eastern branch of this style, especially in China, Korea and Japan, is characterized by considerable glottal embellishment, possibly a clue to its origins in B2. The other branch, B2a2, is characterized by much less embellishment, lack of glottal emphasis, diatonic melody, and strophic (or verse) form of the type most closely associated with the European lyric song and ballad. This is a style that appears to have its origin in Central Asia, where strophic songs are still an important part of the bardic repertoire.

Social Unison

B3, "Social Unison," is an especially important musical "superfamily," characterized by a type of group vocalizing where all parts share the same rhythm, as in a typical Christian hymn, with no rhythmically independent parts and no leader-chorus antiphony. They may be singing either polyphonically (i.e. harmonizing) or in unison. It's easy to take this type of relatively simple group coordination for granted as a reasonable or logical way for any group to organize itself when singing together. It is, however, relatively rare in sub-Saharan Africa, and for that reason, it's unlikely that the Out of Africa migrants or their descendents were vocalizing in this manner at any time prior to the bottleneck. So when, and how — and also why — could such a practice have developed?

An interesting clue is provided by the Australian Aborigines, whose history on that continent, according to the fossil evidence, goes back at least 50,000, and very possibly over 60,000, years, not too long after the initial migration out of Africa. All indications, including the genetic research, point to their descent from the original African migrants, yet they have a very contrastive and distinctive physical morphology and a totally contrastive musical style. A clue to their origins could be the existence of so-called "Australoid" peoples in southern India, many of whom, such as the Vedda of Sri Lanka, bear a strong morphological resemblance to Australians.

Geneticists Alan Redd and Mark Stoneking have reported genetic results that "link Aboriginal Australian populations with populations from the subcontinent of India," whereas their findings "do not support a close relationship between Aboriginal Australian and PNG (Papua New Guinea) populations...", as many assumed would be the case (Redd and Stoneking 1999:808).

While the genetic picture remains complicated and controversial, with no one clear interpretation dominating, it is possible, nevertheless, to speculate that the Australian Aborigines may have originated in southern India as one small band of bottleneck survivors, some of whom remained in India while others eventually made their way to Australia. In other words, it looks as though their musical style could have resulted from the same genetic and cultural "bottleneck" that appears to have produced B1 and B2. Only in this case, the break with the original P/B style seems to have been more complete, as there is little the two would seem to have in common. Since it's difficult to say when a group of Australoids from India might have begun their migration to Australia (assuming that's what actually happened), and since there is no evidence of this style among any group currently living in South Asia, I enclosed B3 in parenthesis in map three.

Style family B3 is subdivided into two main branches, B3a, "Unison Iterative One Beat" and B3b, "Polyphonic Iterative." What both have in common is the "iterative" aspect, i.e., a tendency to reiterate the same note, often several times in a row, and especially at phrase endings. Since this type of melody is so distinctive and unusual, and since it is so often associated with social unison, it makes sense to treat all instances as stemming from the same root.

As indicated in the phylogenetic map, B3 subdivides into a polyphonic and a unison branch, conveniently separating the iterative social unison found so commonly in western Polynesia, predominantly polyphonic and open throated, from what I've called "Unison Iterative One-Beat," a relatively harsh, tense-voiced unison style, often supported by a very simple one-beat accompaniment on drums or idiophones such as boomerangs, sticks or rattles. This is an approach to musical organization characteristic of two geographically very distant groups, Australian Aborigines and Native Americans. The two families, labeled B3a1 and B3a2, have a great deal in common, strongly suggesting that despite the truly enormous geographical distance, they could stem from a single root, that would have formed very early after the bottleneck event, most likely in or near India – though no trace of either style remains in the region today.

In the same map, we see B3 splitting off in two directions, one toward Australia, another pointed northeast, in the direction of Bering Strait. In the following map, "Later Migrations," we see B3a1 spreading throughout the Americas, where it is currently the dominant style. The polyphonic variant, B3b is shown safely ensconced in Melanesia, from whence it has made its way eastward to the islands of western Polynesia, accompanied by a variant form, B3b1, in which iteration on single tones has been replaced by lyrical, mostly diatonic, melodies and harmonies of a type not too different from what we find today in Eastern Europe.

Indeed, on the same "Later Migrations" map we see a distant branch of the same style family (B3b1) centered in Russian Asia, spreading to northern, eastern and southern Europe, where we find types of traditional vocal polyphony surprisingly similar to certain Melanesian and Western Polynesian traditions. Whether there is a historical connection at work, or simply a case of convergent evolution, is at this point impossible to determine, but there are some striking points of similarity well worth further examination.

Europe, Old and New

The fourth map, "Early Migrations," depicts A3&4 spreading the African Signature from the trans Caucasus into every corner of Europe, implying an association with the initial migrations into that continent by direct descendants of HMP. The following map reflects a much later migration into basically the same region by a very different group, post-bottleneck survivors out of Central Asia. This newer group of immigrants — or invaders — possibly a branch of the proto-Indoeuropean speaking "Kurgan" horse nomads posited by archaeologist Marija Gimbutas, may have disseminated an essentially monophonic vocal style, closely wedded to poetic texts in verse, or "strophic" form, the basis of what has come to be known as the lyric song and ballad.

This second population, far more successful than the first, appears to have defeated and marginalized the original Europeans ("Old Europe"), whose P/B-based, polyphonic vocal traditions (A3&4) can still be found in remote refuge areas. The solo-oriented strophic ballad form, possibly originating with the proto-Indo-European horse nomads of Central Asia, has become the norm for traditional folk singers in just about every European country. Since the latter style shows signs of being an offshoot from the much older B2, and a counterpart to the equally solo-oriented but far more elaborate, predominantly Asiatic B2a1, I've categorized it as a sister clade, B2a2.

The last map in the series summarizes the distribution of all the haplogroups discussed above, according to where they can now be found – and by "now" I'm referring to field reports and recordings collected mostly during the 19th and 20th Centuries, since many of these traditions have, very sadly, been lost in recent years. Note the presence of B2, principally associated with Paleosiberian peoples, in two isolated parts of South America, where "breathless" vocalizing has been noted among the Ona of Tierra del Fuego and the Guahibo of Venezuela. Whether these are simply anomalies or might have some broader historical significance is at this time very difficult to say.

What's Been Left Out

My musical tree and the maps derived from it admittedly represent a somewhat subjective, hypothetical view of musical evolution and early human migrations. And some important musical practices have been omitted, largely because of difficulties in assigning them to particular traditions. For example, leader-chorus antiphony, sometimes referred to as "call and response," is commonly found in a great many musical traditions, both indigenous and modern. Since African call and response seems so clearly an offshoot from P/B, I included the two major African variants (A5 and A6) in the tree. However, we also find less distinctive types of leader-chorus response all over the place, Europe, the Middle East, India, China, Southeast Asia, Polynesia, etc. The practice is so common and so simple that it's more easily explained, in my view, as the result of independent invention than archaic survival.

One of the most common types of polyphonic vocalizing worldwide is drone polyphony, where some voices hold or reiterate a single note while others sing a melodic part against it. Various types of drone polyphony can be found widely distributed, usually in refuge areas, in both Europe and Southeast Asia, as well as Island Southeast Asia, Melanesia and Polynesia. Since the practice is so widespread, I've found it almost impossible to assign it a particular root, though its almost total absence from Africa suggests that it's likely to be a post-bottleneck phenomenon.

An especially distinctive type of drone polyphony, popularly associated with Bulgaria, is paralleled by roughly similar traditions to be found in many more or less remote enclaves of Serbia, Montenegro, Bosnia, Croatia,

Macedonia, and Greece. This can be considered a true style area, rather than simply a region of drone polyphony, as it involves several highly idiosyncratic features in addition to drone. Most prominent is the stress on extreme dissonances, based on major and minor seconds, and sometimes even smaller intervals, characteristically emphasized and often sustained, generating acoustic "beats" that can produce a powerfully resonant bodily vibration, in which the singers clearly take pleasure. Other characteristics of this very distinctive style include extreme glottalization (possibly related to yodel), tremulo, free rhythm, extreme volume, and a characteristic upward glissando "glide" prominent especially at phrase endings.

So what's the problem? Couldn't such a style, so clearly localized largely in one region of Europe (the Balkans) have developed as an offshoot of certain other types of polyphony in one particular corner of southeastern Europe and spread from there? Yes, I suppose it could have. The problem is that essentially the same style of singing can be found in totally different parts of the world, most notably on the island of Flores, in Indonesia; but also Manus and Fiji, in addition to other groups in Melanesia; Taiwan; the Afghan province of Nuristan; and even in Tibet.

It's possible that the bottleneck I've been pointing to could have led to the development of this style, perhaps among a group of Toba survivors in India, followed by a three-way split, with one group migrating northward to Afghanistan and Tibet, one eventually finding its way to the Balkans, and a third to Indonesia and Oceania. But it's very difficult to understand why there are such huge gaps in its distribution, and for this reason I was unable to include it in my musical tree.

Partial Bibliography

Ambrose, Stanley. 1998. Late Pleistocene Human Population Bottlenecks, Volcanic Winter, and the Differentiation of Modern Humans. Journal of Human Evolution 34:623-51.

Ambrose Stanley and Williams, M. 2009. Supervolcano Eruption — In Sumatra — Deforested India 73,000 Years Ago. *ScienceDaily* (Nov. 24, 2009).

Amor Potest. 2004. Medieval motet. Transcribed by N. Nakamura from the Montpelier Codex. Available via the Maucamedus website, at *http://maucamedus.net/PDF/amor-p*otest.pdf. Last accessed December 20, 2008.

Arom, S. 1976. The Use of Play-Back Techniques in the Study of Oral Polyphonies. *Ethnomusicology* 20(3), 483-519.

— — — -1991. *African Polyphony and Polyrhythm: Musical Structure and Methodology*. Cambridge: Cambridge University Press.

— — — - 2002. *Musical Anthology of the Aka Pygmies*. Two audio CD's with accompanying pamphlet. Ocora C560171.

Barnard, Alan. 1992. *Hunters and herders of southern Africa:a comparative ethnography of the Khoisan peoples*. Cambridge University Press.

— — — — — — —-. 2006. Kalahari revisionism, Vienna and the 'indigenous peoples' debate. *Social Anthropology* 14 (1):1-16.

Batini, C. et al. 2011. Signatures of the pre-agricultural peopling processes in sub-Saharan Africa as revealed by the phylogeography of early Y chromosome lineages. *Molecular Biology and Evolution*.

Behar et al. 2008. The Dawn of Human Matrilineal Diversity, *The American Journal of Human Genetics*, doi:10.1016/j.ajhg.2008.04.002

Berghaus, Günter. 2004. New Perspectives on Prehistoric Art. Greenwood.

Biesele, Megan and Kxao Royal-/O/OO. 1999. The Ju/'hoansi of Botswana and Namibia. In *The Cambridge Encyclopedia of Hunters and Gatherers*. Richard Lee and Richard Daly, eds. Pp. 205-209. Cambridge:Cambridge University Press.

Birdsell, Joseph. 1967. Preliminary data on the trihybrid origin of the Australian Aborigines. *Archaeology and Physical Anthropology in Oceania*, 2 (2), pp 100-55.

Bishop, Douglas. 2005. A Worldwide History of the Pan Flute. www.panflutejedi.com/pan-flute-history-page.html, accessed April 13, 2006.

Blench, Roger. 1999. Are the African Pygmies an Ethnographic Fiction? In *Challenging Elusiveness*. Biesbrouck, Elders and Rossel, eds. Pp. 41-60. Leiden:Research School for Asian, African, and Amerindian Studies, the University of Leiden.

————————. 2002. Reconstructing African Music History. Unpublished draft.

Boas, Franz. 1940. *Race, Language and Culture*. Macmillan: New York.

Brown, Steven. 2000. The Musilanguage Model of Musical Evolution, in Wallin, Merker & Brown, eds., *The Origins of Music*. Cambridge, MA: MIT Press.

Buchner, Alexander. 1980. *Encyclopédie des instruments de musique*. Paris: Gründ.

Bukofzer, M. 1940. Popular Polyphony in the Middle Ages, *The Musical Quarterly*, vol. 26, no. 1.

Burstyn, S. 1983. Gerald of Wales and the Sumer Canon, *The Journal of Musicology*, Vol. 2, No. 2.

The Cambridge Encyclopedia of Hunters and Gatherers. 1999. Richard Lee and Richard Daly, eds. Cambridge:Cambridge University Press.

Cavalli-Sforza, Luca, *et al*. 1996. *The History and Geography of Human Genes*. (Abridged paperback edition.) Princeton: Princeton University Press.

Chen, Yu-Sheng et al. 2000. mtDNA Variation in the South African Kung and Khwe—and Their Genetic Relationships to Other African Populations. *American Journal of Human Genetics* 66(4): 1362–1383.

Cordaux, R. et al. 2003. Mitochondrial DNA analysis reveals diverse histories of tribal populations from India. *European Journal of Human Genetics*, Mar;11(3):253-64.

Dissanayake, Ellen. 2008. If music is the food of love, what about survival and reproductive success? *Musicae Scientiae*, Special Issue, 169-195.

Draper, Patricia. 1978. The Learning Environment for Aggression and Anti-Social Behavior among the !Kung. *Department of Anthropology Faculty Publications*, University of Nebraska. Digital Commons. http://digitalcommons.unl.edu/anthropologyfacpub/12.

Du, Shanshan. 2005. Frameworks for Societies in Balance: A Cross-Cultural Perspective on Gender Equality. Societies of Peace: 2nd World Congress on Matriarchal Studies. http://www.second-congress-matriarchal-studies.com/du.html

Eliade, Mircea. 1964. *Shamanism*. Bollingen Press.

England, Nicholas. 1967. Bushman Counterpoint. *Journal of the International Folk Music Council* 19:58–66.

— — —. 1995. *Music Among the Zˉu'ǀ'wã-si and Related Peoples of Namibia, Botswana, and Angola*. New York: Garland.

Erickson, Edwin. 1969-70. *The Song Trace: Song Styles and the Ethnohistory of Aboriginal America*. Ph. D. dissertation, Columbia University.

— — — — — — — — —. 1976. Tradition and Evolution in Song Style: A Re-analysis of Cantometric Data, *Cross-Cultural Research*, November 1976, vol. 11 no. 4, pp. 277-308.

Finkel, Michael. 2009. The Hadza. *National Geographic Magazine*, 12.

Frisbie, Charlotte. 1971. Anthropological and Ethnomusicological Implications of a Comparative Analysis of Bushmen and African Pygmy Music. *Ethnology* 10(3):265-291.

Fukuyama, Francis. 2011. *The Origins of Political Order*. Farrar, Straus and Giroux:New York.

Fürniss, Susanne. 2006. Aka Polyphony: Music, Theory, Back and Forth. In *Analytical Studies in World Music*. Michael Tenzer, ed. Pp. 163–204. New York:Oxford University Press.

Gimbutas, M. 1994. *The Civilization of the Goddess:The World of Old Europe*. New York: Harper-Collins.

Grauer, Victor. 1965. Some Song Style Clusters. *Ethnomusicology* 9:265–71.

— — —. 2006. Echoes of Our Forgotten Ancestors. *The World of Music* 48(2):5-58.

— — —. 2007a. Roots. *Musical Traditions*. MT 207. http://www.mustrad.org.uk/.

— — —. 2007b. Music 000001. Internet Blog. http://music000001.blogspot.com/.

— — —. 2007c. New Perspectives on the Kalahari Debate: A Tale of Two Genomes. *Before Farming* 2(4)1-14. http://www.waspress.co.uk/journals/beforefarming/.

— — —. 2009. Concept, Style, and Structure in the Music of the African Pygmies and Bushmen:A Study in Cross-Cultural Analysis. *Ethnomusicology* 53(3):396-424.

Grinker, Roy. 1994. *Houses in the Rainforest: Ethnicity and Inequality Among Farmers and Foragers in Central Africa*. U. of California Press.

Hewlett, Barry. 1991. *Intimate Fathers: The Nature and Context of Aka Pygmy Paternal Infant Care*. Anne Arbor:University of Michigan Press.

— — — — — —. 1996. Cultural Diversity Among African Pygmies. In *Cultural Diversity Among Twentieth Century Foragers*. Susan Kent, ed. Cambridge, England:Cambridge University Press. http://www.vancouver.wsu.edu/fac/hewlett/cultdiv.html.

Heylighen, Francis. 2005. Occam's Razor. pespmc1.vub.ac.be/OCCAMRAZ.html, accessed April 7, 2006.

Hitchcock, Don. 2009. *Lion Camp: Kostienki/Kostenki on the Don River.*
http://donsmaps.com/lioncamp.html, accessed April 7, 2006.

Hohmann, Gottfried and Fruth, Barbara 1994. Structure and use of distance
calls in wild bonobos (*Pan paniscus*). International Journal of Primatology
Volume 15, Number 5, 767-782, DOI: 10.1007/BF02737430.

Home, Home on the Ridge. Undated. Student Handout. *Poverty Point
Expeditions.*
http://www.crt.state.la.us/archaeology/ppexpeditions/homehandout.html

Ingman, M. and Gyllensten, U. 2003. Mitochondrial Genome Variation and
Evolutionary History of Australian and New Guinean Aborigines. *Genome
Res.* 2003 13: 1600-1606

Izikowitz, Karl Gustav. 1970   *Musical and other sound instruments of the
South American Indians; a comparative ethnographical study.* East Ardsley,
England: S. R. Publishers.

Jones, D. 2003 Kinship and Deep History: Exploring Connections between
Culture Areas, Genes, and Languages. *American Anthropologist* 105(3):501-
514.

Jones, Sacha. 2007. The Toba Supervolcanic Eruption, in *The evolution and
history of human populations in South Asia*, ed. Petraglia and Allchin.

Jordania, J. 2006. *Who Asked the First Question? The Origins of Human Choral
Singing, Intelligence, Language and Speech.* Tbilisi: Tbilisi Ivane Javakhishvili
State University Institute of Classical, Byzantine and Modern Greek Studies.

Kárpáti, J. 1980. Myth and Reality in the Theory of Chinese Tonal System.
Studia Musicologica Academiae Scientiarum Hungaricae, T. 22, Fasc. 1/4.

Kent, Susan, ed. 1996. *Cultural Diversity Among Twentieth Century Foragers.*
Cambridge, England:Cambridge University Press.

Kisliuk, Michelle. 1998. *Seize the Dance.* New York: Oxford University Press.

Kuttner, Fritz. 1965. A Musicological Interpretation of the Twelve Lüs in
China's Traditional Tone System. *Ethnomusicology*, Vol. 9, No. 1.

Layriss M. and Wilbert, J. 1961. Absence of the Diego Antigen, a Genetic Characteristic of Early Immigrants to South America. *Science* 13, Vol. 134 no. 3485, pp. 1077-1078.

Lee, Richard B. 1984. *The Dobe !Kung.* New York: Holt, Rinehart, and Winston.

Liazos, Alex. 2008. *The 1950s Mbuti:A Critique of Colin Turnbull's The Forest People.* http://turnbullandthembuti.pbworks.com/MBUTI.

Locke, David. 1996. Africa/Ewe, Mande, Dagbamba, Shone, BaAka, in J. T. Titon (Ed.), *Worlds of Music,* third edition. New York: Schirmer, 71-143.

Lomax, Alan. 1959. Folksong Style. *American Anthropologist* 61, 927-54.

— — — — — — — —. 1962. Song Structure and Social Structure. *Ethnology* (1)4:425-451.

— — — — — — — —. 1972. An Appeal for Cultural Equity, *World of Music,* XIV [2].

— — — — — — — —. 1976. Cantometrics:An Approach to the Anthropology of Music. Berkeley:The University of California Extension Media Center.

Lomax, Alan, et al. 1968. *Folk Song Style and Culture.* Washington:National Association for the Advancement of Science.

Maji, S., Krithika, S. and T.S. Vasulu. 2009. Phylogeographic distribution of mitochondrial DNA macrohaplogroup M in India. *Journal of Genetics,* Vol. 88, No. 1

Maju. 2009. Mtdna Phylogenetic Tree. *Leherensuge* blog. http://leherensuge.blogspot.com/2009/04/mtdna-tree-version-11.html

Malone, Andrew. 2007. Face to Face with Stone Age Man:The Hadzabe tribe of Tanzania. *MailOnline:News.* http://www.dailymail.co.uk/news/article-469847/Face-face-Stone-Age-man-The-Hadzabe-tribe-Tanzania.html.

Marean, Curtis, and Zelalem Assefa. 2005. The Origins of Modern Humans, in Ann Brower Stahl, ed. *African Archaeology.* Oxford: Blackwell.

Marshall, Lorna. 1999. *Nyae Nyae !Kung Beliefs and Rites.*

Merker, B. 2000. Synchronous Chorusing and Human Origins, in Wallin, Merker & Brown, eds., *The Origins of Music.* Cambridge, MA: MIT Press.

Metspalu M. et al. 2004. Most of the extant mtDNA boundaries in South and Southwest Asia were likely shaped during the initial settlement of Eurasia by anatomically modern humans. *BMC Genetics,* 5:26.

Moreno, Eduardo. 2011. The society of our 'out of Africa' ancestors (I): The migrant warriors that colonized the world. *Communicative & Integrative Biology* 4:2, 1-9.

Nattiez, Jean Jacques. 1999. Inuit Throat Games and Siberian Throat Singing: A Comparative, Historical and Semiological Approach. *Ethnomusicology* 43(3):399-418.

Neves, et al. 2005. A new early Holocene human skeleton from Brazil: implications for the settlement of the New World. *Journal of Human Evolution Volume 48, Issue 4,* pp. 403-414

Ojamaa, T. and Aru, J. 2005. Can Hyperventilation be a trance mechanism in Nganasan ritual dance accompaniment. *Proceedings of the Conference on Interdisciplinary Musicology,* Montreal Canada.

Olivier, Emmanuelle. 1998. Bushman Vocal Music:The Illusion of Polyphony. In *Language, Identity, and Conceptualization among the Khoisan.* Mathias Schladt, ed. Pp. 359–70. Cologne: Rüdiger Köppe Verlag.

Olivier, Emmanuelle and Susanne Fürniss. 1997. Systématique musicale pygmée et bochiman: Deux conceptions africaines du contrepoint. *Musurgia* 4(3):10–30.

———. 1999. Pygmy and Bushman Music:A New Comparative Study. In *Central African Hunter-Gatherers in a Multidisciplinary Perspective: Challenging Elusiveness.* Karen Biesbrouck, Stefan Elders, and Gerda Rossel, eds. Pp. 117–32. Leiden: Research School for Asian, African and Amerindian Studies, University of Leiden.

Olson, Steve. 2002. *Mapping Human History.* New York: Houghton Mifflin.

Oppenheimer, Stephen. 2004a. Journey of Mankind: The Peopling of the World. Interactive web site: www.bradshawfoundation.com/stephenoppenheimer/, accessed September 8, 2005.

————————. 2004b. *The Real Eve*. New York: Carroll & Graf.

Patin, Etienne et al. 2009. Inferring the Demographic History of African Farmers and Pygmy Hunter–Gatherers Using a Multilocus Resequencing Data Set. *PLoS Genetics* 5(4):e1000448:1-13, doi:10.1371/journal.pgen.1000448

Perry, Mark. 1995. Why Socialism Failed. *The Freeman*, Volume 45 (6).

Petraglia, Michael et al. 2007. Middle Paleolithic Assemblages from the Indian Subcontinent Before and After the Toba Super-Eruption. *Science* 6 July 2007, *Vol. 317 no. 5834 pp. 114-116.*

Pinker, Steven. 2007. A History of Violence. *The New Republic*, March 19 issue.

Redd, Alan and Stoneking, Mark. 1999. Peopling of the Sahul: mtDNA Variation in Aboriginal Australian and Papua New Guinean Populations, *American Journal of Human Genetics*, 65.

Redd, A. et al. 2002. Gene Flow from the Indian Subcontinent to Australia: Evidence from the Y Chromosome. *Current Biology*, Apr 16;12(8):673-7.

Robock, A. et al. 2009. Did the Toba volcanic eruption of ~74 ka B.P. produce widespread glaciation? Journal of Geophysical Research, vol. 114.

Roscoe, Paul. Undated. The Hunter-Gatherer Spectrum in New Guinea. *Climate Change Institute*. http://climatechange.umaine.edu/Research/projects/NewGuinea.html

Rouget, Gilbert and Yvette Grimaud. 1956. *Bushmen Music and Pygmy Music*. Long Playing recording, with accompanying essay by Gilbert Rouget, and additional commentary and analysis by Yvette Grimaud. Baltimore: Peabody Museum and Paris: Musée de L'homme.

Sadie, Stanley, ed. 1984. *The New Grove Dictionary of Musical Instruments, vol. 3.* London: Macmillan.

Sahlins, Marshall. 1963. Poor Man, Rich Man, Big Man, Chief: Political Types in Melanesia and Polynesia. *Comparative Studies in Society and History,* vol. 5 no. 3, 285-303.

Sanders, E. H. 1974. The Medieval Hocket in Practice and Theory, *The Musical Quarterly,* Vol. 60, No. 2.

Sapir, E. 1916. Time Perspective in Aboriginal American Culture, a Study in Method, in *Geological Survey Memoir 90: No. 13, Anthropological Series.* Ottawa: Government Printing Bureau.

— — — — —. 1994 (1913). *Collected Works.* de Gruyter:The Hague.

Semino et al. 2002. Ethiopians and Khoisan Share the Deepest Clades of the Human Y-Chromosome Phylogeny. *Am. J. Hum. Genet.* 70:265–268

Silverberg, Robert. 1968. *The Mound Builders.* Ohio Univ. Press.

Sklenar, Karel. 1985. *Hunters of the Stone Age.* Middlesex: Hamlyn.

Soares, Pedro et al. 2009. Correcting for purifying selection: an improved human mitochondrial molecular clock. *American Journal of Human Genetics,* 2009 Jun;84(6):740-59

Solway, Jacqueline and Richard Lee. 1990. Foragers, Genuine or Spurious. *Current Anthropology* 31(2):109-146.

Stahl, Ann Brower, ed. 2005. *African Archaeology.* Oxford: Blackwell.

Stone, Jamie. 2006. The Baka Pygmies of Cameroon. Articlesbase. http://www.articlesbase.com/online-education-articles/the-baka-pygmies-of-cameroon-67733.html.

Stone, Jamie. 2006. The Baka Pygmies of Cameroon. Articlesbase. http://www.articlesbase.com/online-education-articles/the-baka-pygmies-of-cameroon-67733.html.

Tamm, E. et al. 2007. Beringian Standstill and Spread of Native American Founders. *PLoS ONE* 2(9).

Templeton, Alan. 2002. Out of Africa Again and Again. *Nature*, 416.

The Y Chromosome Consortium. 2002. A Nomenclature System for the Tree of Human Y-Chromosomal Binary Haplogroups. *Genome Research* 12:339–348.

Tharakan, George. 2007. The Muduga and Kurumba of Kerala, South India and the Social Organization of Hunting and Gathering. *Journal of Ecological Anthropology*, Vol. 11.

Thomas, Elizabeth Marshall. 1989 (1958). *The Harmless People*. New York:Vintage.

— — — — — — — — — — — — — — —. 2007. *The Old Way*. Picador.

Tishkoff, Sarah et al. 2007. History of Click-Speaking Populations of Africa Inferred from mtDNA and Y Chromosome Genetic Variation. *Molecular Biology and Evolution* 24(10):2180-2195, doi:10.1093/molbev/msm155.

— — — —. 2009. The Genetic Structure and History of Africans and African Americans. *Science* 324(5930):1035 – 1044, doi: 10.1126/science.1172257.

Turnbull, Colin. 1961. *The Forest People*. New York:Simon and Schuster.

— — — — — — — — —. 1965. *Wayward Servants*. Garden City, New York:The Natural History Press.

— — — — — — — — —. 1987. *The Mountain People*. Touchstone.

Urquhart, Alvin W. (1963?). *Patterns of Settlement and Subsistence in Southwestern Angola*. Publication 1096. Washington:National Academy of Sciences.

van der Sluys, Cornelia. 2000. Gifts from Immortal Ancestors, in *Hunters and Gatherers in the Modern World*, ed. Biesele and Hitchcock.

Valiulytė, S. 1998. *Sutartinės*. Website: http://ausis.gf.vu.lt/eka/songs/sutartines.html. Recordings performed by the group "Trys keturiose", headed by Daiva Račiūnaitė-Vyčinienė. Copyright 1998. Last accessed 12-2-2008.

Velitchkina, Olga. 1996. The Role of Movement in Russian Panpipe Playing. *Ethnomusicology Online* 2: research.umbc.edu/eol/2/velitch/index.html, accessed December 18, 2004.

Wade, Nicholas. 2006. *Before the Dawn: Recovering the Lost History of Our Ancestors*. Penguin Books: New York.

Wallin, N., Merker, B. & Brown, S. 2000. *The Origins of Music*. Cambridge, MA: MIT Press.

The World Atlas of Language Structures Online (WALS). 2011. http://wals.info/

Wrangham, R. and Peterson, D. 1997. *Demonic Males: Apes and the Origins of Human Violence*. Mariner Books.

Zago, Marco A. *et al*. 1995. Alpha-globin Gene Haplotypes in South American Indians. *Human Biology* 67:535-46.

Žarskienė, Ruta. 2003. Playing Multi-Pipe Whistles of Northeastern Europe: Phenomenon of Collective Musical Performance. *Studia Musicologica* 44:163-74.

Zemp, Hugo. 1979. Aspects of 'Are'are Musical Theory. *Ethnomusicology*, vol. 23, no. 1.

Made in the USA
Middletown, DE
16 September 2016